EXPERIENCE,
MEMORY,
AND REASONING

THE ARTIFICIAL INTELLIGENCE SERIES

A Series of Monographs, Treatises, and Texts
Edited by Roger C. Schank

SCHANK AND ABELSON • *Scripts Plans Goals and Understanding:
An Inquiry into Human Knowledge Structures, 1977*

LEHNERT • *The Process of Question Answering:
Computer Simulation of Cognition, 1978*

MEEHAN • *The New UCI LISP Manual, 1979*

CHARNIAK, RIESBECK, AND MCDERMOTT • *Artificial
Intelligence Programming, 1980*

SCHANK AND RIESBECK • *Inside Computer Understanding:
Five Programs Plus Miniatures, 1981*

KOLODNER • *Retrieval and Organizational Strategies
in Conceptual Memory: A Computer Model, 1984*

KOLODNER AND RIESBECK • *Experience, Memory,
and Reasoning, 1986*

EXPERIENCE, MEMORY, AND REASONING

Edited by

Janet L. Kolodner
Georgia Institute of Technology

Christopher K. Riesbeck
Yale University

LEA LAWRENCE ERLBAUM ASSOCIATES, PUBLISHERS
1986   Hillsdale, New Jersey   London

To Mike, Orly, and Joshua
Maxine, Michael, Elizabeth, and Jonathan

Lawrence Erlbaum Associates, Inc., Publishers
365 Broadway
Hillsdale, New Jersey 07642

Library of Congress Cataloging-in-Publication Data

Kolodner, Janet L.
  Experience, memory, and reasoning.

  (The Artificial intelligence series)
  Includes index.
  1. Reasoning (Psychology) 2. Memory. 3. Experience
— Psychological aspects. 4. Artificial intelligence.
I. Riesbeck, Christopher K. II. Title. III. Series:
Artificial intelligence series (Hillsdale, N.J.)
BF441.K57 1986   153   85-20721
ISBN 0-89859-644-0

Printed in the United States of America
10 9 8 7 6 5 4 3 2 1

Contents

PART II: MEMORY-BASED HYPOTHESIS
FORMATION

PART III: MEMORY-BASED NATURAL LANGUAGE UNDERSTANDING

List of Contributors

WILLIAM M. BAIN • Department of Computer Science, Yale University

B. CHANDRASEKARAN • Department of Computer and Information Science, Ohio State University

KURT P. EISELT • Department of Computer Science, University of California, Irvine

RICHARD H. GRANGER • Department of Computer Science, University of California, Irvine

JENNIFER K. HOLBROOK • Department of Computer Science, University of California, Irvine

JANET L. KOLODNER • School of Information and Computer Science, Georgia Institute of Technology

MICHAEL LEBOWITZ • Department of Computer Science, Columbia University

STEVEN L. LYTINEN • Department of Computer Science, Yale University

CHARLES E. MARTIN • Department of Computer Science, Yale University

DALE M. McNULTY • Department of Computer Science, University of California, Irvine

BRIAN J. REISER • Department of Psychology, Princeton University

CHRISTOPHER K. RIESBECK • Department of Computer Science, Yale University

EDWINA L. RISSLAND • Department of Computer and Information Science, University of Massachusetts

ROGER C. SCHANK • Department of Computer Science, Yale University

V. SEMBUGAMOORTHY • Department of Computer and Information Science, Ohio State University

JEFF SHRAGER • Department of Psychology, Carnegie-Mellon University

ROBERT L. SIMPSON, Jr. • Program Manager, Intelligent Systems, Defense Advanced Research Projects Agency

ROBERT WILENSKY • Computer Science Division, University of California, Berkeley

Preface

Several years ago, during a reunion banquet at the national Artificial Intelligence conference in Washington, DC, some of us were commiserating over the fact that the national and international AI conference had grown too big. The largeness and diversity of the conferences made it hard to do two things: to learn in detail about what others were doing and to present our own work at a satisfying level of detail. It seemed obvious that the thing to do was to begin having a series of smaller, more intimate thematic workshops devoted to presenting research ideas in detail.

The First Annual Workshop on Theoretical Issues in Conceptual Information Processing (TICIP) grew out of that. It was held in Atlanta, Georgia in March 1984 and included 50 people with roughly the same world view. In particular, all of us were interested in content-based theories of conceptual information processing. Despite this, our call for papers for the workshop elicited papers on a wide variety of topics: learning, parsing, creativity, problem solving, representation, and memory organization are just some of the topics that were discussed. Although topics were diverse, everyone was interested in a set of basic issues: What do people know? How do they use that knowledge to reason?

What we didn't know before we set up the workshop was that a majority of the papers would converge on a theme: the relationships between memory, experience, and reasoning. It has long been acknowledged that reasoning depends on heuristics or knowledge gleaned through experience. Thus, one relationship between reasoning and experience is already well-defined. We now add memory to the duo of experience and reasoning. How does memory fit in? The knowledge coming from experience that is used for reasoning must be gleaned from an accumulation of many experiences. Those experiences do not necessarily come in the right order for learning. Yet, we, as people, learn from experience anyway. A memory stores experiences to allow learning to happen on the basis of several experiences. Furthermore, reasoning capabilities evolve as new knowledge is learned.

In addition, heuristic knowledge compiled from many experiences is not the only way we use experience in reasoning. Often, a *particular* previous experience acts as a guide in allowing us to construct a solution to a new problem. If we are *reminded* of a previous case similar to one we are trying to solve, we can use it as a guideline for solving the new one. Memory also stores experience, then, to be recalled to guide later processing. When we consider the role of a memory holding experiences, we also begin considering additional reasoning processes, namely those that consider previous individual cases to make new decisions. The name that has been coined for this view of intelligence is *memory-based reasoning.*

The chapters in this collection are based on presentations made at the First Annual TICIP Workshop. Each chapter addresses some issue associated with the relationships between memory, experience and reasoning. In considering representation, for example, the representation of episodes (experiences) is a major issue, as is their organization in a long-term memory for experience. Chapters in the understanding section consider the relationships between understanding processes and the memory store, including how we can expect knowledge to be organized in that store for access by understanding processes, how it can be updated as part of the understanding process, and what new processing considerations become important when we look at understanding in its relationship to memory. In the hypothesis generation section, a framework explicitly citing the relationships between problem solving, learning, and memory processes is presented, and other chapters explore issues associated with explaining why things have happened and justifying decisions, two reasoning processes that depend heavily on experience.

This book presents a first view of the issues associated with memory-based reasoning. There is much research currently being done along the lines presented in this book, both by those whose chapters are in this book and by others. This book presents an introduction to what we believe will prove to be an important approach to unraveling the mysteries of cognition and AI.

ACKNOWLEDGMENTS

Special thanks go to several people and agencies who helped with the First Annual TICIP Workshop: Shoshana Hardt, who was on the program committee along with us; Dana Eckart, Kirt Pulaski, Robert Simpson, and Katia Sycara, students at Georgia Tech who served as the local arrangements committee; the Georgia Tech School of Information and Computer Science, which provided their copying machines and administrative support; the National Science Foundation, who paid for secretarial time under Grant No. IST-8116892; and especially, Jean Early, who put in much time making sure everything ran smoothly. Funding that supported work on this book came from the National Science Foundation under Grant No. IST-831171, the Army Research Office under Contract No. DAAG-29-85-K-0023, and the Air Force Office of Scientific Research under Contract No. F49620-82-K-0010.

Janet L. Kolodner
Christopher K. Riesbeck

1 Introduction

The chapters in this volume, though different in topic, style, and even scientific discipline, all share a common theme: that knowledge is first and foremost the product of experience. This obvious truth about human knowledge has significant ramifications for artificial intelligence (AI) and cognitive science. It means that to understand human knowledge and how it is organized and applied, we have to understand how it was acquired. It means that to claim that a representation of knowledge is adequate, we have to show how that knowledge could be learned and how it could be updated in the face of new experience.

KNOWLEDGE AND AI

The importance of knowledge for intelligence is one of AI's few consensual beliefs. Knowledge, in large quantities organized into usable chunks, is an essential ingredient of a great deal of intelligent behavior. How to chunk knowledge about the world to make it usable for reasoning is an unavoidable problem in AI research. The real world is full of objects and tableaux that have no identifying labels to help the visitor. To understand the world, we must carry around in our heads a field guide, a guide so large that the quality of its index is a major factor in the usefulness of the guide.

The metaphor is incomplete, however, until we make one further point: the guide is really a notebook that each of us writes and maintains. We are born with pencil and paper and have to take it from there. As a result, we each have a different field guide, in our own handwriting, with illegible scribbles, mistakes, corrections, and redundancies, and at no point can we stop and say that the book is complete.

What does this imply about the organization of our knowledge? First, our knowledge is most likely a redundant, jumbled, inconsistent mess of cross-referenced partially formed concepts, rather than a neatly organized and indexed structure of scientifically respectable categories. Second, our knowledge has to be organized in such a way as to allow for the insertion of new information and indices and the correction and emendation of existing information.

These implications in turn imply that our reasoning and learning processes have to be able to deal with flaws and gaps and shifting information from both within and without. Not only is our knowledge of the outside world often wrong, but our knowledge of our own knowledge is often inaccurate. In spite of this, we seem to able to reason quite well, certainly better in most situations than any AI model of reasoning. Failures do not stop us; we either work around them or learn from them.

It is this ability of ours, to deal with and grow from failure, that most intrigues many AI researchers. We will simply not be able to hand-program all the knowledge our AI programs are going to need. Even if some subset of technical knowledge could be incorporated into a useful system, that knowledge would become obsolete quite quickly. We see this in the real world, where the information explosion has called for the development of AI tools to help human experts who cannot keep up with the latest developments in their fields. An intelligent system, too, must be able to incorporate new knowledge in a natural way if it is not to become obsolete. Hence, there is a practical need for models of knowledge that are robust, flexible, and extensible.

KNOWLEDGE AND COGNITIVE PSYCHOLOGY

Unfortunately, we know very little about how humans organize, use, and acquire knowledge. For methodological reasons, cognitive psychology has for the most part avoided dealing directly with knowledge and its use. The need for limited testable hypotheses and reproducible experimental results led psychologists to devise theories and experiments that were content free, that is, independent of what the subjects in the experiments knew. Thus, most cognitive experiments studied basic properties of human cognition, such as short-term memory and abstract problem-solving abilities.

Some of the most obvious questions about human cognition, however, have to do with what we know, how we know it, and how we use that knowledge in everyday life. Everyday human experience does not involve novel, unrelated inputs. Most of what we do from day to day is embedded in a rich contextual background, rendering questionable the validity of low-knowledge experiments. Hence, many cognitive psychologists are trying to tackle exactly those situations where knowledge comes into play. The problems in doing this are no simpler than they were before, but the perceived importance of dealing with these issues has increased.

KNOWLEDGE VERSUS MEMORY

We like to call much of the work that deals with knowledge as a learned and evolving entity *memory based* rather than *knowledge based*. The distinction is fundamental, but easy to miss when we consider the data structures involved. A memory is something that remembers. A knowledge base is something that holds information. In their pure forms, a knowledge base is static, a repository of facts; whereas a memory is dynamic, a constantly growing trace of experience.

Most computer programs, including AI programs, are knowledge based. When they use their knowledge, that knowledge is not changed. Consider, however, how people normally use their knowledge. When they read a story, they apply what they know to that story, *and* they change what they know based on what is in the story. When they tackle a problem, they apply what they know to the problem, *and* they learn how to solve problems like that better. Using memory is itself an experience that is added to memory. You have to be very forgetful to solve the same difficult problem twice the same way without remembering something about the previous attempt. A story has to be pretty boring for you to read it a second time and not realize that there's something familiar about it.

In a memory-based model of cognition, learning is not an afterthought, an appendix to the knowledge application process. Rather, a memory-based model starts with memory change as the basic process. Instead of viewing understanding as a process that brings knowledge up from memory and applies it to a situation, we view understanding as a process of storing pieces of the situation in the relevant places in memory. The key question such a model is always asking itself is not "What knowledge applies to this situation?" but "Where should I store this experience?" or, in other terms, "How should I categorize this situation?" This approach means that knowledge representation is only part of what has to be resolved. Another key problem is knowledge indexing.

What do we mean by indexing? Consider our personal field guide that we use to understand the world with, and suppose that one section of it is devoted to wildflowers. A naïve model of using the guide to identify some unknown flower would be to look at the flower, list the features that it has, and look in the index for those features.

Anyone who has used a real field guide to flowers knows that the process is much more interactive than this. When you first try to use the guide, you look at the flower, note the color of the blossom and how big the plant is, and then you look for the section with plants of the same color. Unfortunately, you quickly discover that color is a terrible feature to index with because:

- There are too many plants with blossoms of the same color.
- There are too many plants with blossoms of several colors.
- People disagree as to what color something is, for example, is it a light violet or a bluish pink?

- The blossoms may have already faded or disappeared from the plant you want to identify.

Eventually you learn that it is much better to ask questions, such as how many stamens are there, how many petals, what shape are the leaves, do the leaves pair up or occur singly, is the stem downy or smooth, and so on. Different features are distinctive for different plants, and looking for those features leads to faster and surer identification than choosing such obvious but ambiguous features as color and size.

The key lesson from the previous paragraph is: *Different objects are distinctive in different ways.* Some plants have a very distinctive leaf shape, whereas others have a very special arrangement of petals and stamens. Where a novice would look at the purple blooms and run through the entire list of purple and red flowers in the field guide, an expert would note that the leaves all occurred in pairs and were heart shaped and would thereby correctly identify the plant even though the blossom might not be the normal color or even absent.

A good field guide, written by experts rather than novices, is organized at the top level according to the most common, visible features, such as color of blossoms, because they know that that is what novice users will look for first. After that, however, the guide focuses on the distinctive features for each plant, pointing out that the best way to recognize one flower is to note how the leaves pair up, whereas the best way to recognize another is to note the texture of the stem.

It seems reasonable to suppose that as we keep writing our own internal field guides to the world, we keep reorganizing our indices in much the same direction. That is, we keep re-indexing items as we discover what makes them unique. Clearly, when we first encounter some kind of object, we can only guess at which of its features are shared the least by other similar objects. As our experience grows, we learn that, perhaps, paired leaves and downy stems is fairly distinctive. We amaze our less experienced friends with the quick response, "See how the four petals form a cross? That must be in the mustard family."

Unfortunately, there is a bit of magic in all this that our cognitive models do not yet satisfactorily explain. If we have to know what the object is to know what distinctive features it has, then how can we use distinctive features to index the object? Intuition and everyday reaction times suggest that distinctive features are quickly apparent to the experienced observer, but no computer program currently has the same capability. The answer may lie in the parallel associative models of basic memory storage (Hinton & Anderson, 1981), but connecting these models to more standard inference systems is an unsolved research problem.

The models in this volume assume a less cognitively plausible, but more computationally tractable method of indexing. The method is called the discrimination tree (Charniak, Riesbeck, & McDermott, 1980; Quinlan, 1983). In essence, we always start with the same first question. Depending on the answer we get to that question, we ask another question. Depending on the second answer, we ask a third question, and so on until finally enough questions have been answered for us to determine what it is we think we are looking at.

In this kind of model, page 1 of the index to our field guide might look like this:

Is this a physical object?
    Yes 2
    No 86

Answering yes means we should turn to page 2 of the index, where we see:

Color
    Red 3
    Blue 5

On page 3, we have:

Taste
    Sweet 4
    Tomato . . . . . . It's a tomato

On page 4, we have:

Size
    Small . . . . It's a cherry
    Medium . . . . It's an apple

On Page 5, we have:

Shape
    Round 6
    Square 7

On page 7, we have:

Texture
    Hard 8
    Soft . . . . It's my childhood security blanket

And so on. Notice that we have different questions for red and blue things.

Suppose we encounter some object and want to identify it. Using the guide, we first ask if it is a physical object. If it is, we ask what color it is. If it is blue, we ask what shape it has. If it is soft, we are reminded of the blue blanket we used to curl up with when we were young. It was not just a blue square. It was fuzzy, warm, tasted like dust, was normally stashed under the bed, and so on. We look at the object we have again. Is it warm and fuzzy, too? What does it taste like? We ask these questions, not because they are in the index, but because we are now trying to see what differences, if any, there are between what we remember and what we have in hand. If it turns out that there are differences, then we want to take these differences and add them to the index. For example, if the object in hand is not fuzzy, we might change page 7 to read:

Texture

    Hard 8
    Soft 9

and write on page 9:

Is it fuzzy?

    Yes—. . . . . It's my childhood security blanket
    No . . . . It's this thing I had in my hand

Though this example is not a serious memory proposal, it demonstrates several aspects of the indexing issue.

- The stored memory is richer than the set of indices pointing to it; the blanket has features beyond those currently being used to index it.
- What we look for is influenced by what the index says to look for.
- Indexing is based on classification; different features are attended to based on which class the object is put into.
- A new index is based on the existing set of indices and is chosen to distinguish the input from whatever our indices have retrieved.

This is an EPAM-like model of learning (Feigenbaum, 1963), which has been applied in recent years to models of event memory by Kolodner, (1983) and Lebowitz (1980), criticized by Barsalou and Bower (1984), and defended by Feigenbaum and Simon (1984). Modifications to it to make it more reasonable for organizing long-term memory include: (a) discrimination removing strategies, to prune discriminations that turn out to be irrelevant; (b) generalization strategies, to chunk together events sharing several distinctive features; and (c) multiple-indexing strategies, to offer more than one path to various items.

PROBLEM SOLVING IN MEMORY

The field guide metaphor has served us well so far, but it has one major failing as a metaphor for memory: a field guide tells only what something is, but memory also tells us what to do. That is, we should really think of our personal notebooks not as simple field guides to the world, but as survival manuals, with a healthy dose of etiquette instructions. Our guide has to tell us things like "Don't eat those red berries," "Say 'Thank you' when Uncle Bill gives you a dime," "If at first you don't succeed, try, try again," and "If something looks green and tastes bad, file it under 'Spinach'." The last instruction is one of the most interesting because it manipulates the structure of memory itself. A fascinating question is what kind of rules are there for learning rules?

Finally, the guide book metaphor emphasizes the functional characteristics of memory. It points out what memory has to do. It does not, however, address questions such as what does memory really look like? One of the goals of the cognitive psychologists represented in this volume is to get a handle on what particular kinds of indices people use, how knowledge is chunked together, and so on. One of the goals of the AI people is to produce data structures and algorithms that can feasibly carry out the kinds of functions we have described.

BASIC QUESTIONS

We are still a long way from working models of memory-based reasoning. At best, our AI programs can explain how a particular experience can lead to new understanding, but none of them can support the repeated cycle of experience and learning that people do. The efforts described in this volume are laying the groundwork for memory-based reasoning, by addressing the fundamental questions:

- How is memory organized?
- How are new memories acquired?
- How are memories applied to new situations?

Aspects of these issues are addressed throughout this volume. More details about each chapter are provided in the prefatory material to each section, but we give some rough pointers here.

How is Memory Organized?

Much of the work in this volume arose from the Memory Organization Packet (MOP) theory presented in Schank (1982). This is a hierarchically organized, frame-structured model of knowledge organization, with a central emphasis on the issues of how knowledge is indexed and extended. Relevant aspects of this theory are presented in the chapters by Kolodner, Lytinen, Reiser and Riesbeck.

Three chapters directly attack the structure of memory issue and offer solutions to three complementary concerns. For Chandrasekaran, the question is "How does the task we ask memory to do affect its structure?" For Granger, "How can memory structure be made neurobiologically sound?" For Wilensky, "How can functional adequacy be achieved in a knowledge representation scheme?"

How are New Memories Acquired?

One of the key points of Schank (1982) was that learning is not a special addendum to memory processing, but integral to it. Reasoning and learning go hand in hand, because the formation of hypotheses and explanations is a learning process just as much as it is a reasoning process. The formation of hypotheses and explanations is of central concern in Kolodner, Rissland, Schank, and Shrager. Again, the use of case-based reasoning forms the core of much of this work.

How Are Memories Applied to New Situations?

The use of memory structures breaks down into a number of subquestions. One of the most critical is the indexing issue. How do we find the information we need when we need it? Following on exploratory work by Kolodner (1984), Reiser has done some of the most in-depth research yet on how people retrieve information from very long-term memory.

Another important issue is reasoning. How do we use memory structures to solve problems and derive conclusions? These questions are addressed by Bain, Kolodner and Rissland. The central idea here is *case-based reasoning,* which is offered as an alternative to the *rule-based reasoning* approach found in modern expert systems. Rule-based reasoning requires that knowledge be in the form of "if—then" rules in order to be applied. Case-based reasoning uses knowledge stored as traces of previous problem-solving experiences. If—and this is the hard part—we can solve the indexing problem for memory structures, then case-based reasoning offers a model of reasoning that is highly compatible with our models of dynamic memory and very amenable to understanding how we learn from experience.

Natural language understanding has been a touchstone for modern AI research. Hence, another issue is how memory is used in understanding text. This is the topic of the chapters by Granger, Lebowitz, Lytinen, and Riesbeck. Although Granger and Riesbeck differ from previous conceptual analyzers in their use of parallel processes and marker passing, the ties between Lytinen and Riesbeck are very strong.

ORGANIZATION OF THE BOOK

The book is organized into three subsections. The first, about memory and knowledge representation, includes chapters that address representational issues. Reiser's chapter, the last in that section, introduces the MOPs concept and tells about experimentation regarding the organization of experience in people. The second section, on memory-based hypothesis formation, has five explorations of the use of experience in making decisions. Issues of problem solving and learning are discussed in that section. The last section, on memory-based natural language understanding, includes four chapters addressing the relationship between experience and understanding.

Work on experiential memory and reasoning is one of the fastest changing areas in cognitive science, with new insights and new questions arising daily. What this volume contains is a snapshot of research in progress, blurred no doubt by the speed with which everyone is moving. In fact, it is probably best to view this book as the first chapter in a cliffhanger serial, with many episodes yet to come.

REFERENCES

Barsalou, L. W., & Bower, G. H. (1984). Discrimination nets as psychological models. *Cognitive Science, 8*(1), 1–26.

Charniak, F., Riesbeck, C. K., & McDermott, D. (1980). *Artificial intelligence programming techniques.* Hillsdale, NJ: Lawrence Erlbaum Associates.

Feigenbaum, E. A. (1963). The simulation of verbal learning behavior. *Computers and thought.* New York: McGraw-Hill.

Feigenbaum, E. A., & Simon, H. A. (1984). EPAM-like models of recognition and learning. *Cognitive Science, 8*,(43), 305–336.

Hinton, G. E., & Anderson, J. A. (1981). *Parallel models of associative memory.* Hillsdale, NJ: Lawrence Erlbaum Associates.

Kolodner, J. L. (1983). Reconstructive memory: A computer model. *Cognitive Science, 7*(4), 281–328.

Kolodner, J. L. (1984). *Retrieval and organizational strategies in conceptual memory.* Hillsdale, NJ: Lawrence Erlbaum Associates.

Lebowitz, M. (1980, October). *Generalization and memory in an integrated understanding system* (Research Rep. No. 186). Unpublished doctoral dissertation, Yale University, Cambridge, MA.

Quinlan, J. R. (1983). Learning efficient classification procedures and their application to chess endgames. In R. Michalski, J. Carbonell, & T. Mitchell (Eds.), *Machine learning.* Palo Alto, CA: Tioga Press.

Schank, R. C. (1982). *Dynamic memory: A theory of learning in computers and people.* New York: Cambridge University Press.

KNOWLEDGE ORGANIZATION AND REPRESENTATION

The history of AI is rife with attempts to develop knowledge representation schemes. Semantic networks, frames, and if–then rules are typical of structural formalisms that have been developed; conceptual dependency and scripts are typical of content-oriented approaches. There are several deficiencies in all the existing approaches to knowledge representation when we consider it in support of memory-based processing. First are the twin issues of *knowledge indexing* and *memory search*. How can the right chunk of knowledge be found at the right time without irrelevant pieces of knowledge getting in the way? Next is the issue of acquisition of an appropriate *knowledge organization*. How can an organization for knowledge be built up over time and with experience? Related to that, we must also ask whether any one representation is appropriate or if experience using the same knowledge to perform several different tasks may make it more appropriate to represent that knowledge in several different ways, each amenable to a different type of processing. We must also consider the representation of events, the basis for experiential reasoning processes and case-based reasoning. How can they be represented in a uniform and canonical way? The chapters in this section address these problems.

Wilensky begins by asking what a representation needs in order to be functionally adequate. In conceptual dependency (Schank, 1975), for example, semantic primitives have been singled out as different from other concepts. Wilensky asks whether they are different, decides they are not, and proposes a uniform way of representing concepts in particular events. In looking at frames, he notices that there are no constraints on what can be slots and often no good definitions within the frame system of what any particular slot "means." Based on these critiques, he proposes a representational system in which the "links" between concepts are restricted to a small set of primitive relationships and in which any concept used for representation (including the equivalent of slot-names) must be previously defined. He presents the KODIAK system as an implementation of his ideas.

While Wilensky's assumption is that one uniform and canonical representation system can be found that is adequate for reasoning, Chandrasekaran's basic assumption is that the representation should suit the task. He proposes that the same knowledge is encoded in memory in several ways, depending on whether it is to be used for deep or shallow reasoning. Shallow reasoning, according to Chandrasekaran means the reasoning that can be done on the basis of "compiled" knowledge, similar to the if–then rules of expert systems. In familiar situations, compiled knowledge allows a solution to a problem to be found very quickly, but when the situation becomes novel (e.g., something goes wrong or unfamiliar features manifest themselves), more in-depth reasoning ("deep" reasoning) using causal knowledge is necessary. He therefore looks at how knowledge can be reorganized and re-represented based on the task. In particular, he looks at how "device descriptions" used in deep reasoning about novel situations (e.g., trouble shooting) can be compiled into if–then rules to be used in well-known or familiar diagnostic situations. The device descriptions also serve as explanations for the compiled knowledge, allowing reasoning about hypothetical situations when necessary.

The other two chapters in this section are concerned primarily with knowledge organization and indexing issues. Granger's concern is with creating a neurobiologically sound model of memory. By studying the neurobiology literature, he has been able to propose a set of primitive memory operations that allow acquisition, storage, and retrieval of simple episodic information. His operators allow focus to be directed to appropriate parts of an input, indexing of events as they are being experienced, recall and reconstruction of previous experiences, and creation and refinement of episodic schemata. His computer program, CEL-O, uses these operations in a maze-learning environment and exhibits learning activity as it gains experience walking through in the maze. By comparing the behavior of his model to experimental results found in the neurobiology literature, and by tuning his operators appropriately, his long-term goal is to explain many of the low level memory operations that allow us to learn from experience.

Reiser's chapter explores the strategic searching of memory that people do. After presenting the context-plus-index model of memory organization based on MOPS, (Schank, 1982; Kolodner, 1984), Reiser argues that much of what the memory search people do is directed by features of the retrieval cues. Although indexing of a new experience in memory and recognition of a familiar stimulus may be low level automatic processes, Reiser points out that much of the remembering people do requires strategic processing. He gives several explanations of why strategic processing is necessary and presents the results of a set of experiments that support his claims.

Reiser's and Granger's presentations pull many parts of this book together. If knowledge is acquired as a result of experience, and if previous experiences are the basis for understanding, problem solving, and hypothesis generation, then we need a good explanation of the processes involved in memory access. Kolodner's (1984) model of event memory and Schank's (1982) MOPS provide the start of such an explanation. Granger's endeavor explores low level automatic processing of experience. Reiser explores the strategic components of remembering and presents experimental results supporting his hypotheses.

REFERENCES

Kolodner, J. I.. (1984). *Retrieval and organizational strategies in conceptual memory.* Hillsdale, NJ: Lawrence Erlbaum Associates.
Schank, R. C. (1982). *Dynamic memory: A theory of learning in computers and people.* New York: Cambridge University Press.

2 Knowledge Representation—A Critique and A Proposal

Robert Wilensky
Computer Science Division
University of California, Berkeley

ABSTRACT

We criticize the Conceptual Dependency meaning representation theory for its weakness in dealing with higher level objects, and frame-based systems in general for the inadequate treatment of slots as concepts. We present a new theory of representation, called KODIAK, where slots are full-fledged concepts, and the following epistemological relationships exist: a frame MANIFESTs a slot, a general concept DOMINATEs a specific concept, an instance INSTANTIATEs a concept, a concept can be VIEWed as another with respect to a context, a concept can be defined by a GENERIC-INDIVIDUAL concept, and a concept can be EQUATEd with a coreferential concept.

INTRODUCTION

In this chapter I present some observations about the knowledge representation systems now in common use. To some extent these observations are critiques of these systems. I believe that these critiques are self-acknowledging in that the problems they describe have already made themselves known to the users of these various notations. My purpose here is to bring these problems more out into the open and to recognize their greater implications. Doing so leads to a rather different view of representation.

In reaction to these problems, a new theory of representation is proposed. The theory attempts to encompass representational ideas that have emerged from different schools of thought, in particular from work in semantic networks, frames, frame semantics, and conceptual dependency. The theory has a number of salient characteristics: it promotes a proliferation of concepts, each represented as a distinct entity. In addition, the theory is uniform with respect to different conceptual domains. These features are in opposition to an approach in which an effort is made to keep the number of concepts small and in which different conceptual domains are treated by different representational systems. Nevertheless, the theory still meets certain desiderata for a meaning representation. In particular, it does not support the ambiguities present in natural language, it has canonical form, and it is useful as a memory organization device.

Furthermore, the theory eliminates the frame/slot distinction found in frame-based languages (alternatively, case/slot distinction found in semantic network-based systems). In its place is a new notion called the *absolute/aspectual* distinction. As I attempt to demonstrate, the new theory allows for the representation of some ideas that in the past have only been represented procedurally, informally, or not at all.

THE PROBLEM WITH CONCEPTUAL DEPENDENCY

Conceptual dependency (Schank, 1975) offers semantic primitives, concepts that take "cases" based on primitives, and complex conceptualizations composed of combinations of a small set of primitive concepts. The system is concerned largely with representations for actions. Aside from its pithiness, the purported advantages of the system are efficiency of inference, canonical form, and cognitive plausibility, among others.

The problem presented here is what might be called the need for higher level objects. By this I mean that, even if the meaning of a complex notion can be represented in terms of a simpler ones, the need for a higher level entity persists. Unfortunately, conceptual dependency does not accommodate this need.

This problem can be illustrated in a number of ways. For example, consider the claim that the CD reduces the inference problem by allowing inferences to be organized around conceptual primitives. An example from Rieger (1975) involves the specification inference, that is, the filling in of an unfilled case slot through a primitive-related inference routine. This example presumes the usual conceptual dependency analysis of *buy* as two ATRANS conceptualizations that are in a "mutual causation" relation to one another. Then the representation of "John bought a cake mix," has several unfilled case slots in the underlying ATRANS, in particular, one for the party who sold John the cake mix. The ATRANS specification inference moleucle then proceeds to fill in this slot with the representation of a default filler, in this case, the representation of a grocery store.

The problem is that the inference cannot properly be made by an ATRANS routine. There is, in fact, nothing about the idea of ATRANS, that, is of transferring some abstract quality, that rightly suggests who might have transferred a cake mix to someone else. This is the case because the knowledge required is not knowledge about transferring per se. More properly, it is knowledge about transferring something to someone in exchange for money—it is a fact about *buying*.

To encode this fact properly, we need to associate it with a pattern that looks like the entire representation for *buy*, rather than with any underlying ATRANS primitive. In general, the system requires many such assertions that treat this pattern as an entity in its own right. In effect, the system must presuppose a BUY concept, even if it supports an interpretation of such a concept in terms of an underlying decomposition.

In effect, the only real difference between ATRANS and BUY, as far as CD is concerned, is that the former is explicitly acknowledged by the presence of a LISP atom, whereas the latter is not. However, the way in which they both must be manipulated by the system does not justify this distinction.

Another way to convey this problem is to consider the existence of what I call "unmotivated levels." For example, in CD, *threaten* is not considered to be an action (presumably because it is complex) and is not represented as an object within CD. Instead, it is given the status of a plan on a "knowledge structure level" of representation.

Observe first that an entity that went away on the CD level reappears as an entity on another level. This is as it should be, because, as I have suggested, the explicit acknowledgement of these concepts is eventually necessary. However, there appears to be no good reason to propose two separate levels of representation. This must be done here only because CD is unable to digest such a large concept. In fact, this inability has apparently led to a serious error: The difference between *threaten* and simpler actions, for example, *tell,* is not that one is a plan and the other an action. "John threatened to kill Bill" describes an action just as assuredly as "John told Bill he went home." In addition, intending to tell someone something may be a plan to have that person know something, just as assuredly as threatening someone may be a plan for a less benign goal.

In sum, it makes no sense to classify *threaten* as anything other than an action. It differs from CD actions only in its complexity, not in its epistemological status.

The evidence for the lack of motivation of levels increases as additional levels are considered. For example, scripts are complex forms presumably on a knowledge structure level. However, if one looks at how references to scripts are made in actual systems (e.g., Cullingford, 1978), one usually sees "John ate at a restaurant" represented as something like:

($REST (CUSTOMER JOHN1) (RESTAURANT RES1))

Here the predicate position is occupied by an object that references the restaurant script. However, this is just like a CD form, taking roles for the customer and the restaurant instead of actor and object. The problem here is, if it is all right to use the above representation when talking about eating at a restaurant, then why not say

(BUY (SELLER . . .) (BUYER . . .))

when representing an individual buying event? As I have been suggesting, there is no reason not to do so, other than the otherwise unmotivated claim that these are on different levels.

It is possible to cite many other such cases. However, they each point to the same conclusion. CD tries to do without many conceptual categories, only to find them creeping in through the back door. By not acknowledging this need, however, unmotivated nonuniformity is created where a uniform theory is possible and desirable.

THE PROBLEM WITH FRAMES

Semantic networks, frames, and predicate calculus are candidates for a general, uniform formalism. Predicate calculus is usually thought to be too general to be a theory of representation and in any case is not expressive enough. Most important, it is not usually proposed as a theory that has cognitive plausibility, which is of interest here.

This leaves us with semantic networks and frames. However, the former does not usually meet important constraints on meaning representations (e.g., canonical form). Even according to their advocates (e.g., Woods, 1975; Brachman, 1979), the interpretation of most semantic network formalisms is at best capricious. We are therefore left with frames.

However, many of the criticisms that apply to semantic networks apply to frame-based systems as well. After all, if we add defaults and procedural attachment to semantic networks, it is difficult to differentiate them from a collection of frames. In any case, there are a number of serious problems with both. In particular, as these formalisms are normally interpreted, they would not appear to meet the criteria for a meaning representation. Some of the more important criticisms are given later. These criticisms apply equally to semantic networks, although I speak in terms of frames here.

Problem 1: The Meaning of a Slot is Completely Unconstrained.   Despite the apparent usefulness of frames, what it means to be a slot in a frame is just as ill-defined as what it means to be a link in a network.[1] In particular, the meaning of a slot appears only procedurally, if at all. For example, if we fill the Address slot for some Person with "393 Foxon Road," this presumably means that that person's place of residence is at the location so designated. However, filling in the Name slot with "John Smith" means that the person is called by this name. Unfortunately, this difference in meaning appears only in the way various routines happen to manipulate those slots, that is, it is encoded procedurally, and therefore outside of the formal system of representation.

---

[1]Charniak, Riesbeck, and McDermott (1980) talk about frame systems as "form languages." This nomenclature suggests, I think correctly, that the formalism is more of a form to collect knowledge than a representation of that knowledge.

Problem 2: What May be a Slot in a Frame is Completely Uncon-strained. There also appears to be no "in principle" answer to the question of which frames can support which slots. For example, if we allow Age to be a slot in Person, and Father (to be filled by the Person's father) to be a slot in Person, could we allow Father's Age to be a slot? How about Person's best friends between the ages of 25 and 35? Regardless of our own intuitions, the frame languages do not distinguish the suitability of one from another.

In actual practice, frame systems users appear to represent such knowledge outside the frame system. For example, "best friends between the ages of 25 and 35" might be represented as a conjunction in a predicate calculus-like formalism. The problem with this is that now there are two systems of representation. We have no way to decide what would be represented in which, or what it would mean to represent it one way rather than the other.

Problem 3: Many Concepts Do Not Get Defined.   Most important, what we have been calling slots seem to be perfectly good concepts in their own right. These concepts are not only undefined, they tend to be completely unrecognized in frame systems. For example, *age* has a perfectly well-defined meaning (in fact, more than does "person"). Namely, the Age slot implicitly refers to a concept that is the amount of time since the creation of an object to some other moment in time. Similarly, *address* is a "referring object" for a building; *name* is a "referring object" for a person.

In sum, frame systems allow us a multiplicity of objects but seem to lose some basic criteria of a meaning representation in the process. In particular, they tend to divide the world into frames and slots. Slots do not have true concept status, but they do appear to be full-fledged concepts. Frame systems neither recognize this fact nor allow for the expression of the meaning of these items.

KODIAK

KODIAK (Keystone to Overall Design for Integration and Application of Knowledge) is a knowledge representation language being developed at the Berkeley Artificial Intelligence Research Project. KODIAK is an attempt to redress the grievances just enumerated. The basic idea behind KODIAK is to allow for the multipicity of concepts required by any system, without abandoning the criteria for a meaning representation usually not adhered to by frame-based systems or semantic networks.

We view KODIAK as an extention of frames. However, the system is actually no more frame-like than it is semantic-network-like. This also appears to be the case for the more advanced semantic-network derived languages, such as KL-ONE.

Like KL-ONE, the primary structure of KODIAK is the *Concept*. However, there is no notion of role, slot, or case. Instead, the idea of having a slot or role is replaced by a set of primitive epistemological relations. This relation is called MANIFEST. A concept is in a MANIFEST relation to another Concept when, intuitively, the first Concept "has" the second Concept as a property. For example, if we want to indicate that physical objects have ages, we could assert that the Concept Physical-Object MANIFESTs the Age Concept.[2] Furthermore, once the MANIFEST relation has been asserted to exist between two Concepts, a new relation comes into existence. This relation lets us assert that particular kinds (or instances) of one Concept can MANIFEST particular kinds (or instances) of the other. If *Concept1* MANIFESTs *Concept2*, say, then we name this relationship "*Concept2-of-Concept1*." We call such a relationship an *aspectual*. In contrast, we call all other Concepts, such as Age and Physical-Object, *absolutes*.

For example, if we assert that Physical-Object MANIFESTs Age, then the aspectual relation Age-of-Physical-Object comes into existence. We can use this relation to assert the age of some particular physical object, among other things.

The intuition behind the idea of aspectuals is to capture the dual use of terms like *name* and *color*. When we talk of the *name of* someone or the *color of* an object, the claim is, we are referring to color as an aspectual (more properly, we are referring to the Color-of-Physical-Object aspectual). When we say "red is a color," we are talking about both *Color* and *Red* as Conceptual categories. Similarly, *Age* is the Concept of age, but Age-of-Physical-Object is the *age* implicitly referred to in "John is twelve years old."

In effect, we have split the idea of slot into several parts. One is the idea that a frame can have a slot of a certain type (this is expressed by the MANIFEST assertion); another is the Concept that is the slot (this is represented as another, in principle independent, Concept); finally, there is the fact that particulars or subtypes of the frame and MANIFESTed Concept can be in a relation of this sort to one another (this is enabled by the semantics of MANIFEST, and expressed by a particular derivative aspectual relation assertion).

It is awkward to talk about the assertion of a relation between two Concepts. Therefore, I shall loosely refer to such an assertion as a link, and depict it graphically as such.

The advantage of this formulation is that we can provide explicit definitions for and assertions about Concepts such as Age. In a traditional frame based system, such Concepts could not be predicated about explicitly.

For example, we would like to assert that the Concept Age is the difference between the creation time of an object and some other time (usually Now). To do so, we need to introduce some additional epistemological relations.

---

[2]Of course, we may want to assert this fact about some category more general than Physical-Object, so it would be meaningful to talk about the age of an idea, for example. In this paper, I am not concerned about the correctness any such assertion. Instead, I use categories that are familiar rather than those that may be technically necessary to describe properly a conception of the world.

PRIMITIVE EPISTEMOLOGICAL RELATIONS

In KODIAK, the following set of epistemological relations is supposed:

MANIFEST

The semantics of MANIFEST is described above. We indicate this relation graphically by a directed arrow labelled μ. Formally (i.e., in nonpictorial language) we indicate this by the form (MANIFEST *Concept Property-Concept*). For example, to indicate that a Physical-Object has an Age and a Color, we can draw the following:

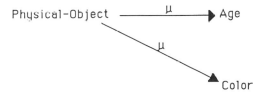

Similar, we can indicate that an Action has an Actor:

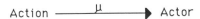

These examples illustrate several different kinds of MANIFESTation. Maida (1984) has suggested that Concepts like Action MANIFEST Actor *definitionally* (i.e., the Concept Actor is defined in terms of the Concept Action), whereas Concepts like Physical-Object MANIFEST Color *assertionally* (i.e., this asserts a true but nondefinitional fact about the world). In addition, we suggest that Physical-Object MANIFESTs Age *derivatively* (i.e., the definition of Age entails this particular MANIFEST relation). See Maida for a further exploration of these ideas.

DOMINATE

This is a structured inheritance relation between Concepts. Its semantics is essentially ISA. We indicate it graphically by a link labelled "D" and formally by an expression of the form (DOMINATE *general-concept specific-concept*).

To indicate the relations between the parts of one Concept and those of a Concept that DOMINATEs it, we use an informal relation called *role-play*. For technical reasons, this relation is implemented in terms of another, so it is not a true relation of the system. Nevertheless, it is convenient for expositional purposes.

As an example, we propose that there exists a type of Event called Causal, which MANIFESTs a Cause and an Effect. If we accept the interpretation that Kill means "cause to die," this can be represented by specifying a Concept Kill

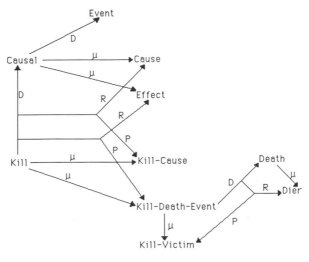

FIG. 2.1.

which MANIFESTs, among other things, a Kill-Victim and a Kill-Death-Event. The latter Concept is represented as meaning that the Kill-Victim died. We want to establish the meaning of Kill now by saying, intuitively, that Kill-Death-Event plays the role of the Cause, when Kill is viewed as a Causal event.

Rather than introduce an explicit role-play relation, however, we take advantage of the fact that the MANIFEST relations between Causal and Effect give rise to an aspectual. In particular, it creates the aspectual Effect-of-Causal. We can then represent the role-play relation simply by asserting that an instance of this aspectual holds between Kill and Kill-Death-Event, that is by asserting (Effect-of-Causal *Kill Kill-Death-Event*). This is shown graphically in Fig. 2.1.

First, note that the terms in Fig. 2.1 refer to the actual Concepts. For example, the term Cause refers to the idea of cause, and the term Effect to the idea of effect. These are not meaningless placeholders in a form.

Second, much has been omitted from this diagram, for example, the semantics of Cause, Effect and Death. These are, of course, a crucial part of the overall system, and are omitted here for simplicity's sake.

Third, note that some Concepts, for example, Kill-Cause, have no additional semantics associated with them. That is, this is an empty *Concept*. Kill could have inherited the general Cause from Causal, so in this case the new name is not strictly necessary. However, it would become necessary if we wanted to make an assertion about the Cause of a Kill event. In contrast, the Concept Kill-Death-Event has an explicit definition as a kind of Death event.

INSTANTIATE

This relation holds when one Concept is to be considered as an instance of another. Its depiction is similar to that for DOMINATE. For example, the fact

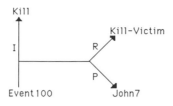

FIG. 2.2.

that some Concept represents an individual human being would be represented by an INSTANTIATE link between that Concept and the Concept Person. Similarly, a particular killing event would be represented by an INSTANTIATE link between the particular event Concept and the Concept Kill.

Like DOMINATE, INSTANTIATE allows for role-play relations between the respective MANIFESTed Concepts. For example, to represent the event in which John was killed, we create a new Concept. We call this Concept Event100, to suggest mnemonically that it is an event, and to indicate that such Concepts are rather numerous. Similarly, John7 denotes the Concept of the person named John. Figure 2.2 indicates that Event100 INSTANTIATEs Kill, and that John7 plays the role of the Kill-Victim: Again, the representation shown is abbreviated. For example, the link between John7 and Person is not shown, nor is the information that the first name of John7 is John.

Note that in KODIAK, there is no such thing as an individual per se. Rather, the notion of an individual is meaningful only with respect to another concept. For example, all the rather general category concepts mentioned earlier may be individuals of other categories. For example, they could all be individuals of the Concept Category, should we introduce such a term in the system. The properties of some individuals that usually lead to typing objects "individual" or "generic," as in KL-ONE, are here considered to be peculiar properties of physical objects rather than something intrinsic to individuals.

As a further example, consider the *War and Peace* problem. The book *War and Peace* is an individual of the Concept Book. However, the particular copy of *War and Peace* sitting on my shelf appears to be in the same relationship to the Concept *War and Peace* as that Concept is to the Concept Book. This situation can be represented in KODIAK by asserting that the Concept *War and Peace* INSTANTIATEs the Concept Book, and that the particular copy of a book INSTANTIATEs the Concept *War and Peace*.

VIEW

An important aspect of the theory underlying KODIAK is that conceptual structure is not monolithic or static. In particular, we want to be able to talk about viewing one Concept in terms of another. This idea was first suggested as a representational technique in KRL (Bobrow & Winograd, 1977). KRL does not admit to a notion of definition, and treats all perspectives as equally valid. We do not adopt this extreme position, but want to allow the flexibility of viewing a

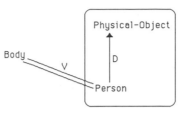

FIG. 2.3.

(possibly defined) Concept as something other than its "ordinary" interpretation.

For example, it is desirable to realize that a person can have properties, such as weight and color, that are generally considered to be general properties of all physical objects. In most representational schemes, to capitalize on this knowledge about physical objects, it is necessary to assert that persons are a kind of physical object. This is peculiar, because such a view of people is at odds with a normal working distinction between people and physical objects.

In KODIAK, we resolve this problem by introducing the relation VIEW. The idea is that one Concept can be viewed as another. In addition, this view of one Concept as another is itself a Concept. For example, in KODIAK, we can assert that Person is DOMINATEd by Living-Thing, or some such Concept. In addition, we also assert that it is possible to VIEW a Person as a Physical-Object. Moreover, the VIEW of Person as a Physical-Object is itself another Concept, namely, the Concept Body.

VIEW is more complicated than the other relations we have seen. This is the case because the VIEW of one object as another may entail a *context*. A context here is a set of KODIAK assertions that are not normally considered to be true, but which are considered to be the case when a particular viewpoint is taken. In general, a context will contain one assertion stating what other concept the given concept is a view of; it may contain other assertions that describe the relations between MANIFESTed Concepts and the like. We depict this graphically with a circle around the context. In the simplest case, we may have something like Fig. 2.3. In Fig. 2.3 the context is simply the assertion that Person is DOMINATEd by Physical-Object.

Formally, we can say that (VIEW *concept viewed-as-concept view-context*), meaning that *concept* is *viewed-as-concept* in the context *view-context*. The last is simply a collection of KODIAK assertions.

As the *viewed-as-concept* may have aspectuals we want to talk about, the context may contain role-play relations as well. For example, consider the application of VIEW to some of the notions that arise in frame semantics (Fillmore, 1982; Fillmore & Kay, 1983; Kay, 1983). In this system, some concepts are defined in reference to a background frame. For example, *buying* and *selling* are defined in reference to the frame for "commercial transaction." We can represent this with VIEW in Fig. 2.4. *Buy* is defined similarly.

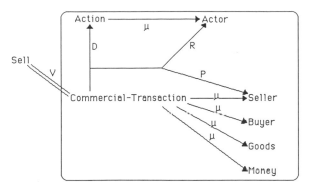

FIG. 2.4.

GENERIC-INDIVIDUAL

This relation is used to define a Concept that acts as an exemplar of another
Concept. Properties that are typically true of a Concept but not strictly necessary
may be asserted about a Concept that is in a GENERIC-INDIVIDUAL relation to
another Concept. Information about prototypes can be accommodated in this
manner. GENERIC-INDIVIDUAL is similar to the *TYPE feature of Fahlman's
(1979) NETL system.

EQUATE

This relation is used to show that two descriptions are coreferential. We shall not
elaborate on its use here.

EXAMPLES

Age

As mentioned earlier, a strong motivation for KODIAK was to be able to represent the semantics of concepts like *age*. Given the foregoing relations, we can
define an Age Concept that is the difference between the creation of a thing and
some other time, as Fig. 2.5 illustrates. In Fig. 2.5, Age is represented as a
Difference-Result of the Difference between Creation-Time and a reference
point. Creation-Time is further defined, although the representations of Object-
Exist and other are abbreviated.

Action

In KODIAK, an Action is just another type of Causal-Event. In particular, it is
the class of such events where the Cause is the Actor willing some intended state.
We represent the general idea of action in Fig. 2.6. Here we neglect to represent
that the Concept Will is a kind of Mental-State.

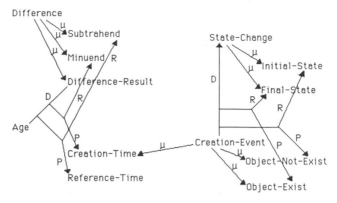

FIG. 2.5.

ADVANTAGES OF THE PROPOSAL

Greater Representational Scope

Most of the power of KODIAK comes from its being an object-oriented system. KODIAK is not unique in this respect; it just tends to provide more objects than other systems do. For example, slots are objects in KODIAK, as is the fact that some Concept has a "slot." So, not only can we define the concepts implicit in slot names, but we can assert information about the kind of *slot,* for example, whether a given Concept can MANIFEST only one such relation, or several.

Uniformity with Canonical Form

KODIAK is rather uniform, making fewer unmotivated and unnecessary distinctions between kinds of concepts, levels of representation, and so forth. This is true not just in comparison with systems like CD, but in contrast to more uniform formalisms like semantic networks, FRAIL and KL-ONE. However, unlike some of these systems, KODIAK supports some basic notions, such as canonical form.

Undefined and Partially Defined Concepts

Although some concepts do have definitions, many apparently do not. For example, the concept *Jew* has many aspects that we know to be true about it, but it is not clear which if any of these are definitional. One may argue that there is a formal definition, that is, a Jew is someone whose mother is a Jew. But this fact is not known to everyone who has a functional use of the concept and therefore seems to be beside the point. Furthermore, we have the classic example of Putnam, who claims that ordinary folk have a functional knowledge of the concept gold, but must appeal to some expert, who really knows what gold is, to determine if some item is truly gold or not. In addition, it has been claimed that

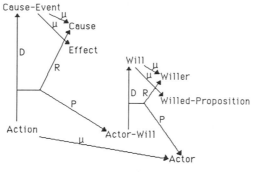

FIG. 2.6.

most natural kind concepts have no definitional information predicated about them. Instead, they are clusters of generally true information.

While KODIAK supports concepts with real definitions, its object-orientation permits concepts that have none. For example, natural concepts can be represented by definitionless objects that have many assertions about their "generic-individual." In fact, any degree of definition is allowable.

Processing Appeal

KODIAK allows for a full and deep meaning representation but, at the same time, has the property that simple linguistic forms (i.e., those that seem to be easily understood) can be easily represented. For example, to represent that "Bill was killed," we need only create a new symbol designating the particular event, a new symbol designating the person, and then grow the appropriate links. To represent "John killed Bill," we could add further links indicating that the symbol designating the new event is also an Action, with the symbol designating "John" being the Actor.

Now, if we wished to represent "John killed Bill intentionally," we would first have to have represented the Concept Intended-Action. This could be represented as a kind of Action in which the Actor Willing something is the actual Cause of that thing. Then the representation of the sentence just entails an additional link to this Concept.

The advantage here is that we capture the full semantics of these sentences, but do not require processing that seems out of line with the ease with which these sentences can be understood.

PROBLEMS AND COMMENTS

An outstanding feature of KODIAK is the proliferation of concepts. Rather than a small set of semantic notions from which all meaning is derived, there will end up being many more concepts in KODIAK than there are words of a given language. This does not appear to be problematic, because, as was argued earlier, more reductionistic systems seem to end up with such concepts one way or another. What we have provided is a uniform means to represent these notions, independent of their particular semantic concept.

There are many details to be worked out in the current system. We have not yet determined how best to assert information about aspectuals. For example, we may want to talk about a MANIFEST relation as being "one-many," or as being transitive, meaning the *Concept* MANIFESTs another, which truly MANIFESTs the one in question.

We are attempting to do without any notion of a variable, and hope that quantification can be accommodated by assertions about general categories. We hope that this will reflect commonsense scoping capability. But we do not yet fully understand the consequences of this assumption.

There is also an organizational notion of association present in KODIAK. I believe that the relation between representational and indexing issues is rather intimate, but this is not reflected in the current system.

In general, these issues appear to be problematic for KODIAK are also problematic for all systems. We are hopeful that the framework established in KODIAK will be able to accomodate solutions to these problems without radical changes, although we have not had enough experience with the system to support such a claim.

REFERENCES

Bobrow, D. G., & Winograd, T. (1977). An overview of KRL, a knowledge representation language. *Cognitive Science, 1* (1), 3–46.

Brachman, R. J. (1979). On the epistemological status of semantic networks. In N. V. Findler (Ed.), *Associative networks: Representation and use of knowledge by computers.* New York: Academic Press.

Charniak, E., Riesbeck, C. K., & McDermott, D. (1980). *Artificial intelligence programming techniques.* Hillsdale, NJ: Lawrence Erlbaum Associates.

Cullingford, R. E. (1978). *Script application: Computer understanding of newspaper stories.* (Research Rep. No. 116). Yale University, Department of Computer Science.

Fahlman, S. E. (1979). *NETL: A system for representing and using real-world knowledge.* Cambridge, MA: MIT Press.

Filmore, C. (1982). Frame semantics. *Linguistics in the morning calm.* Seoul, Korea: Hanshin Press.

Fillmore, C., & Kay, P. (1983). *Final report to NIE: Text semantic analysis of reading comprehension tests.* Unpublished manuscript.

Kay, P. (1983). Linguistic competence and folk theories of language: Two English hedges. *Proceedings of the Ninth Annual Meeting of the Berkeley Linguistics Society.* Berkeley, California.

Maida, A. S. (1984). Processing entailments and accessing facts in a uniform frame system. *Proceedings of National Conference on Artificial Intelligence,* Austin, TX.

Rieger, C. J. (1975). Conceptual memory and inference. In R. C. Shank (Ed.), *Conceptual information processing.* Amsterdam: North Holland.

Schank, R. C. (Ed.). (1975). *Conceptual information processing.* Amsterdam: North Holland.

Woods, W. A. (1975). What's in a link: Foundations for semantic networks. In D. G. Bobrow & A. Collins (Eds.), *Representation and understanding: Studies in cognitive science.* New York: Academic Press.

3

Learning and Memory in Machines and Animals: An AI Model that Accounts for Some Neurobiological Data

Richard H. Granger
Dale M. McNulty
Center for the Neurobiology of Learning and Memory
University of California, Irvine

ABSTRACT

The CEL (Components of Episodic Learning) model of learning and memory (Granger, 1982, 1983a, 1983b) provides a process model of certain aspects of learning and memory in animals and humans. The model consists of a set of asynchronous and semi-independent functional operators that collectively create and modify memory traces as a result of experience. The model conforms to relevant results in the learning literature of psychology and neurobiology. There are two goals to this work: one is to create a set of working learning systems that will improve their performance on the basis of experience, and the other is to compare these systems' performance with that of living systems, as a step towards the eventual comparative characterization of different learning systems.

Parts of the model have been implemented in the CEL-0 program, which operates in a Maze-World simulated maze environment. The program exhibits simple exploratory behavior that leads to the acquisition of predictive and discriminatory schemata. A number of interesting theoretical predictions have arisen in part from observation of the operation of the program, some of which are currently being tested in neurobiological experiments. In particular, some neurobiological evidence for the existence of multiple, separable memory systems in humans and animals is interpreted in terms of the model, and some new experiments arising from the model's predictions are suggested.

INTRODUCTION TO THE PROBLEM

Characterization of Learning Processes

The amnesic patient identified by his initials, H. M., is apparently incapable of learning any new information; since the operation that removed a part of the limbic system of his brain, he has been unable to learn to recognize new people or situations. For instance, he reintroduces himself to his doctor, Brenda Milner, every time she visits him, even though she has visited him many times a week for many years! In contrast, his preoperation memories appear not to be impaired, nor is his ability to carry on a relatively normal conversation or other everyday functions.

However, H. M. can acquire certain categories of new abilities. For instance, he has been tested on the mirror-writing task of writing while seeing only a mirror image of what he writes. Every time the experimenter came in the room, once a day for several weeks, H. M. had to be reintroduced to both the experimenter and the experiment and insisted that he had of course never seen either before and that he didn't know how to do this (mirror-writing) task. Yet his performance on the task improved steadily over the several-week period; in fact, he learned the task at about the same rate that control subjects did. When confronted with examples of his poor early trials compared with his much improved recent trials, he is unable to explain the differences and doesn't remember ever performing those experiments.

These and other results in humans and animals have led inescapably to the hypothesis that there are two memory systems, that is, separable biological systems that semi-independently establish long-term memories from experience. As suggested by H. M.'s behavior, these systems have distinct characteristics; each is capable of learning only certain types of information. An accurate characterization of precisely which tasks are learnable by which mechanism has proved elusive, however, and there currently exist a number of competing neuropsychological hypotheses characterizing the different memory systems (see e.g., Mishkin, 1978; Squire, 1981; Squire, Cohen & Nadel, 1982).

A long-term goal of the research described here is to characterize these different learning systems in terms of the types of learning behavior they produce. Our immediate subgoal is to create a system to characterize learning and memory systems. We hope to be able to build out of similar functional components two different systems, each of which has a particular set of learning abilities. We would then be able to show what differences in the models gave rise to the differences in learning abilities.

Recent research on learning and memory in AI has focused primarily on advanced human abilities (see e.g., Carbonell, 1982; Kolodner & Kolodner, 1983; Langley, 1981, Langley et al.,1982; Lebowitz, 1983; Mitchell et al., 1981; Schank, 1982; Schank & Burstein, 1982). We have adapted some ideas on MOPs (Schank, 1982) and the indexing of E-MOPs (Kolodner, 1983a, 1983b) to the tasks we are modeling. Our focus is on much lower level domains of learning and memory, especially "subcognitive" tasks that lower mammals (e.g., rats) can learn. This has enabled us to concentrate our models on the *processes* underlying learning and memory, rather than on complex memory *structures*. Our approach has been to attempt to identify a candidate set of mechanisms sufficient to allow the acquisition, storage, and retrieval of simple episodic information, and to compare our results against experimental data on learning and memory processes in animals.

A key point here is that these subcognitive learning and memory tasks, as far below higher human abilities as they are, are nonetheless still difficult and elusive and therefore are eminently worthy of being the focus of an AI learning mechanism. These and related tasks have been extensively studied by cognitive psychologists and neurobiologists in their experimental approaches to learning and memory; yet their theories of human and animal learning and memory have been insufficiently precise to allow for the construction of computer models for testing the theories. Still missing is a bridge between AI models of learning and psychological and neurobiological experiments on learning.

Introduction to CEL

The CEL model of learning and memory (Granger, 1982, 1983a, 1983b) provides a process model of the acquisition and operation of certain aspects of learning and memory in animals and humans. The model conforms to constraints provided by relevant results in psychology, neuropsychology, and neurobiology; a number of behavioral data are explained in terms of the model, and certain specific theoretical lesions and modulations of the model predict behavioral effects that correspond to observed behaviors in similarly manipulated animals.

Parts of the model have been implemented in a computer program called CEL-0. CEL-0 takes as input a sequence of experiential sensory events coded in terms of sensory modality and feature sets. The program operates on the inputs, building a memory database of information derived from the input streams. Sample domains that have been worked on include: (a) a simple "feeding" microworld, in which the model learns to predict (via classical conditioning) which events reliably and predictably lead up to its being fed; (b) a "maze" microworld, in which the model explores and learns (operantly) to identify where interesting and rewarding areas of the maze are and to create a simple cognitive map (O'Keefe & Nadel, 1978; Tolman, 1932) of the maze environment; and (c) a "puzzle-solving" microworld, in which the model begins with knowledge of the possible set of moves in a puzzle (currently Towers of Hanoi), and learns to perform the task correctly.

In the maze mocroworld, CEL-0 interacts with MazeWorld, a simulated maze environment program, which receives CEL-0 input moves and returns a value indicating CEL-0's new location in the maze. Hence, each move of CEL-0 causes feedback from the simulated maze, which in turn triggers CEL-0's next move.

Some of CEL-0's unexpected behavior in the MazeWorld has triggered some theoretical ideas, which are presented here. For instance, we have identified seven different categories of learning—seven different ways that new memory traces can be created in CEL-0. Each corresponds to a different "calling sequence" of operators, each of which, in turn, seems to correspond to a logical class of training situations that might arise in the real world. These seven classes of learning are briefly discussed later in this chapter.

Other examples of theoretical ideas that have arisen from working with the program in the MazeWorld include: a mechanism for active exploratory behavior during learning; a mechanism for creating subgoals from goals during learning, acquisition of "landmarks" during learning that serve as useful index points; and a comparison of "efficient" learned behavior with "superstitious" learned behavior. Some of these are described in detail in Granger and McNulty (1984).

Attempts to find detailed correspondences between the model and experimental data in neurobiology have been fruitful. A number of specific predictions arising from work with the model are in the disparate areas of selective attention, modulation of memory, and rapid forgetting and learning deficits associated with certain limbic lesions. Granger (1983b) presents detailed analyses of these three substantive areas of CEL's modeling efforts.

This chapter presents first a description of CEL-0's behavior in the Maze-World simulation, and then a specific neurobiological prediction dealing with multiple memory systems. The prediction is currently being tested in a neuorbiological lab at the Center for the Neurobiology of Learning and Memory at Irvine.

INTRODUCTION TO THE MODEL: THE 12 CEL OPERATORS AND THEIR FUNCTIONS

The CEL model proposes a characterization of the constituent functional operators that comprise learning processes. It is hoped that each of these primitive operators has specific instantiations that can be identified in the neural substrate. The model identifies a set of twelve "primitive" memory operators that operate in parallel to perform collectively five classes of memory manipulation: reception, recording, retrieval, reconstruction and refinement. The model consists of the operation of these 12 operators on memory representations we term *episodic schemata*. Detailed descriptions of the functions of these operators and their (often nonintuitive) interactions are provided in Granger (1982, 1983a, 1983b).

In brief, the 12 operators have the following functions:

- Reception operators:
  - DETECT a set of sensory input channels and any associated hard-wired preprocessing performed by those input channels, such as visual and auditory processing
  - SELECT "tunable" input filter to attend selectively to some inputs over others on the basis of prior experience
- Recording operators:
  - NOTICE matches inputs against known desirable and undesirable states; triggers COLLECT when a match occurs

COLLECT packages recent stream of inputs into a kernel episodic schema

INDEX creates new indices, and hooks into existing indices, for each new episodic schema

- Retrieval operators:

REMIND matches inputs against indices for existing schemas; triggers ACTIVATE when match occurs

ACTIVATE incorporates REMINDed schemas into the currect predictive schema; triggers the Reconstruction operators

- Reconstruction operators:

ENACT performs any efferent actions in the current predictive schema; "tunes" SELECT's filter to attend to predicted afferent events

SYNTHESIZE matches inputs against predicted events in current predictive schema; triggers Refinement operators to modify schema in response to matches and mismatches

- Refinement operators:

REINFORCE incrementally strengthens current schema(ta) according to SYNTHESIZE's judgment of its successful predictiveness (i.e., matches)

BRANCH creates a branch in current schema(ta) according to SYNTHESIZE's judgment of unsuccessful predictiveness (i.e., mismatches)

DETOUR creates a nonpursuable branch in current schema according to NOTICEings of undesirable events, predicted or not

These operators act in parallel, asynchronously and semi-independently in the CEL model, and complex interactions among them at run time enable these relatively straightforward operators to give rise to a rich set of learning and memory behaviors.

A BRIEF EXAMPLE OF THE OPERATION OF THE CEL-0 PROGRAM

Introduction to the CEL-0 Environment

CEL-0 moves through a simple maze by interacting with MazeWorld, a simulated maze environment program. CEL-0 sends a move to MazeWorld and MazeWorld returns CEL-0's new location. This new location triggers CEL-0's next move. Following is a schematic view of the relatively simple MazeWorld maze that we use for the examples in this section; M0 is the entry point into the maze, and M4 contains water, which is used for a reward under circumstances described later.

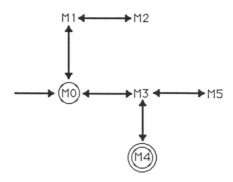

The following sections describe a connected set of examples of CEL-0's operation in this maze. The description are in three phases:

Phase 1 (Exploration phase): CEL-0 uses innate (built-in) episodic schemas to move through the maze, establishing episodic traces corresponding to its 'routes' through the maze.

Phase 2 (Effectiveness phase); CEL-0 has an added desired state (satisfy-thirst) that drives its behavior; it searches for and finds a (not necessarily most efficient) route through the maze to any location of water.

Phase 3 (Efficiency phase); CEL-0 refines its already effective routes through the maze to reward locations. (This phase is actually going on concurrently with the other two).

In each phase, CEL-0's behavior can be described in terms of three lists: a sequence of CEL operators, the corresponding sequence of overt moves in the simulated environment (if any), and the corresponding additions or changes to long-term memory (if any).

CEL-0's Exploratory Behavior in MazeWorld

For the purposes of this example, CEL-0 will start at location M0 in the maze, facing towards M3. The internal representation is described in Granger & McNulty (1984). It consists of information about what views are in front of, to the right of, behind and to the left of the current position of CEL-0 in the maze. Hence, the starting position has a view of M3 in front, walls to the right and behind, and M1 to the left.[1]

---

[1]This is an admittedly huge oversimplification of a realistic maze situation, but it seems justified for two important reasons: (a) selective attention to relevant features is the key element slighted by this oversimplification, and we have already done some analyses of selective attention in complex environments (see Granger, 1983b); and (b) there are a number of interesting and complex processing problems that arise even with this simplification, and these problems would be difficult to present without first simplifying away the selective attention problems for pedagogical reasons.

Because of the extremely simplified inputs for this example, DETECT and SELECT essentially just attend to everything here; see Granger, 1983b and the selective attention section in this chapter for an explanation of how these operators become much more complex in the face of more complex inputs.

Once SELECT has entered a representation into temporary memory, NOTICE attempts to match it against desirable and undesirable states, and REMIND attempts to match it against any existing schemas that might be relevant to the situation. There are three built-in exploratory schemas in CEL-0, two of which get REMINDed by this input. Each of the three schemas (ES1, ES2, and ES3) is two events long, each corresponding to the impetus to move in a particular type of situation, essentially corresponding to the following sequences:

ES1: see front opening $\Rightarrow$ go straight
ES2: see obstruction $\Rightarrow$ look around (360°)
ES3: see side opening $\Rightarrow$ turn towards opening

Therefore at location M0, REMIND will find both ES1 and ES3, and ACTIVATE will have to choose one of them to pursue. For this example, let it choose ES1. (ACTIVATE in fact contains a set of (currently six) "preference metrics" that it uses to decide among proposed (REMINDed) alternative schemas (Granger & McNulty, 1984, describe these in detail). ENACT and SYNTHESIZE then begin to reconstruct ES1. ENACT does so by performing any events in the schema, and SYNTHESIZE by comparing new inputs that result from successive ENACTed events against the predicted inputs in the schema itself. SYNTHESIZE notes that the match between the event and the more generalized representation in ES1 is only a partial match and, because it is not an exact match, calls BRANCH to create a new branch of the schema, and begins recording this new branch.

CEL-0 continues in this fashion, making the following moves through the maze: M0 - M3 - M5 - M3 - M0 - M1 - M2 - M1 - M0 - M3 - M5 - M3 - M4 - M3 - M0 - M1 - M2 - etc. An extensive description and explanation of the operator sequences driving these moves can be found in Granger & McNulty, 1984.

Note that when M4 is arrived at, the fact that there is water there will cause a REMIND of another innate (built-in) schema that essentially says when water is seen, drink it. However, this schema may not be reconstructively ENACTed unless ACTIVATE allows it (or unless there are no alternative schemas that get REMINDed); one of ACTIVATE's preference metrics says not to prefer schemas that do not match any currently desirable state, as specified on the Desirable State List (DSL).

Effective Goal Pursuit in CEL-0

The result of the exploration phase is the creation of a number of schemas describing various routes through the maze, indexed by their starting and ending positions (more detail on INDEX is provided in Granger, 1983b and Granger and McNulty, 1984).

In phase 2, we simply add a desired event to CEL-0's DSL—this is the list that NOTICE matches incoming events against and that ACTIVATE checks to see whether or not to bother to ENACT a REMINDed schema. Hence, if we add "drink water" to the DSL, CEL-0 will now "act thirsty," in the following three senses: (a) it will drink water if it sees any (via REMIND, ACTIVATE and ENACT of the built-in schema that says when water is seen, drink it); (b) it will tend to prefer sequences that lead to seeing water (via ACTIVATEs preference metric for currently desirable states); and (c) it will store any sequences of events that lead to water (via NOTICE and COLLECT). Hence, via all three of these mechanisms, CEL-0's memory will now contain schemas that are 'effective' with respect to the achievement of its goal of finding and drinking water.

Active Exploration by CEL-0: Sensitivity Analysis

A schema that leads to M4 at the end of the exploration phase is: M0 - M3 - M5 - M3 - M4. Note that although effective, this schema is not maximally efficient— it could simply go M0 - M3 - M4. The fact that it doesn't is simply an accident of the exploration phase (see Design Decisions later). CEL-0 has a process that causes schemas to be tested for their sensitivity to changes in the sequence; the process makes multiple variations of schemas by deleting various features or events from the event sequence, and then tests the resulting variations for their effectiveness.

The process effectively establishes a set of multiple internal hypotheses as to which of the features of the episode are the most critical and predictive. Hence, this process amounts to a test of the sensitivity of the new episode to changes in those features. This process of testing episodes for their sensitivity to changes is termed *sensitivity analysis*. The following subsections briefly outline the process.

Introduction to Sensitivity Analysis.   When the model senses an instance of an episode (e.g., a pursuit-type episode such as M0 - M3 - M5 - M3 - M4) that results in some NOTICEd desirable state, that episode is COLLECTed into a long-term memory trace. The INDEX operator then begins to choose features of the events in the episode to use as indices, which will be used as recognition cues at retrieval time, that is, whenever similar events happen subsequently. Depending on which features are chosen as indices, of course, subsequent retrieval either will or will not take place based on the presence or absence of any particular feature in the new input trace. Hence, the effective recognition of any new instance of a learned episode is sensitive to the feature indices that are created at INDEX time during recording of the episode.

During the establishment of these feature indices on a new trace, the INDEX operator performs a multistep process that has the effect of creating multiple traces of the episode, each with a different feature or set of features deleted from the trace. The multiple versions of the episode that result from this process enable CEL-0 to test instances of the episode for their sensitivity to changes in the constituents of the episode: the long-term trace undergoes ongoing modification and refinement depending on which versions of the episode turn out to accurately match subsequent instances of the input stimuli.

Intuitively, what is happening is that the INDEX operator is hypothesizing a series of variations of the instance of the episode, implicitly predicting that these versions might be useful predictors of subsequent instances of the episode. Those predictive hypotheses are tested each time the set of variations of episodes is retrieved and reconstructively compared to a new input instance (via ENACT and SYNTHESIZE). In this way, the sensitivity analysis process allows the model to learn more than was contained in the single instance of the episode: it learns ways in which that episodic instance might be sensitive to changes and variations. Furthermore, the process has the effect of robustly reducing any dependence on the order of presentation of events, making the model eventually learn the same things about the maze regardless of what order it happens to acquire them in.

The Five Steps of Sensitivity Analysis.

1. When a new long-term trace is written, INDEX's first step is to search for any existing feature indices that match any features in the new trace. If they do, then those indices are 'attached' to the trace; that is, each index now points to the new trace in addition to any other traces it may already be pointing to.
2. For each sensory feature in the input, create a new index for that feature, which points to the episode.
3. For each feature index pointing to the episode, either found by step 1 or created by step 2, begin creating variations of the episode by leaving out one or more of the features contained in the initial copy. Each variation is written into memory as a near-miss copy of the episode.
4. For each of the new episode variations, search for an existing index that has the new subset features of the variation; if found, attach it to the episode.
5. For each feature-set index created, attempt to find others with subsets of the same features. For each such index set found, create a new higher–level index (see Granger, 1983b, corresponding to the shared features that point to each of the members of the index set.

The combined effect of these steps is to create a growing set of indices pointing to the episode; each index will be triggered by a different set of feature cues at retrieval time. At the same time, multiple copies of the episode itself are being created, each a slight variation of the others—no two are exactly alike. The indices will slowly become a hierarchical set, because step 5 creates higher level or second-order indices, each of which points only to other indices (see Granger, 1983b). For instance, template indices are examples of higher indexes that contain only event-sequence information, with specific sensory information deleted.

SOME INSIGHTS RESULTING FROM EXPERIENCE
WITH CEL-0

A number of difficulties that have arisen during the programming of CEL-0 present interesting theoretical problems that were not obvious until the implementation difficulties arose. Some of these are discussed here, with the focus on the emergence of seven categories of learning, based on seven different calling sequences of CEL operators. Each calling sequence is capable of establishing or modifying a memory trace, that is, learning.

Seven Ways to Establish a Memory Trace in CEL

The 12 CEL operators do not call each other serially. Hence, although COLLECT is the primary way for episodic traces to be established in permanent memory, there are four distinct calling sequences that may result in the creation of new traces. Each calling sequence constitutes a category of learning in CEL. In turn, these four categories have between them a number of different subcategories, for a combined total of seven. These are listed below, followed by a set of brief descriptions and examples of each subcategory.

1. Goal-based establishment:
   a. pursuit of desirable result (Pursuit-based learning)
   b. avoidance of undesirable result (Avoidance-based learning)
2. Expectation-based establishment:
   a. match between expectation and environment (Success-driven learning)
   b. mismatch between expectation and environment (Failure-driven learning)
3. Exploration-based establishment:
   a. analysis of relevance of schema features (Sensitivity analysis)
4. Coincidence-based establishment:
   a. schema activated simultaneously with newly-created schema (Append-driven learning)
   b. two schemas concurrently activated (Splice-driven learning)

Goal-Based Trace Establishment.   When the NOTICE operator finds that an incoming event matches something on either the Desirable or Undesirable state list (DSL or USL) (Granger, 1983b), NOTICE triggers the COLLECT and

INDEX operator to make a record of the sequence of events that led up to the desirable or undesirable event.

Case 1a: Pursuit-based learning. In the desirable case, the INDEX operator simply indexes the sequence of events by SELECTed features (see Granger, 1983b).

Case 1b: Avoidance-based learning. In the undesirable case, INDEX calls the DETOUR operator to attempt to create a link pointing to potential alternatives to the undesirable result, so that that path won't be pursued in the future.

Expectation-Based Trace Establishment. While a schema is being reconstructively ENACTed after having been triggered (REMINDed and ACTIVATEd) by some cue, the SYNTHESIZE operator is constantly matching incoming real-world events against events in the schema (i.e., it is checking the schema's implicit expectations). Both matches and mismatches can cause new things to be written into memory.

Case 2a: Success-driven learning. If SYNTHESIZE finds a match, then it calls REINFORCE to add strength to the links pointing to the successfully predictive schema.

Case 2b: Failure-driven learning. If a mismatch is found, BRANCH is called to create a new link between the index and the new sequence of events (whatever just actually happened), thereby effectively reducing the relative strength of the link from the index to the previously-expected result.

Exploration-Based Trace Establishment. Apparent exploratory behavior by CEL arises from the operation of the sensitivity analysis procedure just described (and described in more depth in Granger, 1983b), combined with the existence of the set of simple exploratory schemata. Recall that sensitivity analysis causes a number of variations of each schema to be created, each of which will be tested and either strengthened or weakened according to its success or failure. These will operate on the schemas collected during CEL-0's wandering through the maze, to refine the model's representation of pathways through the maze, eliminate some redundancies, and identify some landmarks that make useful indices to the set of pathways (see Granger & McNulty, 1984).

As it collects sequences of paths through pieces of the maze, sensitivity analysis refines them by testing the relevance of their consituent events.

Case 3a: Sensitivity analysis. For instance, if an initial route through the maze is the sequence M0 - M3 - M5 - M3 - M4, a diminution of the route yields M3 - M5 - M3 - M4, which will work when the starting point is M3. Further diminution causes the eventual creation of the route M3 - M4, which is actually an improvement over the original in terms of efficiency, since it can get to the presumably desirable state M4 without bothering to go through M5 and doubling back through M3. Note that in light of this new schema, the initial five-step route can be viewed as "superstitious" behavior; that is, the model is acting as though it "thinks" that just because it went through M5 to get to M4 the first time, it must do so on subsequent trials. It is important to note that efficiency is not always best; in fact, mammals can be trained to repeat long sequences of otherwise superstitious behavior, as long as that behavior is rewarded, and any variations go unrewarded (see e.g., Hilgard & Bower, 1966).

Coincidence-Based Trace Establishment.   There are two cases of coincidence that can arise in the model: either an existing schema gets REMINDed during the COLLECTion of a new schema, or a schema gets REMINDed during the ENACTing of another schema that has been previously REMINDed and ACTIVATEd.

Case 4a: Append-driven learning. If the model is COLLECTing a new schema that leads to, say, an undesirable result such as an unplesant taste, that NOTICEd taste may simultaneously cause a REMIND of, say an innate gag reflex schema (i.e., it says to spit out after sensing a bad taste). In such a case, the INDEX (and DETOUR) operators create index links to both the sequence of events leading up to the bad taste, so that it might be avoided in the future, and to the sequence of events REMINDed by the event, so that this sequence might be substituted for the undesirable sequence the next time it happens; this is an instance of an 'active avoidance' situation.

Case 4b: Splice-driven learning. If the model is currently ENACTing an active schema, for example, running a maze toward a food reward, and during this, another schema gets REMINDed (e.g., a light flash that is known to lead to some different reward), then both schemas are indexed together by the same initiating feature, giving that feature added predictive power.

Note: Design Decisions Affecting CEL-0's Performance

A number of design decisions in CEL-0 (including the specifics of the ACTIVATE preference metrics, the details of the built-in exploratory schemas, and the details of the functions of the operators, notably SYNTHESIZE, REMIND and ACTIVATE) will affect the path it takes through the maze and in many cases will affect whether or not the correct learning takes place at all. We have been experimenting with versions of CEL-0 to see which changes cause which behaviors, but we intend to continue to compare the resulting behaviors against the learning literature wherever possible (see esp. Rescorla & Wagner, 1972), and to suggest new experiments (and their predicted outcomes) when the literature does not provide the necessary data on some specific point about how a rat, for instance, should run the maze. The next section comments about our use of some results in animal learning as a "requirements specification" for CEL-0's performance. Granger and McNulty (1984) discuss this subject in greater detail.

THE NEUROBIOLOGY OF MULTIPLE MEMORY SYSTEMS

The Constellation of Deficits in the Amnesic Syndrome

The patient H. M., like most other amnesics, exhibits a whole constellation of related deficits. The key deficit is the inability to consciously store new information, as described earlier.

Two of the other major components of the overall amnesic syndrome are:

- *Retrograde amnesia:* H. M. not only is incapable of consciously storing new information since his operation, he also has lost some of the memories of what happened to him immediately preceding the operation, up to about 2 years before the operation, whereas memories older than that remain unimpaired. This striking finding (Squire, 1981) is used as evidence that memory consolidation takes time (perhaps up to 2 years) before it becomes a permanent part of memory. Perhaps memories that were still being consolidated at the time of the operation were disrupted and never became firmly established as permanent memories.
- *Rapid Forgetting:* H. M. is able to carry on conversations, and perform other tasks of long duration, as long as the task isn't interrupted. When it is interrupted for more than a few minutes, he completely forgets where he was and starts over again from the beginning: he might have exactly the same conversation all over again without realizing it.

Of Rats and Men

There are recently encountered situations in which rats in a maze exhibit forms of learning previously attributed only to primates and humans. Learning-set learning (LSL) refers to very rapid (usually just a single trial) learning of new situations that are similar to previously learned ones, that is, the animal seems to form a template that it can use to expedite the learning of subsequent situations. The rats' learning-set learning system apparently is entirely separable from its more standard, slower associative learning (AL) system—there are specific drugs and lesions that have been used to eliminate entirely abilities associated with the LSL system without affecting the performance of the AL system, and vice versa. This constitutes evidence that rats have multiple memory systems.

Furthermore, recent experimentation (Staubli & Lynch, 1984) has shown that rats can be given amnesic symptoms strikingly similar to those in humans, by having corresponding lesions made to the hippocampus and another limbic structure, the thalamus. In particular, rats are trained to select one of two odors for a water reward. This initially requires 50–100 trials before a minimal criterion of learning is met (AL). Over successive pairs of odors, the rats' behavior changes such that they come to learn the correct odor in subsequent odor pairs in only 3–4 trials (LSL). Two forms of learning are thought to be involved: (a) abstract "template-driven" (LSL-type) information about the task (e.g., the fact that it contains a correct and an incorrect olfactory cue), and (b) specific memory (AL-type) of which particular odor was correct for a given pair.

One specific type of lesion (lesions of the connection between the dorsomedial nucleus [DMN] of the thalamus and the frontal cortical system) eliminates the animals' ability to go from the many-trial (AL) mode to the subsequent rapid-learning (LSL) mode over successive pairs of odors. This suggests that the rats are learning the specific memories for correct odors but are failing to learn the template information about the existence of correct and incorrect odors in each pair.

Disconnection, or lesions, of the hippocampus, on the other hand, produces an apparent inverse of this result, with a time dependency as well: the rats acquire the rapid learning mode (i.e., they appear to learn the abstract correct-incorrect information), but for any given pair of odors they cannot recall the right specific odor (i.e., cannot perform the task) if delays of more than about 5 minutes are interposed between trials (i.e., a deficit similar to rapid forgetting). It seems that these rats are acquiring the abstract memory but are failing to create a long-term trace of the specific memory.

Interpretation of the Data

What ability—what specific knowledge or process—is available to the rat in the LSL situation, but not in the AL situation, to enable template-driven learning? The problem for CEL (or for any other model of learning and memory) in attempting to provide a consistent account of these results is that apparently the templates are learned but the specific memories leading to those templates are lost. We do not have a complete solution, but we have come up with a set of opposing hypotheses, either of which could potentially explain the data. These opposing hypotheses have been used to design an experiment that is currently being run to help further clarify the the question, and to narrow down the set of possible consistent models of these two learning systems.

In the language of the CEL model, there are two classes of possible explanations: (1) the hippocampal (AL) losses are due to a storage-side failure either to COLLECT or to INDEX the specific information, or else (2) these losses are due to a retrieval-side failure to use correctly the specific odor memory to find the water reward; perhaps REMIND finds both the template memory and the specific-odor memory, but ACTIVATE is not correctly using the specific-odor memory to instantiate the template memory in order to find the reward.

The articulation of these two opposing possibilities has suggested an experiment to try to test whether the specific odor was in fact present in memory at all.

The memory seems not to show up in the odor-choice situation, but if explanation (2) is correct, then the memory may be there but not being used correctly in that situation. It turns out that there is a relatively simple experimental methodology for testing for "raw memories" like this. Details are provided in Granger (1983b). Briefly, the experiment allows us to see whether or not a rat has any memory of a particular event (such as a specific odor). That is, the rat's behavior in the presence of some previously seen event can be reliably distinguished from its behavior in the presence of an unrecognized event; hence, we should be able to tell whether or not the specific odor is in memory or not. This experiment, described in Granger (1983b) is currently being run at the Center for the Neurobiology of Learning and Memory at Irvine.

If it turns out that the memory shows up in this experiment, then we may hypothesize that the deficit is on the retrieval side, that is, the memory is present, but cannot be correctly used to perform the choice behavior. In CEL terms, it is possible that ACTIVATE cannot instantiate the memory into the template that can use it to find the water reward. If, on the other hand, the rats exhibit no recognition of the specific odors, we will hypothesize that the deficit may indeed be a storage-side deficit, and we will have to attempt to alter the model to account for the loss of a specific memory after the creation of a template from it.

Either way, the CEL model will have aided in suggesting a key experiment that can decide the question of whether the rapid-forgetting phenomenon is a storage-side or a retrieval-side deficit. This brings us a step closer to understanding the nature of the multiple (LSL and AL) learning and memory systems.

CONCLUSIONS: ARTIFICIAL AND NATURAL LEARNING MECHANISMS

There exist many theoretical questions in learning and memory that rely on the consistent interpretation of an almost bewildering array of interrelated experimental results. The field of multiple memory systems is a particularly exciting current example of this. A battle over the characteristics of these systems is currently raging among memory researchers in the neurosciences (Mishkin, 1978; Squire, 1981; Squire, Cohen, & Nadel, 1982; Tulving, 1983).

The search for consistent interpretations of these data can be aided by artificial models of learning and memory, and, reciprocally, the development of consistent models can be furthered by the experimental testing of the models' predictions against natural learning systems. Although it is not necessary for an artificial learning system to account precisely for all available psychological data on learning, it has happened time and again in AI that sincere attempts to provide consistent interpretations of problematic psychological results have resulted in both better psychological theory and richer and more productive computer systems.

There are certain specific processing problems that any learning system, natural or artificial, must have a way of solving. We are trying to characterize some of those processing problems in specific learning situations, in hopes of identifying the similarities among, and differences between, different instances of learning systems. The CEL model has so far been helpful in identifying and clarifying some of the possible theoretical interpretations of results in the area of multiple memory systems. We hope that by continuing to iterate the loop from theoretical suggestion to experimental result and back, we can further refine and narrow down the range of possible interpretations of multiple learning and memory systems, so that the study of artificial and natural learning mechanisms can productively use each others' results.

ACKNOWLEDGMENTS

This research was supported in part by the National Science Foundation under grant IST-18-20685, and by the Naval Ocean Systems Center under contract N66001-83-C-0255.

REFERENCES

Carbonell, J. G. (1982). Experiential learning in analogical problem-solving. *Proceedings of the National Conference on Artificial Intelligence,* 168–175, Pittsburgh, PA.

Carbonell, J. (1983). Derivational analogy and its role in problem solving. *Proceedings of the 1983 National Conference on Artificial Intelligence,* 64–69.

Granger, R. H. (1982). *Identification of mental operators underlying the acquisition of simple predictive behavior.* (Tech. Rep. No. 191). University of California, Irvine, Department of Computer Science.

Granger, R. H. (1983a). Identification of components of episodic learning: The CEL process model of early learning and memory., *Cognition and Brain Theory,* 6(1), 5–38.

Granger, R. H. (1983b). *An artificial-intelligence model of learning and memory that provides a theoretical framework for the interpretation of experimental data in psychology and neurobiology.* (Tech. Rep. No. 210). University of California, Irvine, Department of Computer Science.

Granger, R. H., & McNulty, D. M. (1984). *The CEL-0 system: Experience with a computer model that learns to run a maze.* (Tech. Rep. 220). University of California, Irvine, Department of Computer Science.

Hilgard, E. R., & Bower, G. H. (1966). *Theories of Learning.* New York: Appleton.

Kolodner, J. K. (1983a). Maintaining organization in a dynamic long-term memory. *Cognitive Science,* 7(4), 243–280.

Kolodner, J. K. (1983b). Reconstructive memory: A computer model, *Cognitive Science,* 7(4), 281–328.

Kolodner, J. L., & Kolodner, R. M. (1983). An algorithm for diagnosis based on analysis of previous cases. *Proceedings of MEDCOMP 83.*

Langley, P. (1981). Data-driven discovery of physical laws. *Cognitive Science,* 5(1), 137–143.

Langley, P., Bradshaw, G., & Simon, H. A. (1981). BACON.5: The discovery of conservation laws. *Proceedings of the Third International Joint Conference on Artificial Intelligence,* 121–126.

Lebowitz, M. (1980). *Generalization and memory in an integrated understanding system.* (Tech. Rep. No. 186). Yale University, New Haven, CT, Department of Computer Science.

Lebowitz, M. (1983). Concept learning in a rich input domain. *Proceedings of the 1983 International Machine Learning Workshop.* 177–182, Champaign-Urbana, IL.

Mishkin, M. (1978). Memory in monkeys severely impaired by combined but not by separate removal of amygdala and hippocampus. *Nature, 283,* 297–298.

Mitchell, T. M., Utgoff, P. E., Nudel, B., & Banerji, R. (1981). Learning problem-solving heuristics through practise. *Proceedings of the Seventh International Joint Conference on Artificial Intelligence,* 127–134, Vancouver, B.C.

O'Keefe, J., & Nadel, L. (1978). *The hippocampus as a cognitive map.* Oxford: Clarendon Press.

Rescorla, R., & Wagner, A. R. (1972). A theory of Pavlovian conditioning: Variations in the effectiveness of reinforcement and non-reinforcement. In A. H. Black & W. F. Prokasy (Eds.), *Classical conditioning II: Current research and theory.* New York: Appleton-Century-Crofts.

Schank, R. C. (1981). Failure-driven memory. *Cognition and Brain Theory, 4,* 41–60.

Schank, R. C. (1982). *Dynamic memory: A theory of learning in computers and people.* New York: Cambridge University Press.

Schank, R. C., & Burstein, M. (1982). *Modelling memory for language understanding* (Tech. Rep. No. 220). New Haven: Yale University, Department of Computer Science.

Simon, H. A., Langley, P., & Bradshaw, G. (1981). Scientific discovery as problem solving. *Synthese, 47,* 1–27.

Slotnick, B. (1974). Olfactory learning in rats. *Science, 185,* 796–798.

Squire, L. R. (1981). Two forms of human amnesia: An analysis of forgetting. *Journal of Neuroscience, 1,* 635–640.

Squire, L., Cohen, N., & Nadel, L. (1982). The medial temporal region and memory consolidation: A new hypothesis. In H. Weingartner & E. S. Parker, (Eds.), *Memory Consolidation,* Hillsdale, NJ: Lawrence Erlbaum Associates.

Staubli, U., Ivy, G., & Lynch, G. (1984). Hippocampal denervation causes rapid forgetting of olfactory information in rats. *Proceedings of the National Academy of Sciences (USA), 81,* 5885–5887.

Tolman, E. C. (1932). *Purposive behavior in animals and men.* New York: Century.

Tulving, E. (1972). Episodic and semantic memory. In E. Tulving & W. Donaldson (Eds.), *Organization of Memory.* New York: Academic Press.

Tulving, E. (1983). *Elements of episodic memory.* New York: Oxford University Press.

4

Functional Representation of Devices and Compilation of Diagnostic Problem-Solving Systems

V. Sembugamoorthy
B. Chandrasekaran
Department of Computer and Information Science
The Ohio State University

ABSTRACT

Most of the diagnostic systems that have been developed in medicine and in other domains can properly be called "compiled" knowledge systems in the sense that the knowledge base contains the relationships between symptoms and malfunction hypotheses in some form. However, in human reasoning, an expert's knowledge of how the device "functions" is often used to *generate* new relationships during the reasoning process. This deeper level representation, which can be processed to yield more compiled diagnostic structures, is the concern of this chapter. Using the example of a household buzzer, we show what our functional representation of a device looks like. We discuss the nature of the compilation process that can produce the diagnostic expert from this deeper representation. We also outline how another form of problem solving, predicting consequences to device functionality of changes in the structure of a device, can also be supported by this representation.

MOTIVATION

The work described in this chapter can be motivated by reference to a number of issues that have recently attracted attention in knowledge-based reasoning. Three of them are:

1. What does it mean to understand how a device works, in particular, to understand how its *function* is related to and arises from its *structure?* How to represent the result of this understanding in such a way that this representation can be used to support problem solving, such as troubleshooting a malfunction-

47

ing device, or to predict consequences to device functionality of changes in its structure? With human beings at least, it seems reasonable to expect a person who claims to understand how a device works to be able to engage in these forms of problem solving tasks. Some recent work in artificial intelligence (deKleer & Brown, 1981; deKleer & Brown, 1982a; Forbus, 1982; Kuipers, 1982) deals with these issues. In the context of this set of research issues, our goal in this chapter is to present a framework for approaching this problem, to describe a language for representing functioning of a class of devices, and to show how this representation can support problem solving of the types just mentioned.

2. A related concern, especially in the literature on systems for medical diagnosis, has been with *causal reasoning*. Typically this has meant representing detailed causal relationships between pathophysiological states that underlie a disease process and using this information to make conclusions about disease entities, given symptomatic information. The work in Patil (1981) and Weiss, Kulikowski, Amarel, & Safir (1978) exemplifies this approach. Such representations have been called *deep* models (Hart, 1982; Michie, 1982), in contrast to systems such as MYCIN, whose knowledge base contains the evidentiary relationships between disease hypotheses and symptoms directly, without specifying the causal pathways between them. From this viewpoint, the functional representation advanced in this paper can be thought of as a proposed form of deep model for diagnostic expert systems. It can yield causal chains of behavioral states at several levels of detail, and can also generate evidentiary relationships just mentioned to the extent that they are derivable from causal models.

3. Related to the notion of a deep model of a domain is the idea of *compiling* from it different forms of knowledge structures useful for different kinds of reasoning (Chandrasekaran & Mittal, 1983a). For example, for diagnostic reasoning, we need malfunction hypotheses and pieces of knowledge that relate symptoms to these hypotheses (the evidentiary knowledge of the previous paragraph); for reasoning about consequences of actions that may be performed on a system, we keed knowledge that relates state changes at different levels of system description. The intuition is that an agent with an appropriate deep model can generate from it knowledge in these forms, and then use them directly for the relevant problem solving task. An adequate deep model can give rise to different compiled structures for different tasks. If the tasks are *generic* in some sense, then one might look for compilation processes that are device independent. (A theory of generic types of knowledge-based problem-solving tasks is developed in Chandrasekaran, 1983.) In this perspective, the work presented here proposes an approach for compiling diagnostic problem-solving structures from deep models corresponding to a knowledge of how devices function. We also outline how another problem-solving structure for predicting consequences of proposed actions can also be compiled from the same representation, but the major emphasis is on diagnostic reasoning. In these cases, compilation is meant to capture the idea that knowledge in a certain more general form is transformed into knowl-

edge of a more particular form, suitable for particular classes of uses. (Whether a complete diagnostic structure is compiled initially or portions needed for particular diagnostic problems are compiled as these problems are encountered is not of concern in this research; the word *compilation* is not used to contrast the process with *interpretation* in the computer science sense of the terms.) Whereas the functional representation will be more economical in storage, the compiled structures will be more efficient for the particular problem-solving tasks.

COMPONENTS OF A FUNCTIONAL REPRESENTATION

We envisage that an agent represents the functioning of a device in many dimensions, which include *causal, temporal,* and *interaction.* In the causal dimension a "unit of functioning" (e.g., buzzing of a household buzzer) is represented as a causally related sequence—a genetic, not a temporal sequence—of device (or component) states. In the temporal dimension, these units obey time constraints. For example, two units of functioning should happen sequentially or overlap, or their duration cannot exceed a certain amount of time, and so forth. In the dimension of interaction, they interact through feedback or by communicating information. For example, kidneys and lungs interact with the "acid-base" buffer system by communicating through changes in the concentration of bicarbonate and carbonic acid in blood. The functional representation of a device is an integrated whole of these various dimensions.

In this chapter we briefly describe the salient features of the causal dimension of our functional representational scheme, and how it can be used for automatically compiling a diagnostic expert structure by using a device-independent diagnostic compiler. The compiled diagnostic structure has an architecture similar to the MDX system (Chandrasekaran & Mittal, 1983b; Gomez & Chandrasekaran, 1981), that is, it is a hierarchical collection of diagnostic (more specifically, classificatory) specialists.

Our representational scheme is rich in the number of primitives it employs to represent many aspects of functional knowledge. This richness is necessary to capture all the uses to which this representation can be put. Although we attempt to be complete in describing the causal dimension of the scheme in this chapter, only a portion of the scheme is utilized by the diagnostic compiler described.

A REPRESENTATIONAL SCHEME FOR THE FUNCTIONING OF DEVICES

One of the significant tools available to both humans and machines to combat complexity is abstraction. Accordingly, our scheme for functional representation allows one to represent functional knowledge at many levels of abstraction. Each level recursively describes the functioning of a device or component in terms of the abstractions of, and relations between, its components. At each level there are five significant aspects to an agent's functional knowledge:

- STRUCTURE: This specifies relationships between components, and abstractions of these components from lower levels.
- FUNCTION: This specifies WHAT is the response of a device or a component to an external or internal stimulus.
- BEHAVIOR: This specifies HOW, given a stimulus, the response is accomplished.
- GENERIC KNOWLEDGE: Chunks of deeper causal knowledge that have been compiled from various domains to enable the specification of behavior; for example, a specialized version of Kirchoff's law from the domain of electrical circuits.
- ASSUMPTIONS: Using which the agent chooses a behavioral alternative over other possible ones.

Next we describe how these five aspects together represent the functioning of devices at each level of abstraction. Following de Kleer and Brown (1981, 1982a), we use the household buzzer (shown in Fig. 4.1) to illustrate our ideas.

Function

The functional specification of a device is illustrated by describing one of the functions of the buzzer, namely *buzz*.

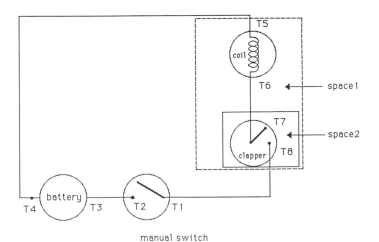

FIG. 4.1. A schematic diagram of a household buzzer.

FUNCTIONS:
  buzz: TOMAKE buzzing (buzzer)
  IF pressed (manual-switch)*
PROVIDED assumption1
BY behavior1
  stop-buzz: . . . .
END FUNCTIONS

In the preceding description *buzzing(buzzer)* is a state description.[1] * denotes repetition of a state. The buzzer is represented as having a number of functions, for example, *buzz, stop-buzz.* That the initial states, t7 and t8, (refer to figure 4.1) are electrically connected, is specified by *assumption1* (more about assumptions later). The BY clause relates the function with its behavior, that is, the manner in which the function is accomplished (behavioral specification is described below). As we shall see later, this association between function and behavior is useful during compilation. Note that primitives such as TOMAKE trigger specific subprocesses during compilation, and thus the compiler (described later) can be said to "understand" them (and their syntactic constraints on their arguments). On the other hand, names such as *behavior1* are used for indexing; state descriptions are treated as strings and used to synthesize pieces of diagnostic knowledge.

Structure

The structure of a device (component) is represented by the abstractions of its components (subcomponents) and relations between them. As an illustration, consider the structure of the buzzer. In this illustration *t1, t2,* are terminals of components. Relations such as *serially connected* are not understood by the compiler. t1, t2, etc. are local terminals. The function *magnetic* is defined at the next level as a function of the clapper in the same way as the functions of the buzzer are described. Its function is to disconnect t1 and t2 electrically if space is magnetized.

It is important to note first that the functional knowledge of a component is specified independent of that of a device that comprises the component. An abstraction of a component inside the specification of a device represents the role of the component in the functioning of the device. This not only concurs with the manner in which we store functional knowledge (e.g., we know the function of a battery independent of its role in a car, camera, etc.) but also has an important practical significance, namely storage efficiency. Second, what is carried over from one level to another are not behavioral specifications but names of func-

---

[1]More precisely, they are partial state descriptions of the device as a whole. We use the term *state* for simplicity.

tions. This is important when an agent needs to replace a malfunctioning component by a functionally equivalent but a behaviorally different one.

> STRUCTURE:
> COMPONENTS:
>   manual-switch (t1, t2), battery (t3, t4),
>   coil (t5, t6, space1), clapper (t7, t8, space2)
> RELATIONS: serially-connected (manual-switch,
>   battery, coil, clapper)
>   AND includes (space1, space2)
>
> ABSTRACTIONS-OF-COMPONENTS:
> COMPONENT clapper (t1, t2, space)
>   FUNCTIONS: magnetic, acoustic, mechanical
>   STATES: elect-connected (t1, t2),
>   repeated-hit (clapper)
>   ASSUMPTIONS: assumption 2, assumption3
> END COMPONENT
>
> COMPONENT coil (t1, t2, space)
>   . . .
> END COMPONENT
> END ABSTRACTIONS-OF-COMPONENTS
> END STRUCTURE

Behavior

The behavioral specification of a device describes the manner in which an agent has composed the functions of the components to obtain the functions of the device. This specification also has pointers to any generic domain knowledge and assumptions (relating to behavioral alternatives) used by the agent in the process of composition. Figure 4.2 illustrates how the buzz function discussed earlier is realized. We have made use of three conceptually important notations in behavioral specification.

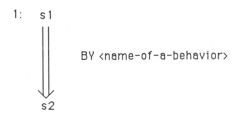

Consider step 1 in Fig. 4.2. This is intended to represent that the state s1 (more specifically a state complex; see the states in step 1 of Fig. 4.2) causes the

BEHAVIOR:

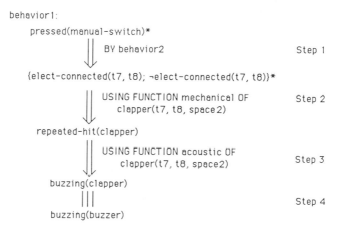

Notes:
   1. "≡" equivalences two states.
   2. s1; s2 means s2 follows s1.

FIG. 4.2.   An illustration of behavioral specification.

state s2, and the details are in another behavioral specification (*behavior2*). This relation enables a behavioral specification of a device (or a component) to be made at many futher levels of detail, but still within the overall level of the device (or component). We call this hierarchy the *Hierarchy of Details*.

For example,

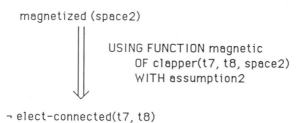

The specification in *assumption3* is to represent the idea that if space2 is magnetized, the resulting force will be greater than the spring force. The notation in step 2 means that state s2 is caused from s1 by making use of a function (*magnetic*) of the component (*clapper*). (Recollect the comments on the magnetic function in the specification of STRUCTURE of the buzzer.) This makes it possible to glue the functions of the components together to obtain a behavior. In other words, it enables causal knowledge at the level of device (component) to be represented in terms of causal knowledge at the level of its components (subcomponents). This hierarchy of causal knowledge is called *Component Hierarchy*.

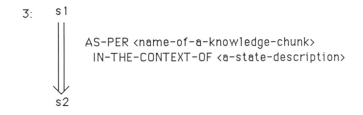

For example,

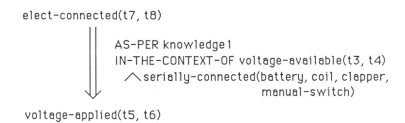

The piece of understanding "if the terminals t7 and t8 are electrically connected, then voltage will be applied between t5 and t6," is true as per the knowledge chunk called *knowledge1* when it is applied in the context of battery, coil, clapper, and manual switch being serially connected and voltage being available at the battery's terminals. (*knowledge1* is specified in the next section.) This primitive enables causal knowledge (i.e., s1 causes s2) to be represented using more general causal knowledge (i.e., knowledge1) and as described later, the latter to be represented using still more generic knowledge (i.e., Kirchoff's law). We call this hierarchy the *Generalization Hierarchy*.

Generic Knowledge

The generic knowledge specification of a device (component) describes all chunks of deeper knowledge used in its behavioral specifications. The following is a specification of knowledge1. There are types of generic knowledge requiring notations other than the ones used below.

```
GENERIC KNOWLEDGE:

    knowlege1:
```

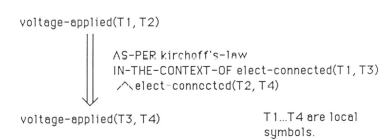

```
        voltage-applied(T1, T2)

                    AS-PER kirchoff's-law
                    IN-THE-CONTEXT-OF elect-connected(T1, T3)
                    ∧ elect-connected(T2, T4)

        voltage-applied(T3, T4)          T1...T4 are local
                                         symbols.

END GENERIC KNOWLEDGE
```

We draw particular attention to the notion of generic knowledge in our representation. It enables us to capture the relation between functional representation and deeper causal knowledge such as Kirchoff's law. This link will be useful when the correctness of an application of a generic knowledge in a functional representation is checked. Moreover, an agent using the functional representation can justify a step in a behavioral specification by quoting the generic knowledge employed.

Assumptions

All assumptions made use of in the behavioral specifications of a device (component) are described in ASSUMPTIONS as illustrated with reference to the clapper:

ASSUMPTIONS:

assumption2: IF magnetized(space) THEN magnetic-force $>$ spring-force
assumption3: IF ⌐ magnetized(space) THEN magnetic-force $<$ spring-force

END ASSUMPTIONS

de Kleer and Brown (1982a) state that one difference between a novice and an expert is that the expert has made explicit all the assumptions underlying behavior of devices. Our functional representation has constructs to represent assumptions and their role in behavioral specification. It is worth restating here that though the compiler does not understand strings like *magnetic-force,* it can use them to compose pieces of diagnostic knowledge.

COMPILATION OF A DIAGNOSTIC PROBLEM-SOLVING SYSTEM

Now we can proceed to a discussion of how a diagnostic problem-solving system can be generated from the functional representation by using a device-independent complier. As a prerequisite for this compilation, the compiler needs to check the correctness/consistency of those portions of the functional representation that it will use. An example of incorrect specification is: A behavioral specification may specify that s1 causes s2 as per some knowledge chunk in some context. But when the knowledge chunk is applied in the context, s1 may not cause s2. We have not yet investigated this form of reasoning. The compiler described here assumes that the representation is correct/consistent in those aspects that it uses.

The Structure of a Generated Diagnostic System

As shown in Fig. 4.3, the generated expert system is a hierarchy of specialists. The structure and problem solving of the diagnostic system are similar to those of a medical diagnostic system called MDX (Chandrasekaran & Mittal, 1983b; Gomez & Chandrasekaran, 1981). Each specialist corresponds to a malfunction in the device at a certain level of abstraction, for example, a bad clapper or bad serial connection. Specialists corresponding to more general or abstract malfunctioning are higher in the hierarchy. For example, node 2 corresponds to the following malfunction: the buzzer does not buzz when the manual-switch is pressed. One of its subspecialists (node 7) corresponds to acoustically bad clapper. Every specialist has knowledge to establish the associated malfunctioning. As shown in Fig. 4.3, the knowledge is in the form of two types of rules: confirmatory and exclusionary rules. A malfunction is diagnosed top-down by establishing a specialist and refining the malfunction represented by it by calling its subspecialists (see Gomez & Chandrasekaran, 1981).

We have identified three types of malfunctioning, namely, a violated assumption, faulty function, and faulty relation. The corresponding specialists can be viewed as assumption checker, function checker and relation checker.

The Compilation Process

The compiler first generates the root specialist, which corresponds to a *malfunctioning buzzer*. The root specialist contains no rules. Invocation of the diagnostic

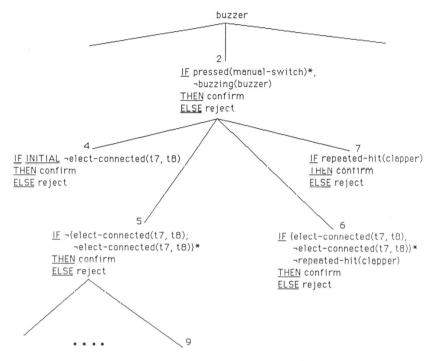

FIG. 4.3.   An example of a generated diagnostic expert.

expert will automatically establish the root specialist. The compiler then generates a function checker for each function of the device (since the malfunctioning
must be due to one or more of the faulty functions). For example, given the *buzz*
function described earlier, the compiler will generate a function checker with the
following rule:

IF pressed(manual-switch)* ∧ ⏋ buzzing(buzzer)
  THEN confirm
  ELSE reject

(How the compiler operates on the PROVIDED clause is discussed later.) The
function checkers thus generated will be attached to the root specialist. After-
wards the compiler, using the BY clause in the functional specification, obtains
the behavior associated with each function and compiles it. For example, if the
behavior is specified in the form (we do not discuss here multiple causes and
multiple effects):

$s1 \Longrightarrow s2 \Longrightarrow \ldots\ldots\ldots \Longrightarrow sn$

The compiler will generate a set of n-1 function checkers. (This is because if the function is faulty, then one of the steps in the corresponding behavior may be malfunctioning.) The rules for the ith specialist will be: IF $S_{i-1} \wedge \neg S_i$ THEN confirm ELSE reject. For the *buzz* function example, *behavior1* (given in Fig. 4.2) will be used to generate nodes 5, 6 and 7 (in Fig. 4.3). Another possible reason for a function's not working is that the condition in the PROVIDED clause may not be holding. Therefore, the compiler will generate an assumption checker using the PROVIDED clause, if any. For example node 4 corresponds to the PROVIDED clause in the buzz function. Also, the condition in the rule associated with node 5 does not include *pressed(manual-switch)** because it is checked at the parent node.

Further processing of a behavioral specification depends on the kind of composition of behavior. The following cases arise:

1. Step 1 in Fig. 4.2 will result in compiling *behavior2* (behavior2 is specified in the Appendix) as described earlier, and attaching the generated specialists to node 5.

2. Step 2 in Fig. 4.2 will result in obtaining the behavior associated with the function *mechanical* from the functional representation of clapper and compiling it. If there is no behavioral specification for the function, the specialist will be a tip specialist (e.g. node 6). Also, if a function is used in a behavioral specification under an assumption (as illustrated earlier), say assumption1, and the specification of assumption1 is of the form IF S_3 THEN S_4, then the additional specialist with the rule *IF $S_3 \wedge \neg S_4$ THEN confirm ELSE reject* will be generated (because the function may be faulty due to a violated assumption).

3. The piece of causal knowledge

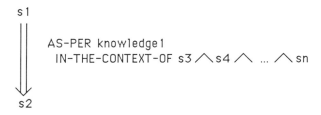

will result in n-3 sub-specialists with the rule for the ith $(3 < i < n)$ specialist being IF $\sim Si$ THEN confirm ELSE reject. The reason the above step does not hold is that the context of the application of *knowledge1* is different (note that the compiler assumes the representation to be correct/consistent). The ith specialist will turn out to be a relation checker if si corresponds to a relation.

We have implemented the compiler just described in ELISP on a DECsystem 20/60. The compiler is being tested extensively in the medical and electromechanical domains.

Meaning of Function in the Representation

In what sense can the proposed representation be said to correspond to understanding how the device works? We can point immediately to several aspects of understanding that are not meant to be incorporated in the representation: it does not understand *buzzing* or *electrically connected* or any of the terminals that are treated as strings of symbols, not to speak of any common sense substratum of knowledge such as objects and actions. What the functional representation really does is *organize* the agent's understanding of how the device's *functions* result from *behaviors* made possible by the *structure* of the device, and contains explicit pointers to *generic domain knowledge* and *assumptions about behavioral alternatives* used by the agent in this process. Thus this representation is a piece in the total understanding structure, and is responsible for elucidating the role of the structure in the functioning of the device.

There is a need to distinguish between the intrinsic function of a device and the variety of functions to which it may be put as part of a larger system. Consider the example[2] of a steam valve that opens and lets steam escape when the steam pressure goes over a certain limit. One designer may use this to make a high-pressure alarm by attaching it to a whistle, and another may use it as an explosion-preventer in a steam engine. But the typical functional representation of the steam-valve will not have either of these functions represented in it, since representing them goes beyond the intrinsic function of the device itself. An intrinsic function of a device is related to the no-function-in-structure (NFIS) principle suggested by de Kleer & Brown (1981) and Kuipers (1981) as a way of ensuring that the agent's representation of a component is specified independently of the contexts in which the components may be used. Thus, this principle forbids representing the battery's function in the buzzer as something that will help it to buzz, or that it is to be connected in series with a clapper in a buzzer, etc.

THE DIAGNOSTIC TASK AND THE STRUCTURE
PRODUCED BY THE COMPILER

Diagnostic reasoning in general needs strategies and knowledge that go beyond what is obtainable from considerations of functioning of the device alone. The final form of the diagnostic problem solver will reflect an integration of the diagnostic structure obtained from the functional representation and these addi-

---

[2]Ben Kuipers, personal communication. Note that the scheme permits representation of "negative" functions; the TOMAKE construct can be followed by the negation of a partial state: e.g., "TOMAKE~explode(engine)BY $<$ .. $>$ .... ."

tional strategies and knowledge. Some of this additional sources of complexity in diagnostic reasoning are given in the following:

1. Not all diagnostic knowledge about a system is derived from a functional understanding of the system in question. This is especially true of complex systems such as the human body, where a sizeable portion of the diagnostic knowledge of physicians comes from empirical and statistical means, rather than by a device-based understanding of the body. Our approach can account for those portions of the diagnostic knowledge base that are derivable from a deeper functional model.

2. The diagnostic system in Fig. 4.3 has diagnostic rules that use results of some tests as evidence for or against malfunction hypotheses. Often, however, these tests cannot be performed, or their results cannot be observed. For example, one of the functions of the liver is to secrete bile into the duodenum, and our functional compiler will produce, *Check if there is bile secreted in the duodenum* as a test to be performed for a liver malfunction. *Bile in the duodenum* is not directly observable, and thus additional information-gathering processes will need to be launched to infer this datum. There are several strategies typically available for this. One is to regard the presence or absence of bile as state changes in another functional system that characterizes the action of bile in the body, derive the consequences (e.g., bile not secreted into the duodenum - - - > high bilirubin in blood), and use the latter data as evidence about the unobservable test values, and thus about the hypothesis. Sometimes, such an iterated reasoning process will be able to give only probabilistic evidence. For example, the test *Check if <organ> is enlarged* may not be directly observable, but pain in that region may result from the enlarged organ. However other organs in that region, if enlarged, may also result in pain. Thus *pain in <region>* may give a probabilistic evidence for the hypothesis for which *Check if <organ> is enlarged* was to be a test.

3. Another strategy useful when the functional compiler produces nonobservable tests is illustrated by the following example. Assume that a certain input, say s1, to a device will produce action a1 if the device is in mode m1, and action a2 if it is in mode m2. Consider the function corresponding to action a1, and let us assume that the behavioral sequence that results in a1 can be simply diagrammed as follows:

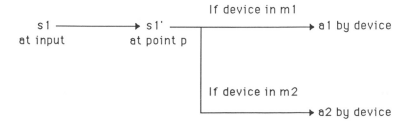

The fragment of the diagnostic hierarchy for function a1, with the attached rules, will be as follows:

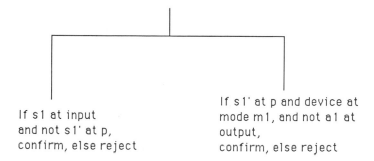

If s1 at input
and not s1' at p,
confirm, else reject

If s1' at p and device at
mode m1, and not a1 at
output,
confirm, else reject

Let us now assume that s1' at p is not observable, but s1 is at the input and the device is not outputting a1 as action. A typical strategy in diagnostic reasoning is to ask what other functions s1' at participates in, (in this case it will be a2 at output if device is in mode m2), and use it for ruling out. In this situation, the strategy will call for trying to get the device in mode m2, send s1 at input, and see if action a2 takes place.

The point about this and the previous strategy is that they are external to the functional representation and the compilation process. The diagnostic structure produced by the compiler has extracted the diagnostic knowledge directly derivable from functional knowledge, and other strategies need to be called upon to transform it further.

4. Another transformation of the diagnostic structure is quite common but also beyond the responsibility of the functional representation and the diagnostic compiler. This transformation involves incorporating knowledge about costs of malfunctions and their relative probabilities into the diagnostic process so that certain malfunctions may be considered before others. For example, in many electronic applicances, the first thing to check when it malfunctions is the battery, since that is the most common source of failure. Similarly, some malfunctions may be more costly, or tests for them may be more economical, so they may be investigated before others. This form of knowledge, and its incorporation within the diagnostic structure, is not related to how the device's function arises from its structure, and thus requires processes outside of the compiler described earlier.

5. Because of the simplicity of the device, all the nodes in Fig. 4.3 could be established or rejected on the basis of one test. Typically, however, the knowledge needed for confirmation or rejection of a malfunction hypothesis in complex systems would consist of a number of pieces, each contributing some evidence for or against the hypothesis, and these pieces of evidence may need to be combined in a complex way. This complexity in the knowledge needed for confirmation or rejection of a malfunction hy-

pothesis arises from a number of sources mentioned earlier: the fact that some of the knowledge is empirical and needs to be integrated; and the introduction of probabilistic aspects due to the need to convert the tests to observables.

6. Another example in which additional knowledge and reasoning beyond the functioning of the device is called for in reaching interesting diagnostic conclusions is illustrated by the following example. Assume that the manual switch in the buzzer example has been so altered that the circuit is closed when the switch is open, and vice versa.[3] Now both the *buzz* and the *stop buzz* functions are not being fulfilled by the device. The diagnostic structure will be able to recognize this and will make two sets of diagnoses: buzz function blocked because the Switch is not on when pressed, and the stop buzz malfunction happens because the switch does not go off when not pressed. To go from these correct conclusions to hypothesize that possibly the same structure change is causing both the malfunctions involves a form of reasoning distinct from the task of the diagnostic compiler.

7. In our approach, we define the diagnostic task as finding the structure change that is responsible for an observed failure of a function of a device. This is the diagnostic task handled by the compiled problem solver, such as the one in Fig. 4.3. Note that this explicitly does not include having to account for how the observed (malfunction) behavior is generated from the changed structure. Human problem solvers sometimes do the latter as part of their diagnostic reasoning; sometimes they do not. The latter process may generally require a form of qualitative simulation, called envisioning (de Kleer & Brown, 1982b), in order to reason from structure to behavior. In this paper we do not address the problem of envisioning, which is also related to how an agent may construct a functional representation from the structure and functions of components. Some theories of how this may be done are proposed in (de Kleer & Brown, 1982b; Forbus, 1982; Kuipers, 1982).

8. A malfunction may be caused by introduction of alternate causal pathways, without any particular component being faulted. In the buzzer example, imagine that some form of leakage or short circuit exists between terminals t5 and t6, thus depriving the coil of any current. There is nothing in the functional description specifically stating that such a short circuit should not be present for the device to work, nor would it be reasonable to expect it to say so, since such a statement will need to be made about every component. This is general electrical knowledge that is implicit in an agent's understanding of how a whole class of such devices work. During diagnosis, hypothesizing such short circuit for every component would be

---

[3]Example from Wendy Lehnert, personal communication.

prohibitive. The diagnostic system in Fig. 4.3 would identify the problem as one of transiting from elect-connected(t1,t2) to voltage-applied(t5,t6) in behavior3 (see appendix 4.). Under normal conditions this can be interpreted as a failure of the coil (say an open circuit in it), indicating that it should be replaced. However, when that fails to solve the problem, other (typically precompiled) causes of no voltage across the coil terminals can be tested, and one would assume that such a list will include short circuits around the component. Note that, while this portion of the diagnostic reasoning is itself not driven by any functional knowledge about the device, the problem solver in Fig. 4.3 derived from functional knowledge has nevertheless strongly focused the problem. Without this focusing, the number of alternate pathway hypotheses that will need to be considered will be prohibitively large.

"WHAT WILL HAPPEN IF" PROBLEM SOLVING USING THE FUNCTIONAL REPRESENTATION

It is natural to expect an agent who understands how a device works to be able to say what consequences to functionality a change in the structure of the device will produce. This task has two components: one is to know which of the intended functions will be affected by a proposed structure change, and the other is to deduce what new behavior will follow. For example, given an understanding of how amplification is produced in an electronic amplifier and given a change in the value of some resistors, an agent may be able to say "The device will fail to amplify," whereas another agent may be able to augment this with "Instead, the device will oscillate." Our functional representation can support the former component (as we show shortly). The latter, as in the case with the diagnostic task, will in general require construction of a new functional representation.[4]

We can view this WWHI problem solving as being performed by a problem-solving structure that is compiled from the functional representation, similar to the diagnostic problem solving described earlier. Although we have not implemented this compiler, we can outline this process in a fairly straightforward manner. Let us motivate the discussion with the following concrete questions

---

[4]However, when alternative functions (such as oscillation) are the consequence of certain *assumptions* in the functional representation being violated (such as the value of certain resistors being greater than a certain amount), it is possible to construct an augmented representation that essentially encodes the functions that would result from alternative assumptions. In such a case both parts of the WWHI task can be answered from the augmented functional representation. This augmented representation bears the same relation to our functional representation that the "intrinsic mechanism" of deKleer and Brown (1982a) does to their causal state sequences.

about the buzzer that we might wish such a structure to answer. (These questions are slightly modified versions of those given in de Kleer and Brown, 1981.)

1. What happens if we reverse the leads of the battery?
2. What happens if we switch the leads of the coil?
3. What happens if we remove the battery from the circuit?
4. What happens if we make the clapper spring tension lighter?

The general procedure is that given a proposed change in the structure, the compiler looks to see in which behaviors the component affected by the structure change participates. Referring to the appendix, which gives complete description for the *buzz* function, we see that the battery participates in *behavior2* and *behavior3*. For question 1, then, the relevant issue with respect to *behavior2* and *behavior3* is whether *FUNCTION voltage OF battery* is still delivered and whether relation *serially-connected (battery, coil, clapper, manual-switch)* is still valid. The functional representation itself cannot answer these questions, but points to the questions that need to be answered by further domain knowledge. We know from domain knowledge that for question 1 the answer is that neither the voltage function of the battery nor the serially connected relation is affected; thus the two behaviors are not affected, and the buzz function is not affected. For question 3, a similar analysis will result in the following sequence of reasoning steps. In behavior3, the transition from *elect-connected (t1, t2)* to *voltage-applied (t5,t6)* will fail, which will cause *behavior3*, namely, the transition from *pressed (manual-switch)* to ⅂ *elect-connected(t7,t8)* to fail. This will result in *behavior2*'s failing, which will in turn result in *behavior1*'s failing in the first transition; continuous pressing of manual switch will not result in the alternate connection and disconnection of t7 and t8. As a result, function buzz will fail, because *behavior1* is used to realize this function.

Answering question 2 is quite similar. Question 4, however, is worth considering in some detail. The compiler will note that this part of the structure (i.e., spring tension) plays a role in *assumption2* and *assumption3* (see Assumptions subsection earlier). Again, further domain knowledge is used to conclude that spring tension, if sufficiently weak, will violate assumption3. The clapper's functional representation describes its magnetic function as consisting of:

FUNCTION: magnetic: TOMAKE ⅂ elect-connected(t7,t8)
                     IF magnetized(space2)
                     PROVIDED assumption2
                     AND
                     TOMAKE ⅂ elect-connected(t7,t8)
                     IF ⅂ magnetized(space2)
                     PROVIDED assumption3

Possible failure of *assumption3* will imperil the second part of the above magnetic function, which will endanger the

$$\neg \text{ magnetized(space2) - - - - - - - -> elect-connected(t7,t8)}$$

transition in *behavior4* in buzz function (see appendix 4.), thus putting the *buzz* function into question. The final conclusion is that for sufficiently weak tension (or sufficiently light arm), the *buzz* function will not be delivered by the device.

In the preceding description, we have used the word *compilation,* but in fact actually described the problem solving. More precisely, we should show that the compiler actually builds a problem-solving structure (like the diagnostic structure in Fig. 4.3) that then solves the WWHI problem. However, for purposes of this discussion, our aim was only to show how the functional representation can support this type of problem solving.

Note that the WWHI problem solving just described moves through behavioral levels of abstraction made possible by the hierarchical structure in the functional representation. This is consistent with the nature of information processing for this generic task as described in Chandrasekaran (1983).

RELATION TO OTHER WORK

Our research differs from that of de Kleer and Brown (1981, 1982a, 1982b) Patil (1981), and Davis et al. (1982) in the following three significant respects:

1. Our representation identifies and relates the five aspects of functional knowledge, namely function, behavior, structure, assumptions, and generic knowledge in a specific scheme.
2. We have refined the notion of causation in terms of three hierarchies, namely Hierarchy of Details, Component Hierarchy, and Generalization Hierarchy, and used it to represent the functional knowledge of devices.
3. We have been directly concerned with compilation of expert problem solving structures from the functional representation.

Kuipers (1982) discusses a form of envisionment about changes to an equilibrium condition in a physiological system and proposes this as a kind of understanding of the human body that may be incorporated in medical expert systems. The issues discussed by him are orthogonal to our concerns here. Kuipers (1981) critiques the representation proposals of de Kleer and Brown.

The Work of de Kleer and Brown

We were originally motivated in our work by our concern with deep models for problem solvers, and thus we were searching for mental models of devices that would permit compilation of problem-solving systems. Once we formulated our theory, we noted that the work of de Kleer and Brown (1981) which proposed using envisioning to produce such a mental model, had some elements in common with our idea, but the representation was significantly different. The desire to understand the points of contact and departure between our points of view was in fact one of the reasons we chose the same device they had used, namely, the buzzer. In this section we compare the representation and the underlying points of view.

The mental model proposed by de Kleer and Brown (1982a) for the understanding of devices consists of representing qualitatively the causal sequence of behavioral states that the device needs to pass through during its functioning. In the buzzer example, a portion of this mental model can be stated as follows: ''The clapper being open results in no current through it, which results in no current into the coil, which results in no magnetic field, which results in clapper being closed, which results in current flowing through its input and output, which results in current into the coil, which results in a magnetic field, which results in the clapper being open.'' The alternative representation proposed in Kuipers (1981), although different in a number of details, is also essentially a sequence of behavioral states. In our approach, however, the function is distinguished from the behavior of the device to accomplish it. Our functional representation is a hierarchical organization of behavioral segments of components into a representation which itself is not a causal sequence of partial states, but can be processed to obtain such a sequence. Further, unlike the causal sequence of de Kleer and Brown (1982a), the sequence that can be produced by our representation can be in varying levels of detail, because its hierarchical structure reflects the component hierarchy in the device. The hierarchical nature of the functional description is very important; otherwise describing the functioning of a complex system would involve an excruciatingly long sequence of causal states at a low level of abstraction. Simply, we distinguish an agent's description of the causal/behavioral sequence device undergoes from the representation used by the agent to produce such a description, and identify the latter with the functional representation or the mental model of the agent.

Another advantage of distinguishing between function and behavior as we do is that we are able to represent functions that prevent certain things from happening. (See footnote 2 on explosion-preventer). This would be difficult to do if function is represented as the actual causal sequence followed by the device: prevented situations would hardly occur unless the device were malfunctioning!

Historically, de Kleer and Brown (1981) have been concerned with how an agent composes the behavior of the components of a device to obtain the behavior of the device itself. This process they have called *envisioning*. While this is an important part of the comprehension process, we feel that understanding the functioning of the device consists of a further activity of constructing a functional representation along the lines advanced in this paper. How an agent constructs such a functional representation by combining envisioning, functional representation of components of the device, some global properties of the device, and assumptions about the device itself is an open question.

We have said several times that a test of a functional representation is its ability to support different types of problem solving such as trouble-shooting. Although, to ourf knowledge, de Kleer and Brown have not reported on any implementation of a diagnostic reasoning system based on their causal sequences as mental models, they have described how such a process may work (de Kleer & Brown, 1982a), and it is instructive to compare that process with our approach.

de Kleer and Brown (1982) regard diagnostic reasoning as a task of accounting for how an observed behavior that differs from an intended behavior is actually produced by a malfunctioning device. They indicate that if the malfunctioning device essentially follows the same causal sequence (with some of the attributes of the states or assumptions possibly being different) as the one corresponding to the functioning device, then the structure causing the difference in behavior can be identified relatively easily. (For large systems, this might require following an equally large state causation chain.) If the structure change is such that the device is not undergoing essentially the same causal chain, this task calls for a new envisioning for each structure change hypothesis. The causation chain itself is not useful for generating structure change hypotheses efficiently, or for the new envisioning that would be needed for each candidate structure change hypothesis. They correctly point out that the diagnostic process would now face a prohibitively combinatorial search.

The diagnostic task, as mentioned earlier, can be decomposed into two components: first, identifying the part of the structure that is responsible for the original function (for which the agent has a functional representation) not being delivered, and, second, explaining, if possible, how the changed structure produced the observed malfunctioning behavior. To use an example well known in electronics, amplifiers may sometimes malfunction and behave as oscillators. The first part corresponds to saying, "Amplification is not taking place because resistor R1's value is less than required," and the second part explains how the change in the value of the resistor resulted in the device acting as an oscillator. If one can do the former without being able to do the latter, one would still have accomplished a significant diagnostic act. It is not clear that most trouble-shooting situations necessarily require the latter part in any case, since the goal of the trouble-shooting process is often to identify the components that are causing the malfunction and to replace them.

The first part is not subject to a combinatorial search problem in our theory: the functional representation and the compiler in principle can identify the component at fault[5] because of the hierachical structure of the resulting diagnostic

---

[5]See item 8, The Diagnostic Task, for some qualifications for this statement, but it entails no essential change in the argument here.

system as well as because the representation encodes the relation between structure and the intended function. The second part, expaining how the new behavior is produced, may or may not be subject to combinatorial search, depending on the degree of change to the structure and the resulting need for new a functional representation.

CONCLUDING REMARKS

As we have indicated, the task of accounting for how complex systems and devices are understood has many components. We have developed a framework in which this comprehension process and its relation to problem solving can be investigated. In particular, we have proposed a language for the representation of what we call the causal component of this comprehension that captures some aspects of how a function of a device arises from its structure, and shown that this structure can support problem solving for diagnosis and some kinds of prediction.

Directions for future research include the following. First, we need to develop methods to check the correctness/consistency of a given functional representation. This requires domain knowledge for interpreting state descriptions as well as the relations such as serially connected. Second, we need to investigate the design of the other two dimensions of our representational scheme, namely, temporal and interaction. Also, the causal dimension has to be integrated with the other two in a disciplined, partically useful and cognitively meaningful framework. Third, we need to identify the compilation processes that come into play to generate other types of expert problem solving structures, such as predicting functional and behavioral consequences of changes in structure or assumptions. Finally, it is a matter of singificant theoretical and practical interest to ask how an agent can incrementally acquire a functional representation of a device from its structure, generic knowledge, inadequacy of the current representation for supporting the compilation of adequate problem systems, and so on.

In broader terms, this research is part of our ongoing effort to uncover the multiplicity of generic structures and processes involved in knowledge-based problem solving. Whether or not one accepts the hypothesis of homogeneous and unitary architectures, such as production systems, as adequate at the level of symbol processing in the mind, we feel we need a richer collection of generic knowledge structures and a correspondingly rich collection of knowledge-processing mechanisms that operate on them, in order to account for knowledge-based problem-solving activity at the information-processing level. In expert systems work especially, we feel there is a need to explore richer architectures that capture the information-processing activity. From this perspective, the functional representation is one of the information-processing level theories that are needed for understanding knowledge-based reasoning.

ACKNOWLEDGMENTS

This research was supported by National Science Foundation grant MCS-8305032 and by Air Force Office of Scientific Research grant AFOSR 82-0255.

APPENDIX

Details of the functional representation of FUNCTION: *buzz* of the buzzer

NOTE: We have represented only the buzzer;
       Battery, coil, clapper and manual switch have NOT been represented.

    DEVICE buzzer
       FUNCTION:
          buzz: TOMAKE buzzing (buzzer)
                IF pressed (manual-switch)*
                PROVIDED INITIAL elect-connected (t7,t8)
                BY behavior1

          stop-buzz: TOMAKE ⌐ buzzing (buzzer)
                     IF ⌐ pressed (manual-switch)
                     PROVIDED INITIAL buzzing (buzzer)
                     BY behavior5

       STRUCTURE:
          COMPONENTS:
             manual-switch (t1,t2), battery (t3,t4),

             coil (t5,t6,space1), clapper (t7,t8,space2)

          RELATIONS:
             serially-connected (manual-switch,battery,coil,clapper),

             includes (space1,space2)

          ABSTRACTIONS-OF-COMPONENTS:
             COMPONENT clapper (T1,T2,SPACE)
                FUNCTIONS: mechanical,acoustic,magnetic
                STATES: elect-connected (T1,T2),
                        repeated-hit (clapper)
             COMPONENT coil (T1,T2,Space)
                FUNCTIONS: magnetic

                STATES: magnetized (SPACE), voltage-applied(T1,T2)

             COMPONENT manual-switch(T1,T2)
                FUNCTIONS: connect

STATES: elect-connected (T1,T2),
pressed (manual-switch)

COMPONENT battery (T1,T2)
FUNCTIONS: voltage

BEHAVIOR:

behavior1:

pressed(manual-switch)*

⇓ BY behavior2

{elect-connected(t7, t8); ¬elect-connected(t7, t8)}*

⇓ USING FUNCTION mechanical OF
clapper(t7, t8, space1)

repeated-hit(clapper)

⇓ USING FUNCTION acoustic OF
clapper(t7, t8, space2)

buzzing(clapper)

|||

buzzing(buzzer)

behavior2:

{ pressed(manual-switch)

⇓ BY behavior3

¬elect-connected(t7, t8)

⇓ AS-PER knowledge1 IN-THE-CONTEXT-OF
serially-connected(battery, coil, clapper,
manual-switch)
∧FUNCTION voltage OF battery

¬voltage-applied(t5, t6)

⇓ BY behavior4

elect-connected(t7, t8) }*

behavior3:

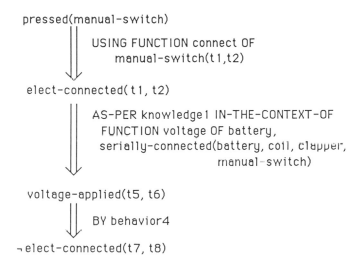

pressed(manual-switch)

USING FUNCTION connect OF
manual-switch(t1,t2)

elect-connected(t1, t2)

AS-PER knowledge1 IN-THE-CONTEXT-OF
FUNCTION voltage OF battery,
serially-connected(battery, coil, clapper,
manual-switch)

voltage-applied(t5, t6)

BY behavior4

¬elect-connected(t7, t8)

behavior4: IFF

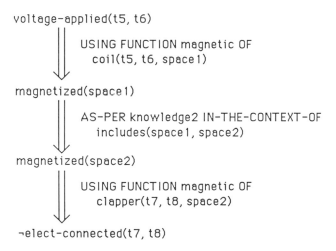

voltage-applied(t5, t6)

USING FUNCTION magnetic OF
coil(t5, t6, space1)

magnetized(space1)

AS-PER knowledge2 IN-THE-CONTEXT-OF
includes(space1, space2)

magnetized(space2)

USING FUNCTION magnetic OF
clapper(t7, t8, space2)

¬elect-connected(t7, t8)

NOTE: IFF (S1 ⟹ S2⟹S3) is the same as
S1 ⟹ S2 ⟹ S3   and   ¬S1 ⟹ ¬S2 ⟹ ¬S3

GENERIC KNOWLEDGE:

knowledge1:

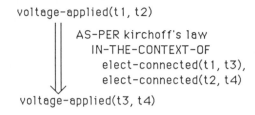

voltage-applied(t1, t2)

AS-PER kirchoff's law
IN-THE-CONTEXT-OF
    elect-connected(t1, t3),
    elect-connected(t2, t4)

voltage-applied(t3, t4)

knowledge2:

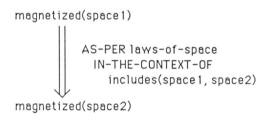

magnetized(space1)

AS-PER laws-of-space
IN-THE-CONTEXT-OF
    includes(space1, space2)

magnetized(space2)

END-DEVICE buzzer

REFERENCES

Chandrasekaran, B. (1983). Towards a taxonomy of problem-solving types. *AI Magazine, 4*(1), 9–17.

Chandrasekaran, B., & Mittal, S. (1982). Deep versus compiled knowledge approaches to diagnostic problem-solving. *Proceedings of the National Conference on Artificial Intelligence* (pp. 349–354). Pittsburgh, PA.

Chandrasekaran, B., & Mittal, S. (1983a). On deep versus compiled approaches to diagnostic problem-solving. *International Journal of Man-Machine Studies, 19,* 425–436. (A summarized version appears in Chandrasekaran & Mittal, 1982).

Chandrasekaran, B., & Mittal, S. (1983b). Conceptual representation of medical knowledge for diagnosis by computer: MDX and related systems. In M. Yovits (Ed.), *Advances in computers* (pp. 217–293). New York: Academic Press.

Davis, R., Shrobe, H., Hamscher, W., Wieckert, K., Shirley, M., & Polit, S. (1982) Diagnosis based on description of structure and function. *Proceedings of the AAAI-82* (pp. 137–142). Pittsburgh, PA.

de Kleer, J., & Brown, J. S. (1981). Towards a theory of qualitative reasoning about mechanisms. In J. R. Anderson (Ed.), *Cognitive skills and their acquisition.* Hillsdale, NJ: Lawrence Erlbaum Associates.

de Kleer, J., & Brown, J. S. (1982a). *Assumptions and ambiguities in mechanistic mental models.* (CIS 9). Xerox Palo Alto Research Center, CA.

de Kleer, J., & Brown, J. S. (1982b). Foundations of envisioning. *Proceedings of the AAAI-82* (pp. 434–437). Pittsburgh, PA.

Forbus, K. (1982). *The role of qualitative dynamics in naive physics.* MIT Lab Report.

Gomez, F., & Chandrasekaran, B. (1981, January). Knowledge organization and distribution for medical diagnosis. *IEEE Transactions on Systems, Man, and Cybernetics, SMC-11*(1), 34–42.

Hart, P. E. (1982). Directions for AI in the eighties. *SIGART Newsletter, 79,* 11–16.

Kuipers, B. (1981). De Kleer and Brown's 'mental models': A critique. *Working papers in cognitive science* (17). Boston, MA: Tufts University.

Kuipers, B. (1982). Commonsense reasoning about causality: Deriving behavior from structure. *Working papers in cognitive science.* Boston, MA: Tufts University.

Michie, D. (1982). High-road and low-road programs. *AI Magazine, 3,* 21–22.

Patil, R. S. (1981). *Causal representation of patient illness for electrolyte and acid-base diagnosis.* Unpublished doctoral dissertation, Massachusetts Institute of Technology.

Weiss, S. M., Kulikowski, C. A., Amarel, S., & Safir, A. (1978). A model-based method for computer-aided medical decision-making. *Artificial Intelligence, 11,* 145–172.

5 Knowledge-Directed Retrieval of Autobiographical Memories

Brian J. Reiser
Carnegie-Mellon University

ABSTRACT

Many cognitive processes, such as case-based reasoning and problem solving, rely on the retrieval of representations of individual experiences stored in memory. In the "context-plus-index" memory model, retrieving an experience involves accessing a context, then traversing an index or link describing that experience's unique features. Typically, the initial cues do not contain enough information to fully enable this discrimination. Instead, strategic reasoning mechanisms direct the memory search, examining the partial products of retrieval in order to decide which paths are likely to lead to the target event. This model is supported by several types of empirical evidence.

ACCESSING AUTOBIOGRAPHICAL EXPERIENCES

Other chapters in this volume have addressed the organization of general world knowledge and its effects on various types of cognitive tasks, such as reasoning, language processing, decision making, and learning. In addition to generalizations learned from experience, many cognitive processes also rely on representations of the individual experiences themselves that are stored in memory. Accessing these individual instances plays an important role in case-based reasoning (see chapters by Kolodner, Rissland, and Bain, this volume), and are also utilized to guide problem solving (Ross, 1984). It is therefore important to address the nature of the search mechanisms that access individual experiences from memory. How are the relevant experiences found from the enormous data base of stored experiences? How are these experiences organized?

Most memory research has focused on modeling "automatic" retrieval processes. For example, most models of automatic memory retrieval propose that when a cue is presented, the representation of that cue in memory is accessed, and then associated paths in the memory network are followed until the target node is reached. Strategic components of a retrieval are often considered only in order to rule them out as explanations for an empirical result. However, the types of memory retrieval we do in everyday life typically present more complex demands than memory for simple verbal material presented in a psychology laboratory. In this chapter, I argue that a model containing only automatic processing is insufficient to account for the type of memory search involved in retrieving memories of individual experiences. I describe a model of this directed search process, and present arguments and psychological evidence to support the role of strategic search mechanisms in autobiographical memory.

A MODEL OF DIRECTED RETRIEVAL

In previous papers, we have described a context-plus-index model of autobiographical memory organization and retrieval (Reiser, 1983; Reiser, Black, & Abelson, 1985; Reiser, Black & Kalamarides, in press) that builds on earlier proposals by Schank (1982) and Kolodner (1983, 1984) concerning the connection of individual experiences to general knowledge structures in memory. To retrieve episodic information, one must access the mental context used to encode the event (Tulving, 1983). In the case of real-world experiences, this encoding context consists of the knowledge structures activated to process that experience originally, namely, those utilized in planning and comprehension processes. Knowledge structures contain generalizations about events that can be used to plan a course of action to effect one or more goals. These same generalizations can be used to interpret the behavior of others in terms of their goals and plans. For example, the Going to the Movies activity contains knowledge about what one is expected to do in that situation, the expected behavior of others, the goals achieved by that activity, the physical objects likely to be found in that setting, and other details. This knowledge structure is accessed to figure out what actions to perform and to understand the behavior of others in that context. Therefore, this structure is accessed during the encoding of an experience, and consequently representations of particular movie experiences become associated with the structure in memory. In order to retrieve one of those experiences, it is first necessary to access one of these contextualizing knowledge structures.

After a retrieval context has been selected, the next step involves isolating the target experience from among the many events associated with that structure. This process involves specifying a set of features that uniquely discriminate an experience with the target properties. Hence, retrieval involves accessing a context, then traversing an index or link describing the experience's unique features.

Typically, the cue does not contain enough information to fully enable this discrimination. Instead, the possible set of experiences is continually narrowed down as more and more features of the experience are proposed and tested (Kolodner, 1983, 1984; Norman & Bobrow, 1979; Reiser, 1983; Williams & Hollan, 1981). Partial information retrieved on one probe of memory can be used to predict further features of the target, thus elaborating the retrieval description until an individual experience is retrieved. An example of these incremental retrieval mechanisms is shown in the following verbal protocol: (Subjects in these protocols were asked to think aloud as they tried to recall a personal experience with the stated characteristics.)

[1] E: Think of a time when you felt cold at an exam.

S: Cold at an exam . . . . Wow, I keep thinking how most of my exam rooms have been really well heated! I remember being really hot in exams but never really cold, which I guess is pretty lucky. 'Cause most . . . I mean, at Christmas it's usually been really well heated.

E: What's going through your mind now . . . what can you think of?

S: Um, I was trying to start thinking through the exams I've taken at Christmas. Um, going through the different classes but they're not really coming . . . I think maybe my Bio exam freshman year I was cold 'cause I had to walk all the way up to Science Hill to go take it, but the room was heated. But they gave us lollipops in the exam, which I thought was kind of nice! But it was a long walk and it had snowed.

This retrieval protocol exhibits some interesting evidence for a focused search process. The subject concentrated his processing on the Taking Exams activity, rather than the feeling cold state. For example, the subject managed to recall experiences matching the activity that do not fit the state, although it is reasonable to expect that he had more feeling cold experiences in memory than exam experiences. The subject also appears to have added a constraint to the search representing a likely component of the target experience, namely that the exam took place at Christmas rather than spring term. Finally, the protocol exhibits an explicit stragegy for enumerating instances of an activity. The strategy involves searching an organization of information external to the activity, that is, classes the subject had taken, selecting elements of that organization that satisfied the generated constraint (Christmas exam), then testing the retrieved instances to see whether they contained the target attribute (feeling cold). As in this protocol, Reiser et al. (in press) found that subjects tended to focus on activities rather than mental or physical states when trying to recall experiences. In fact, subjects queried about such states often transformed the question into one about a related activity, and then generated experiences involving that activity.

What is the role of strategies in these mechanisms? Is it possible to access a context when given a cue and then automatically follow paths or probe associated structures at random until the target experience is successfully retrieved, or are these types of memory searches necessarily directed by reasoning mechanisms? For less complex tasks such as recall of simple verbal material, memory models focusing on automatic undirected probing of memory have been effective in characterizing memory retrieval. For example, Raaijmakers and Shiffrin (1981) proposed an incremental search model that utilizes partial products in an undirected probabilistic fashion. At each stage of the search, associated nodes are probed and accessed randomly. In an attempt to apply memory retrieval theories to real-world cognitive tasks, the context-plus-index model expands on this type of retrieval model in two important respects. First, as I argue in the next section, purely automatic processing is unlikely to yield the target items in memory. Instead, strategic reasoning mechanisms are required to *direct* the memory search, examining the partial products of retrieval in order to decide which paths are likely to lead to the target event. Furthermore, the directed retrieval model addresses the organization of the data base, left unspecified by these automatic processing models and yet of central importance when world knowledge is called upon to direct the search.

An important distinction between directed search and automatic retrieval is in the use of information associated to a search cue. In one class of models of automatic processing, memory retrieval is achieved by first perceiving and parsing the cue and then accessing associated information by spreading activation to connected nodes in a memory network, thus extending the search to other nodes until a target is reached (Anderson, 1976; Collins & Loftus, 1975). In these models, activation decreases as a function of the number of associations it spreads across and increases if activation converges on a node from multiple sources. Thus, if multiple cues are presented, the search can intersect on a node with sufficient activation to retrieve it. In contrast, directed search can be defined as the selected use of associated information to determine which paths to follow in memory. Reasoning mechanisms are employed to use associated information to construct a likely scenario for an event with the target characteristics. This type of search is thus controlled rather than automatic (Schneider & Shiffrin, 1977). For example, in protocol [1], the subject was queried about both a feeling and an activity, and yet focused processing primarily on the activity, presumably because of a directed search strategy. Furthermore, he possessed much knowledge about both that state and the activity, and only some of that knowledge was called into play in this retrieval. Strategies are called upon to decide which dimensions are relevant in finding the particular target experience (e.g., participants in the event, reasons for engaging in the event, time of year, varieties of an activity), and then to generate plausible values for the chosen dimension. A directed search model can account for this by describing the reasoning mechanisms that focus attention on the associated information accessed. To explain this type of retrieval, we must first account for the reasoning mechanisms that reformulate the query to direct search to profitable contexts. Second, to explain why these strategies are both necessary and effective, we must characterize the organization of the memory system storing these experiences.

There are two stages of autobiographical memory search that require strategic direction. First, a context for search must be selected. This search context is sometimes provided in the query, as when one is asked to recall an experience involving a particular common activity, such as going to movies or dining at restaurants. However, more typically a search is initiated in response to an incomplete cue. For example, one may be trying to remember a conversation, seeing a friend, or some other type of event that could occur in many different contexts. In such cases, it will be necessary to access a context based on information related to the concepts in the query. For example, if one is trying to remember an experience involving a particular friend, one could use information about that friend to predict circumstances in which that person would have been a participant (e.g., "We usually go to science fiction movies together," "She loves spicy Chinese food," etc.). Activities rather than feelings or more general event descriptions appear to be the primary organizers of autobiographical memories (Reiser, 1983; Reiser et al., 1985; Reiser et al., in press). Activity structures are essential in many types of planning and provide a great deal of information about the motivations, behavior, and consequences in common situations. Retrieval strategies have developed to take advantage of this organization, directing search to access activity categories and then utilizing information contained in those structures. Thus, in protocol [1], the search strategies focused attention on the presented activity rather than the feeling, and subjects queried about feelings and nonactivity-specific actions (e.g., picked out what you wanted, paid for something) often infer an activity to use as a search context (Reiser, 1983; Reiser et al., in press).

A second use of retrieval strategies occurs during search within the chosen context. Frequently the search cue does not contain enough information to discriminate an experience from the others in the context, and thus retrival strategies must be employed to infer plausible features of the target experience. These retrieval mechanisms rely primarily on general information represented in the knowledge structure in order to make these inferences. Thus, the original cue is elaborated to develop a more complete description of the type of experience likely to contain the target features. Such strategies are called *elaboration strategies* (Kolodner, 1983, 1984). Information that is ineffective in enabling further predictions about the event is of little use for the search process. In order to effectively predict circumstances that would include an event with the target features, strategies must utilize social knowledge about the causes, motivations, and results of behavior. Thus, an important role of the directed component is to find the type of associated information that will be useful for predicting likely values for those features. If one is trying to remember a conversation that occured with a business associate, one could first use knowledge about the interactions of business associates to generate a candidate list of contexts, for example, cocktail parties, business meetings, and business lunches. After one of these contexts, say business lunches, is selected, general knowledge contained in that context could be used to restrict the search further, considering Fancy Restaurants as a more likely context than College Bars for the target experience. Then, the information in that more specific context can be used to direct further probes of memory.

ARGUMENTS FOR DIRECTED SEARCH MODELS

Several arguments support the necessity for a directed component of autobiographical retrieval. These arguments rely on considerations of the organization of autobiographical memory, the nature of the information typically provided in search cues, the correspondence between information in queries and that used to encode experiences, and finally the types of information that are predictive of experience features.

Too Many Paths

The first argument is that there are simply too many paths to follow for an undirected search process to be successful. After selecting a context, it is necessary to elaborate the query in order to traverse the indices to an individual experience. Most contexts contain many associated experiences that must be discriminated in order to find one possessing the target attributes. This elaboration draws on the information associated with a knowledge structure in order to generate candidate features. Thus, accessing the Dining at Restaurants context provides information about the motivations for eating at a restaurant (e.g., being too busy to cook, celebrating), the standard varieties of restaurants (e.g., college hangouts, Chinese restaurants, pizza places, French bistros), probable participants of the activity, and perhaps some memorable exemplars of that activity. These types of features are commonly used to refine the retrieval description (Reiser et al., in press). Yet if all this information, or even only the most highly accessible information, were combined with the original context, it would result in quite a large number of potential paths. If search were to randomly traverse all these paths, the chance of successfully reaching an experience with the target characteristics seems slim indeed. There would simply be too many paths for search to efficiently access and check all of them for the target event. For example, in spreading activation terms, the spread of processing (or activation) is too diffuse, and something is required to direct the search to relevant paths in memory. The purpose of the predictive mechanisms is the use of generalizations encoded about events to direct the search in this fashion (perhaps adding activation to the appropriate paths). The search is thus reconstructive or inference

driven, because information not explicitly provided in the original retrieval specification is required to select among the numerous paths available for search.

One might argue that information learned in typical laboratory experiments is
also connected to a great deal of information in the memory system, and yet
automatic processes provide a good model of memory for verbal material in these
cases. However, in these types of experiments, the experimental situation itself
becomes a retrieval cue. That is, the list of words or facts are encoded or labeled
in memory associated with the particular experimental context in which they
were learned. Although a common word learned in an experiment contains a rich
set of associates, the experimental context can be used to constrain search for that
item during recall, and thus strategic directed search may not be necessary. In the
case of studies of pre-experimentally learned material (e.g., semantic memory),
these studies have tapped general world knolwedge (i.e., facts about common
objects and events) that is likely to be more easily retrieved than individual
events.

Retrieval protocols often reveal a predictive search that considers plausible
memory paths (Reiser et al., in press; Whitten & Leonard, 1981; Williams &
Hollan, 1981). For example, after a general context has been selected, subjects
often use knowledge about that context or bring in related knowledge in order to
further refine the query, thus restricting the paths to be searched. In general, the
additional features that are selected are plausible components of the target experience, as shown in this protocol:

> [2] E: Think of a time when you went to a restaurant and didn't get what
> you wanted.
>
> S: Never happened. [Pause]
>
> E: What's going through your mind now?
>
> S: Um, I'm thinking about a restaurant in New Jersey I used to go to all
> the time and get pizza and it was, you know, really crazy but I always got
> what I wanted. It was in Morristown, Jersey, it was called Cutter's, and it
> was probably near around '77, '78, and it's a really hectic place but I
> always got what I wanted.

Here the subject considered a particular restaurant that was a "hectic place,"
presumably because this type of situation would have resulted in the target event.
Similarly, our subjects also considered variations of restaurants (e.g., college
hangouts vs. "fancy" restaurants) in order to restrict the search to a plausible
subset of restaurant experiences. To guide search within an activity context,
processing may utilize subclasses of the activity, probable participants of the
event, portions of their lives in which such an event was likely, motivations,
probable causes, and results of the experience.

Effectiveness of Retrieval Features

Given the enormous number of potential search paths that could result, the importance of reasoning mechanisms to restrict the search becomes clear. There are several reasons why these additional features that restrict the search could not simply be generated "at random" from concepts associated with the original cues. First, not all feature dimensions are equally useful in elaborating the retrieval cue. For example, features of low causal salience are unlikely to be related in systematic ways to other attributes of the experience, and thus are poor retrieval cues, because they will not enable search to further specify related featuees of the target. Furthermore, different dimensions will be relevant for different types of targets. Thus, when the query concerns feeling cold during an exam, the semester for the course will be a relevant dimension, and search can focus on an organization such as a time map to generate winter courses. If a query concerns lunch with a friend who is a college student, then the variety of activity will be relevant, and college hangouts can be selected over elegant New York restaurants as a plausible constraint on the search, and time of year is less relevant for this retrieval.

After a relevant dimension has been selected, not all possible values for that dimension will be equally likely to lead to a target experience. For example, if the search mechanisms were considering reasons for engaging in the target activity, it would be ineffective to consider all possible reasons. If at each branch point in the search all possible values for the attribute were considered, it is difficult to see how the search could converge on the target experience. Instead, a retrieval strategy can be called upon to infer a *plausible* motivation for the target activity and focus search on the most likely path. Finally, it is unreasonable to expect that each feature dimension will always enable easy access of a list of possible values. Instead, causal reasoning will often be necessary to generate those features.

These arguments suggest that retrieval strategies tend to consider those experience features that have predictive value, selecting those that are judged to be plausible in a situation with the target properties. Thus, those knowledge structures rich in predictive power will play a principal role in directing retrieval of autobiographical memories. As suggested earlier, information contained in activity structures is likely to be more useful for inferring features of an individual event during retrieval, such as causes, results, and associated contexts of events. Activities provide information about the overarching goal for the events (the reason these particular general actions are being placed together in this sequence), and the actors and props in the event. For example, one expects salespeople, merchandise, a cash register, a counter, and shoppers in the Shopping in Department Stores activity. An activity is an inference-rich structure; therefore, its access allows many features of an event to be predicted. Consistent with these arguments, studies of retrieval protocols and the effectiveness of retrieval cues reveal a tendency, as shown in protocol [1], to focus search on these more effective activity concepts (Reiser et al., 1985; Reiser et al., in press).

Incompleteness of Retrieval Cues

Another important factor requiring directed search is the nature of the retrieval cues themselves. Retrieval cues typically do not contain enough information to specify an event completely (Kolodner, 1983, 1984; Norman & Bobrow, 1979; Reiser, 1983; Williams & Hollan, 1981). In some cases, the retrieval cue simply underspecifies the target event, describing a subclass of experiences. To retrieve one experience matching those features, it is necessary to generate additional features to discriminate it from others in that subclass. In the following protocol, the subject has narrowed the search context to a subclass of experiences involving the activity and then must import additional information external to the activity in order to further constrain the search.

[3] E: Think of a time when you went to a public library. [pause] What's going through your mind?

S: That I always go to the library like a mile away from my home in Colorado, and it's hard to think of one particular time so I'm trying to figure out if I can think of like going for one book. And if I can remember doing like one research project, then I could put it together. Well, okay I remember going to get a book on running, but I didn't have my card so I was talking to a man about running because I had ran up there and it's two miles back. And he was saying "Oh well, if you can do it man." That's as close as I can get to my public library.

After narrowing the search context Public Library to one in his home town, the subject decided to focus on plausible motivations for performing that activity. By considering other events that might generate goals achieved by going to a library (e.g., reading for classes and hobbies), he was able to isolate an individual public library experience. Focus on motivations of experiences is common strategy in autobiographical retrieval (Reiser, 1983; Reiser et al., in press).

Another type of incompleteness in retrieval queries occurs when the the cue specifies a target attribute but does not specify features that must be considered before that attribute can be used. The next protocol provides an example of this type of strategy.

[4] E: Think of a time when you felt impatient.

S: Felt impatient. Those are always the tough ones to answer. Um, I'm trying to think of times I felt impatient . . . um . . . um . . . impatient always seems to mean when you're waiting in line for something or waiting for something to happen. . . . I can think of times when I felt frustrated waiting but not really impatient, and I think there's a difference. I remember waiting for someone who didn't show up for 4 hours, and it wasn't really that I was impatient, I was just frustrated with the fact that I didn't know whether this person was going to show up or not . . .

E: Was this waiting in line?

S: No this was waiting to meet someone in front of a museum in Hartford. And he didn't come for about 4 hours, and mostly the reason that I was frustrated or maybe it even is impatient is that I didn't know whether he was actually coming . . .

In this protocol the subject used her knowledge about impatience to generate a set of circumstances in which she was likely to have experienced that mental state. This process led to thinking about situations involving waiting, and ultimately to an experience where she was waiting for someone who was very late. Interestingly, the subject's hesitation in classifying this experience as impatience supports the claim that it was accessed in memory using waiting, as a search context, rather than simply using impatience as a cue. Although a mental state such as feeling impatient has many different types of information associated with it (e.g., related emotions such as anger or guilt, behavior such as pacing, reactions such as yelling or arguments, etc.), retrieval strategies focus search on related situations that might cause that state (e.g., waiting for someone) and then generate instances of that type of event. In order to direct the search and find this nondistinctive event attribute, a more predictive context must be found; search begins by accessing an activity. As in this protocol, subjects queried about mental states or very general action descriptions often reformulate those cues into questions concerning types of events (Reiser et al., in press).

Mismatch between Indexing Features and Retrieval Cues

It is not sufficient merely to characterize uniquely an experience in memory. If the stated features do not correspond to those features that index the experience, they will not be effective retrieval cues. Thus, a further need for reformulation of the query arises when the given cues do not correspond to the way the event is encoded. In these cases, retrieval strategies are employed to infer an appropriate context by reasoning about causes, results, or events related to the concepts in the query. Strategies designed to access related contexts are called *alternate context searches* (Kolodner, 1983, 1984). The incompleteness of retrieval cues and a mismatch in encoding between the retrieval cue features and those used to index experiences both indicate the importance of strategically adding features during search. The next protocol exhibits a typical method for adding features, namely considering the consequences of an event:

[5] E: Think of a time when you felt hungry on the train.

S: I remember the last time I was on a train. Have I ever been hungry on a train? I usually feel sick to my stomach on a train. Yeah, I was visiting my friend Chris coming back early with her friend Ann to get to work on time. We bought breakfast so I must have felt hungry, but I don't recall ever feeling hungry on the train.

Interestingly, the subject recalled an experience that did not include the particular feeling specified, but instead included another, related event (buying food) presumably inferred to aid search.

Retrieval is Reunderstanding

As I have argued, retrieving an event requires constructing a plausible scenario for an occurrence of that type of event. Finding plausible connections to other features that elaborate the original description is essentially the process of explaining this hypothetical event. To find an event in memory, one might consider the motivations for the event, the behavior of others that would have provoked the event, larger episodes in which this event may have occurred, and new states or events that might have been motivated by or resulted from the target event. Retrieval therefore entails reunderstanding the event and can rely on the same causal inference mechanisms used in comprehension.

One might question whether a model with so many different retrieval strategies that relies on such a rich indexing and organizational scheme for experiences is a parsimonious model. There are several reasons to believe that it is not only a plausible, but also a parsimonious model. First, the data support this complex indexing scheme. For example, examination of autobiographical retrieval protocols reveals a set of reasoning mechanisms employed to direct search that rely on a rich representation of general world knowledge (Kolodner, 1983, 1984; Reiser et al., in press; Whitten & Leonard, 1981; Williams & Hollan, 1981). Second, it is important to point out that we have not proposed these complex structures solely to account for autobiographical memory phenomena. Instead, this memory organization is motivated also by considerations of the use of these same knowledge structures for planning and performing actions, comprehension of texts and real world events, and memory retrieval of general and specific information learned from texts and from real world experience. As I argued earlier, knowledge about the motivations and results of behavior in common situations is used in order to plan behavior, understand behavior during an experience, and in various types of discourse. Furthermore, the same causal reasoning mechanisms are brought into play in order to construct explanations, generate plans, and guide memory search. Therefore, the context-plus-index model of autobiographical memory organization and retrieval is more sensible and parsimonious than models that rely on different knowledge structures and organizations for different cognitive tasks.

PSYCHOLOGICAL EVIDENCE FOR DIRECTED SEARCH

There are several types of empirical evidence for the role of directed search mechanisms in autobiographical retrieval. The first type of evidence is found in verbal protocols taken during the retrieval process. Verbal protocols of complex retrievals often exhibit the explicit use of retrieval strategies to direct search (Kolodner, 1983, 1984; Reiser et al., in press; Whitten & Leonard, 1981; Williams & Hollan, 1981). The use of retrieval strategies to reformulate queries and predict additional features is often explicit in these protocols. For example, the subject in protocol [3] indicated his focus on motivations for the experience, then generated several possibilities in order to pin down an experience; and the subject in protocol [1] described his use of a mental time map of exams to generate possibilities that could be tested for the target properties.

There are several other types of evidence for directed search in retrieval protocols found by Reiser et al. (in press). Subjects often elaborated the original query, describing these new retrieval contexts before they were effective in accessing particular experiences. Features present in a remembered experience are not strong evidence that those features were used in the retrieval process, because they may merely have been components of an experience that was retrieved by focusing on other features. However, a general description of the experience that is an elaboration of the original query indicates the manner in which reasoning mechanisms have altered the query in order to construct a new search context. For example, in protocol [4], the subject described the new search context (waiting) that was generated by considering the original query (impatient), and then proceeded to search experiences within that new context. Subjects often describe general types of experiences that are refinements of the original query but not narrowed down to the individual experience level.

[6] E: Think of a time when you went shopping and couldn't pay for the item you wanted.

S: Oh, that's happened a couple of times too. Normally, I'm very careful about that because I . . . there must have been a couple of times way way long ago when I had gone, you know, with my mother's money in my hand and then just not looked at items I was buying and overcharged and had to go through that embarrassing procedure of giving back things and deciding what one could do without for this week's shopping. . . . But that doesn't happen anymore, because I always count things up as I go along the supermarket aisles.

E: Can you think of one particular experience?

S: Well . . . there was one, but I can't really locate it anymore than probably about ten years ago or twelve or something. But, yeah, Grand Union in my hometown where all the checkers knew me because I was this cute kid that always traipsed along after her mother and here was I . . . it was probably pretty much at the beginning of when I started out going shopping on my bicycle which I did ever since then and all through high school and everything . . . and going again to get a week's supply of food and then just sort of running around the aisles piling things together with only an eye to what would fit in my knapsack as opposed to what would fit in my . . . the bill I was carrying . . .

Here the subject first reasoned that the experience would have to have occurred when she was shopping for food for her mother rather than recently, while she was in college. When probed, the subject then was able to pin down an experience within that refined context.

Reformulations of queries can also be observed in two types of failed searches. False starts occur when the subject articulates a new category for search, but then discovers that the category does not contain a suitable experience. Protocol [2] is a good example of a false start—the subject decided a particular restaurant was a likely setting for the target event, but, on searching that subclass, discovered that there were no experiences matching the criteria. Near misses occur when the subject remembers an experience that doesn't match the presented description but is similar in some respects to the target experience. The ways in which the near miss is similar to the target event suggest the type of inferences made during retrieval to modify the query. The following protocol presents a typical case of a near miss.

[7] S: Think of a time when you went to a bank and didn't have proper identification.

E: Identification . . . They always ask me for identification, but I usually have something. Uh, thinking . . . when you said bank . . . I was sort of thinking, well, last time I went to the bank and it was closed and not being . . . and being annoyed that it had closed rather than not having enough money and still not being . . . able to get money out.

Although the intermediate steps are not explicit, it appears that the subject inferred the result of the described problem and then searched memory for an experience with that particular result. The subject may have searched for an experience where he was unable to withdraw money, and then accessed an experience where the bank was closed instead of one where he didn't have proper identification. This near miss demonstrates the type of causal reasoning used to add features (e.g., unable to withdraw money) to the retrieval set.

Further evidence for directed search comes from several experiments examining the effectiveness of different types of cues in eliciting autobiographical experiences. In one series of experiments, Reiser et al. (1985) found that activity cues represent an optimal level of description for autobiographical retrieval. We compared retrieval for experiences given activity cues (e.g., went to the movies), general action cues (e.g., paid at the ticket booth), and combinations of those cues (went to the movies/paid at the ticket booth). Activities enable a rich set of inferences to be made about the target experience; in contrast general action cues can be performed in a diverse set of activities and thus were expected to be inferior retrieval cues. Interestingly, cues that were less constraining than activities (the general actions) elicited longer retrieval times as expected, but cues that involved an activity plus the additional constraint of the action also elicited longer retrieval times than activities. Furthermore, when searching within an activity, less frequent variations of the activity were more difficult to retrieve (see also Reiser & Black, 1983). These results suggest that activities represent an optimal level of constraint for an autobiographical retrieval cue. We argued that providing the activity is an essential component of retrieval, and thus cues less constrained than activities are more difficult because an activity must be inferred on those trails. However, providing more constraint than the activity only slows search, because it requires more careful search within that category, entailing a greater reliance on strategies to access an experience matching those additional constraints.

It would be difficult to account for this nonmonotonic effect of constraint using an undirected search model. Suppose one proposed a search process that randomly samples paths to events within a category, testing each retrieved event to see whether it contains the target attributes. In this model, more frequent event types (described by less constraining cues) are more likely to be retrieved in a given sampling and thus would be faster to retrieve. This accounts for the faster retrieval times for activities than for more constrained cues, but it does not account for the effectiveness of activities over less constrained cues. If search were completely undirected within some very large category (e.g., social events), then experiences matching general actions (e.g., paid at the ticket booth) would be easier to retrieve simply because there are more of them. Organizing experiences by activity appears to be one way in which experiences are stored in memory. The function of the search mechanisms when given a nonactivity cue is to find a candidate activity that might contain the experience.

Additional evidence for the use of causal reasoning to direct search was provided by Reiser (1983). If search were undirected within a category, then events of equal probability should be equally accessible. Cues describing events that do not differ in how frequently they tend to be performed should be equally effective retrieval cues. However, I found that retrieval cues describing actions constituting more central components of activities elicit faster retrieval than actions that are equally probable but of lower causal importance in the activity. For example, the action Receive the Money is a more central component of the activity Cashing a Check than the action Write Down Date, although both actions are equal in how frequently they tend to be executed in performances of the activity (as judged by subjects' ratings reported by Galambos, 1983). I argued that cues describing highly central components provide more of the required information for the inference mechanisms, because they provide access to the causally important features used to discriminate experiences. Cues describing low salience details do not provide sufficient direction for retrieval. Greater elaboration of the retrieval specification is therefore necessary, and the retrieval mechanisms must search for other information in the context to assemble features necessary to discriminate an experience.

Two additional experiments examined the features of events important in organizing and searching memory (Reiser, 1983). The first experiment used a priming, or cue-repetition, methodology to examine the effects of prior retrievals on subsequent memory searches. Demonstrating that a particular feature can be used in later searches suggests that a search strategy was able to use that feature in both retrievals. If elements of the same context are used by strategies in a subsequent search, this should be observable by noting commonalities between the two remembered experiences. Subjects were asked to recall experiences matching cues that repeated some type of information from the preceding cue. The best situation for reusing features should be when search is required to stay within the same context. To evaluate this condition, cues were constructed using an activity and general action (e.g., went shopping / stood in line). Each target trial either (a) repeated the activity from the preceding trial with a different general action, (b) repeated the general action from the preceding trial with a different activity, or (c) concerned a different action and activity. Subjects were required to recall a different experience from their own past in response to each trial. As expected, repeating the activity phrase enabled more features of the remembered events to be reused on the next memory search. This is consistent with other results indicating that activities provide the principal source of direction for autobiographical memory search.

Subjects' remembered experiences were examined to find commonalities between the features mentioned in each experience and those from prior recalls. The repeated experience features were classified in an attempt to characterize the event components used to discriminate experiences in memory. Rather than simply being a set of related associates, the repeated features fell into systematic classes.

These features correspond to the results of a second study, in which subjects were asked to recall experiences involving a particular activity and then to sort those experiences into groups of similar experiences (Reiser, 1983). The subjects' labels for those groups were used to infer the event features salient in discriminating these experiences. Most of the event features found in the cue repetition experiment were used by subjects to determine the clustering of their experiences. For example, two frequent types of groups of experiences were determined by common Activity Subclasses (e.g., a group of Museum experiences all involving Museum Libraries) and common Participants (e.g., a group of Museum visits all involving the same school friends). Furthermore, the set of retrieval features suggested by these results is consistent with those used in strategies found by Reiser et al. (in press). These features concerned choices about goals in the event (determining subclasses of activities), relationships between goals, descriptions of outcomes and their affects on goals, and connections to other experiences that motivated or resulted from the experience. Taken together, these experiments support the role of strategies to elaborate retrieval cues during memory search.

EFFECTIVE SEARCH STRATEGIES

In previous sections, I have presented arguments and empirical support for a directed component of autobiographical memory retrieval. This section briefly summarizes the nature of those strategic mechanisms.

The strategies described by Reiser et al. (in press) and Kolodner (1983, 1984) indicate the various reasoning mechanisms that direct memory search in order to find an event matching a target set of features. The search begins by constructing a scenario for the event's occurrence to constrain and guide the search. In some cases, this context is provided in the set of target features, but often strategies are employed to consider people's motivations or prior events that would lead to the event, particular variations of events in which the target event would be likely, and possible consequences of the target event. Activities are the most frequently selected search contexts, because these structures are rich sources of information for elaborative search mechanisms. After a context has been selected, elaborative mechanisms are employed to generate and test additional features of the target experience, until enough features have been predicted to isolate a single experience. Reasoning about the characteristics of activity subclasses as well as plausible causes, motivations, and consequences of the event may be invoked in order to generate additional features.

These retrieval strategies rely primarily on causal reasoning. The principal reason for this is that experiences are indexed according to those features that are causally relevant to the goals and course of action taken by the person in the activity, and thus the representations of experiences are causally based. Experiences concern deliberate actions. The mental structures active during an experience are those comprehension and planning structures containing information required to select actions and activities to achieve some desired results, and to understand the actions of others in terms of the interacting motivations of the various participants (Black, 1984; Reiser & Black, 1982). It is therefore reasonable to expect that experience features relevant to these goals and their outcomes will determine how the experiences are represented and stored in memory. For example, when one decides to perform an activity, one must decide on particular goal objects or standard varieties of the activity. Hence, considering the type of food desired in a restaurant, the type of atmosphere desired for going out drinking, or the type of movie desired would each result in the selection of a particular activity subclass. Similarly, other choice points in an experience represent discriminations concerning goal-relevant features such as participants or location, as well as the particular motivation for performing the activity. In general, the relevant features will be those that represent the motivations of the people involved, the actions undertaken to achieve those goals, the outcomes of the goals (whether they were achieved, were thwarted, or led to new subgoals), and the consequences of the actions for the states of the participants and affects on their future behavior. These types of features are used to represent experiences in memory, and strategies have developed that process this organization, using these features to direct search for experiences.

A second consideration is the necessity of the knowledge structures to guide the elaboration of the query. The type of planning structures that serve as contexts in autobiographical memory are rich in predictive power. These structures contain much information useful for predicting likely settings for the event. Clearly causal reasoning is an effective strategy for constructing a plausible scenario for an event. Retrieval strategies cannot rely on merely accessing highly associated information. As we have seen, the particular nature of the target experience determines which types of information are relevant for that search. Information that does not enable causal connections will not be effective for directing search.

In conclusion, these retrieval strategies are suggested as general reasoning mechanisms. These strategies are used to predict the characteristics of a target event given certain cues and thus are useful for searching memory for an experience. However, the inference mechanisms that are useful in inferring causal relationships between events and goals are also essential for comprehension. That is, the same strategies are also used to access relevant features from memory in order to understand an event currently being considered. Similarly, these mechanisms can also be used to answer questions by searching memory for relevant knowledge structures or individual experiences. In fact, Walker and Kintsch (1985) attempted to apply the Raaijmakers and Shiffrin (1981) model to the task of idea generation, recalling general information about a target topic. In trying to fit this model to their data, they found it was necessary to add controlling mechanisms that access related information for use as retrieval cues, much like the notion of directed search strategies I have presented in this chapter. Thus, such strategies appear to be general mechanisms for reasoning about experiences and the generalizations one has learned based on those experiences.

ACKNOWLEDGMENTS

This research was supported by a grant from the System Development Foundation to the Cognitive Science Program at Yale University and by ONR contract N00014-84-K-0064. I am grateful to John Black and Robert Abelson for helpful discussions on the issues addressed in this chapter, and to Albert Corbett for comments on an earlier draft. Portions of these analyses were included in a dissertation submitted to Yale University by the author.

REFERENCES

Anderson, J. R. (1976). *Language, memory, and thought.* Hillsdale, NJ: Lawrence Erlbaum Associates.

Black, J. B. (1984). Understanding and remembering stories. In J. R. Anderson & S. M. Kosslyn (Eds.), *Essays on learning and memory.* San Francisco: W. H. Freeman.

Collins, A. M., & Loftus, E. F. (1975). A spreading-activation theory of semantic processing. *Psychological Review, 82,* 407–428.

Galambos, J. A. (1983). Normative studies of six characteristics of our knowledge of common activities. *Behavior Research Methods and Instrumentation, 15,* 327–340.

Kolodner, J. L. (1983). Reconstructive memory: A computer model. *Cognitive Science, 7*(4), 281–328.

Kolodner, J. L. (1984). *Retrieval and organizational strategies in conceptual memory.* Hillsdale, NJ: Lawrence Erlbaum Associates.

Norman, D. A., & Bobrow, D. G. (1979). Descriptions: An intermediate stage in memory retrieval. *Cognitive Psychology, 11,* 293–331.

Raaijmakers, J. G., & Shiffrin, R. M. (1981). Search of associative memory. *Psychological Review, 88,* 93–134.

Reiser, B. J. (1983). *Contexts and indices in autobiographical memory* (Tech. Rep. 24). Cognitive Science Program, Yale University.

Reiser, B. J., & Black, J. B. (1982). Processing the structural models of comprehension. *Text, 2,* 225–252.

Reiser, B. J., & Black, J. B. (1983). The roles of interference and inference in the retrieval of autobiographical memories. *Proceedings of the Fifth Annual Conference of the Cognitive Science Society.* Rochester, NY.

Reiser, B. J., Black, J. B., & Abelson, R. P. (1985). Knowledge structures in the organization and retrieval of autobiographical memories. *Cognitive Psychology, 17,* 89–137.

Reiser, B. J., Black, J. B., & Kalamarides, P. (in press). Strategic memory search processes. In D. C. Rubin (Ed.), *Autobiographical memory.* Cambridge, England: Cambridge University Press.

Ross, B. H. (1984). Remindings and their effects in learning a cognitive skill. *Cognitive Psychology, 16,* 371–416.

Schank, R. C. (1982). *Dynamic memory: A theory of learning in computers and people.* New York: Cambridge University Press.

Schneider, W., & Shiffrin, R. M. (1977). Controlled and automatic human information processing: I. Detection, search, and attention. *Psychological Review, 84,* 1–66.

Tulving, E. (1983). *Elements of episodic memory.* New York: Oxford University Press.

Walker, W. H., & Kintsch, W. (1985). Automatic and strategic aspects of knowledge retrieval. *Cognitive Science, 9,* 261–283.

Whitten, W. B., & Leonard, J. M. (1981). Directed search through autobiographical memory. *Memory and Cognition, 9,* 566–579.

Williams, M. D., & Hollan, J. D. (1981). The process of retrieval from very-long term memory. *Cognitive Science, 5,* 87–119.

II

MEMORY-BASED
HYPOTHESIS FORMATION

Nearly everybody agrees that experience is an integral part of knowledge acquisition and development of expertise. Through experience, people learn how to focus on important details of a problem, ignoring extraneous information. Through experience, people become better at judging the appropriateness of plans or responses to a given situation. Certainly, experiences that are very similar to a new one can aid in making judgments about a new case. The first time a doctor sees a mysterious combination of symptoms, for example, he may have to work hard to make a diagnosis. The second time he sees the same set of symptoms, however, he has a working hypothesis available to him from the beginning, namely, the diagnosis he made the first time. Similarly, if a lawyer trying to analyze a case has similar precedents available to him, his judgments will be a lot easier than if his case is very different from anything he has experienced before.

Experiences that on the surface are different from a new one may also help in understanding and explaining the new situation if they have some common underlying thread. An experience of plans being cancelled unexpectedly may cause a reminding of another time that happened, even if the plans are very different: an explanation can be formulated for the second case based on the first.

The chapters in this section examine the uses of *case-based reasoning* in problem solving and hypothesis formation. Case-based reasoning is a reasoning process that relies on analogies to previous or hypothetical situations. People have been observed to make use of cases in their reasoning in areas as diverse as medical diagnosis, legal judgment, advice giving, trouble shooting of mechanical devices, learning simple algebra, and everyday, common-sense reasoning. The cases used in case-based reasoning may be previous personal experiences, carefully constructed hypothetical cases, precedent-setting cases, or the experiences of other people. Case-based reasoning is used during problem solving to direct focus to appropriate parts of a problem, to flesh out a problem description, and to create a plan for problem resolution. It is used in learning to generate hypotheses for testing. Previous cases also contribute to the generation of explanations necessary to justify decisions in problem solving and to understand another person's actions. Cases used in case-based reasoning may be almost identical to the situation being considered or may be similar along only one important dimension.

The chapter by Kolodner and Simpson gives an overview of case-based reasoning as it is used in problem solving. In order to use previous cases in problem solving, a memory process must work alongside the problem solver providing cases to use in case-based reasoning. Kolodner and Simpson present a framework that includes both processes. To use previous cases in problem solving, the problem solver must be able to examine and evaluate the results of its previous decisions and be able to update its knowledge as appropriate. Thus feedback and the capability of learning based on failure are also presented as part of their model.

The framework presented by Kolodner and Simpson presents the uses of previous cases very similar to a current case in several processes involved in problem solving. Rissland's work concentrates on the role of cases in one part of the problem solving framework: understanding or interpreting the problem. Rissland concentrates on argumentation in legal reasoning. The task here is to create an argument in support of a particular understanding or analysis of a case. A standard method for such argumentation is the use of hypothetical cases to support one's point. Although precedent cases are used as a standard for determining judgment in a new case, it is often not clear exactly which precedent should be applied. Hypothetical cases are often created by massaging some aspect of the current case to a point where the case obviously corresponds to some precedent or by massaging a precedent until it corresponds to the current case. The hypothetical case is then available for comparison to the current case to see if the current case conforms to the precedent too. Arguments are made one way or the other. In this chapter, Rissland provides examples of how hypothetical cases are used to shape understanding of a presented case.

Bain, too, concentrates on legal reasoning. Like Rissland, he explores the roles of cases in creating explanations. In particular, he looks at the use of experience in understanding the motives of defendants in criminal cases. Because motives or intentions drive the actions of individuals, a judge must determine the intent of a defendent before passing judgment and sentencing. Bain shows how the motives of defendants can be justified or not, based on the circumstances of the case and known "justification units" built up from experience. Justification units provide explanations for the actions of defendants, allowing judgments about the ethics of a situation to be made.

Whereas Bain's justification units and Rissland's hypothetical cases provide means of creating explanations in understanding in two specialized circumstances, Schank provides the beginning of a process model of explanation. For several years, researchers in Schank's lab at Yale have been collecting and analyzing remindings. One of the observations is that, often, reminding seems to be a result of explaining what went wrong in the current situation and then being reminded of the basis of the explanation. Key to reminding, then, is the generation of explanations in understanding and problem solving. Often reminding itself is just a verification that an explanation has been derived correctly. Schank presents examples of remindings, the explanations that caused those remindings, and his explanation of how those explanations were derived. He offers a list of items that, in general, need to be explained, such as aberrant behavior, strange plans, and strange goals. He constructs a taxonomy of explanation types, the kinds of explanations we accept (e.g., alternate beliefs, laws of physics). He also considers how we can tell if an explanation is acceptable. His final message is that "there is no learning without explanation." We can learn only when we can explain why something happened the way it did. Only then can the content of a situation be rendered useful for later reasoning.

The concluding chapter in this section is about learning. Shrager explores the learning cycle when a person is presented with something new. In this case, the new item is a toy called BigTrak, and people have to figure out how it works without instructions. He shows how a model of the way the device works can be created purely from the explanations created while its behavior is being tested. The learning cycle he presents is a process of (1) creating an initial explanation (hypothesis), (2) testing some part of it, (3) adapting the hypothesis based on an explanation of the results of the test and (4) going back to (2). Whereas Schank concentrates on explanation, Shrager shows us explicitly how it contributes to learning.

6 Problem Solving and Dynamic Memory

Janet L. Kolodner
Robert L. Simpson, Jr.
School of Information and Computer Science
Georgia Institute of Technology

ABSTRACT

Most research into problem solving has considered each problem to be solved as a unique event. Our observations have led us to conclude that much of the problem solving people do is based on previous experience. Analogies to previous, similar problems help in solving new problems. Each problem-solving experience also contributes to refinement, modification, and confirmation of the problem-solving knowledge already available. This chapter presents a framework for those components of problem solving that make use of previous experience. The processes involved and the organization of experience that supports them are considered. Examples are drawn from two problem domains: diagnosis and treatment of mood disorders, and plan selection for resolution of disputes.

EXPERIENCE'S ROLES IN PROBLEM SOLVING

Problem solving is a widely studied area in both psychology and artificial intelligence (e.g., Hayes-Roth, 1980; Newell & Simon, 1972; Sacerdoti, 1977). Yet, with few exceptions (Ross, 1984), there has been little study of experience's role in the process. Our observations have led us to believe that experience plays two important roles in problem solving (Kolodner & Kolodner, 1983). First, experience contributes to refinement and modification of reasoning processes. Successful experiences reinforce already known rules or previous hypotheses, whereas failures require reanalysis of the reasoning and knowledge that was used, and modification of faulty rules and knowledge. Experience thus plays a

major role in enhancing problem-solving knowledge, in the process turning novices into relatively more expert reasoners. Experience's second role is equally important. Individual experiences act as exemplars upon which to base later decisions. Analogies to previous cases guide and focus later decision making.
An example from medicine illustrates our claims:

> Dr. X sees a patient who shows classic signs of Major Depression. She has previously been diagnosed as Depressive and was treated in a mental hospital with antidepressants. She was sickly as a child, has had a drinking problem, and has had some unexplained physical illnesses. Dr. X concludes that she is suffering from Major Depression, Recurrent, without Melancholia and treats her with antidepressants. They seem to work, but the woman comes back complaining of additional major physical disorders. Taking a further history, the doctor finds that her unexplained medical problems have been numerous. Realizing that this is an important consideration, he makes a second diagnosis of Somatization Disorder (adapted from Spitzer, Skodol, Gibbon, & Williams, 1980, case #125).

Dr. X should learn from this case that it is important to consider medical history in choosing predominant clinical features and that Depression can camouflage Somatization Disorder. Using the first fact, he can refine his rules for choosing predominant clinical features. The relationship between Depression and Somatization Disorder will be helpful in diagnosing and treating later cases. This shows the first role of experience: the modification of reasoning processes.
To illustrate experience's second role, providing exemplars, consider Dr. X's capabilities on seeing a second patient diagnosed for Major Depression who also has unexplained medical problems. We expect him to transfer his knowledge from the previous case to the new one and consider whether the new patient might also have Somatization Disorder.
Experience plays the same role in common-sense domains (Simpson, 1984), as is shown in the following example:

> Two sisters are quarrelling over an orange. Their mother surveys the situation, and proposes that each sister take half of the orange. One of the sisters complains, since she wants to use the whole peel for baking. Realizing the real nature of the conflict, the mother suggests that the sisters divide the orange agreeably: one will take the fruit and eat it, while the other will take the peel and use it for baking.

Analysis of this example shows that although the mother thought that both sisters had the same goal, she was mistaken. Their subgoals were in conflict, but their goals were not. Stepping back and considering the real goals rather than the manifest ones resulted in a concordance. The following shows how this analysis is transferred in understanding and making a prediction about another situation. Here, we imagine the mother reading the following story in the paper:

> Egypt and Israel both want possession of the Sinai. The US suggests they cut it down the middle. Both Egypt and Israel complain.

Analogy to the orange dispute should allow her to conclude that possession of the Sinai is merely a subgoal, that the real goals of the two countries should be considered, and that a mutually agreeable split based on those goals be sought.

In building a framework for problem solving that includes experience, we must consider a number of issues:

1. What knowledge is available as a result of experience?
2. How does experience change the structure of knowledge in memory?
3. Which reasoning processes use experience?
4. How is experiential knowledge integrated into reasoning processes?

Before discussing the answers to these questions, we present a model of a problem-solving process that uses experience. There are two key points in the interaction of problem solving and experience. First, using experience in problem solving requires a problem-solving framework that includes feedback. Any reasoning system that is going to use its experience to solve problems must be able to both make decisions and evaluate their outcomes. A system that never knows the outcome of its suggestions has no basis for evaluating its decisions and cannot be expected to suggest new solutions based on old ones. We therefore suggest the model in Fig. 6.1 for problem solving, which includes follow-up procedures for the evaluation of decisions.

Second, the interaction of problem solving and experience requires the services of a *dynamic memory* (Kolodner, 1983; Schank, 1982), that is, a memory that itself is changing with each new experience. As the memory receives feedback about its decisions and evaluates them, it records its experiences and modifies any knowledge that might have been faulty. Because memory changes with experience, the results of asking a particular memory to solve the same problem at two different times will be different, as will the results of asking memories with two different sets of experiences to solve the same problem. In the first case, the combination of having solved the same problem once before and the set of experiences that came between the two episodes will result in the differences. If the previous experience on the same problem can be recalled, for example, the second instance of solving the same problem will require only recall. If the set of experiences encountered by the memory between the two cases of solving the same problem shed new light on some aspect of the problem, then the second solution will take advantage of the new knowledge. In the case of asking two different memories to solve the same problem, even if both started with the same

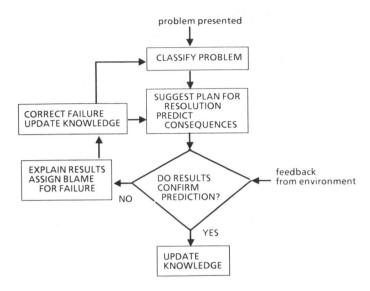

FIG. 6.1.   Problem solving with follow-up.

"facts," their varying experiences mean that each will have different areas of "expertise"—the memories will have evolved differently and will have learned different things.

We present a model of the organization of a dynamic memory for events, and then present the set of learning processes, driven by experience, that evolve the knowledge the memory starts with. We then present a set of case-based analogical reasoning processes that use previous experiences to aid later decision making, and show where these processes fit into each of the steps in the problem-solving process pictured earlier. Our examples come from two task domains: diagnosis and treatment of psychiatric disorders, and resolution of common-sense disputes.

ENCODING AND ORGANIZING EXPERIENCE IN A
DYNAMIC MEMORY

A prerequisite for learning from and using experience is the capability of retrieving relevant past experiences applicable to a new situation. The memory structure we describe is based on MOPs (Kolodner, 1983; Schank, 1981), also referred to as the context-plus-index model (Reiser, Black, & Abelson, 1985). In this model, generalized episodes (previously called E-MOPs (Kolodner, 1983) or MOPs (Schank, 1982) hold generalized knowledge compiled from the individual experiences they organize, and individual experiences are indexed in these structures according to features that differentiate them one from another. Features of events used for indexing are not explicitly predicted by the generalized episode but are contextually related to it. When two experiences differ from the generalized episode in the same way, a collision, which we call *reminding* (Kolodner, 1983; Schank, 1981) occurs. Analogy occurs when predictions based on the first episode are used to analyze the new one. Generalization occurs when similarities between the two episodes can be compiled to form a new memory schema.

Reminding happens through a traversal procedure. When a new experience (e.g., problem-solving case) is encountered, appropriate generalized episodes are chosen for it. Features that differentiate it from others in the same generalized episode are extracted from it, and indices associated with those features are traversed. In the process, the new case collides with previous ones already indexed in memory. It is those cases that are now available for further evaluation. New cases are added to memory by the same process.

In the psychiatric domain, diagnostic categories (e.g., Major Depression), for example, form one type of useful generalized episode. The medical example mentioned earlier is differentiated from other cases of Major Depression by (among other things): (a) the fact that there were unexplained physical disorders in addition to those symptoms considered in the original diagnosis, and (b) treatment failed in that the patient seemed cured of depression but complained of additional physical disorders. Figure 6.2 shows the memory organization that results from this experience.

When a second patient identified as having recurrent Major Depression also exhibits unexplained physical illnesses, this first case can be recalled, and the suggestion that the second patient also has Somatization Disorder can be made. Similarly, if a second patient diagnosed for recurrent Major Depression complains of new, unrelated symptoms after being treated with antidepressants, then

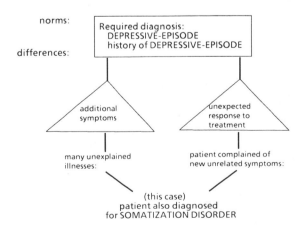

FIG. 6.2. Recurrent major depression.

this case will be recalled. If, after this case is recalled, suggestions made by it for the second case are effective (e.g., the second case with unexplained physical illnesses also has Somatization Disorder, and the same treatment works for both patients), then the place in memory where this case is stored is replaced by a generalization compiled from the similarities between the cases indexed to this point—patients with recurrent Major Depression who also have Somatization Disorder should be treated in the way that has worked for the previous cases comprising the generalization. The cases used to compile the generalization are then indexed from it by the features that differentiate them from each other. In this way, a hierarchy of generalized episodes is created, and memory's generalized knowledge becomes more specialized as similar experiences are encountered.

Another task domain we have worked on is dispute resolution. In the mediation domain, one type of generalized episode we have found useful in problem solving (Simpson, 1984) is the dispute type (e.g., physical, economic, political). Each type predicts which characteristics of the disputed object are more salient (e.g., aspects that determine value in economic conflicts, or size and sets of parts of objects in physical disputes), and which mediation tactics are likely to be applicable (e.g., divide equally for physical disputes over divisible objects). Features for indexing include object characteristics, actor characteristics, and additional goals of each party not predicted by the chosen dispute classification. Indexing of the orange dispute as a physical dispute is shown in Fig. 6.3. This dispute is recalled when the Sinai dispute presented earlier is processed, because both are cases classified as physical disputes in which the plan "divide equally" failed.

EXPERIENCE CONTRIBUTES TO CHANGE IN MEMORY'S STRUCTURES

Within the memory structure and problem-solving process we have presented, learning happens in three ways. The first type of learning we identify is *adding a new experience to memory*. As explained earlier, when a case is encountered, it is indexed in appropriate memory structures by those of its features that differentiate if from other cases in the same structure. As later cases are being evaluated, they will also be indexed in memory by their differentiating features. In the process, there will be collisions with, or remindings of, previous cases. Those cases already in memory and recalled through reminding are used for analogical reasoning. A previous case recalled during problem solving may suggest a solution to the current problem without the need to "reason from scratch." Thus, learning a case results in being able to solve a similar problem more quickly later. If numerous attempts were made to resolve the first problem, and if after a series of failures a solution was found, then that good solution can be attempted

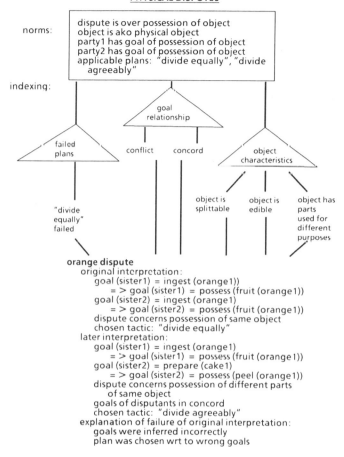

PHYSICAL DISPUTES

norms:
dispute is over possession of object
object is ako physical object
party1 has goal of possession of object
party2 has goal of possession of object
applicable plans: "divide equally", "divide
    agreeably"

indexing:

goal
relationship

failed
plans

conflict   concord

object
characteristics

"divide
equally"
failed

object is
splittable

object is
edible

object has
parts
used for
different
purposes

orange dispute
    original interpretation:
        goal (sister1) = ingest (orange1)
            = > goal (sister1) = possess (fruit (orange1))
        goal (sister2) = ingest (orange1)
            = > goal (sister2) = possess (fruit (orange1))
        dispute concerns possession of same object
        chosen tactic: "divide equally"
    later interpretation:
        goal (sister1) = ingest (orange1)
            = > goal (sister1) = possess (fruit (orange1))
        goal (sister2) = prepare (cake1)
            = > goal (sister2) = possess (peel (orange1))
        dispute concerns possession of different parts
            of same object
        goals of disputants in concord
        chosen tactic: "divide agreeably"
    explanation of failure of original interpretation:
        goals were inferred incorrectly
        plan was chosen wrt to wrong goals

FIG. 6.3.   Physical disputes.

in a later similar case without first having to try previously unsuccessful options. Recording in memory and using them during problem solving can help avoid further failures. The procedures involved in reasoning analogically from a previous case are discussed in the next section.

Two other learning processes result in refinement and modification of the domain-specific and strategic knowledge already in memory: similarity-triggered generalization and failure-triggered explanation. Both occur in the problem-solving framework we propose after enough feedback has been encountered to evaluate the results of a decision made previously in the problem-solving cycle.

Similarity-triggered generalization (Kolodner, 1983) occurs when two cases already assigned to the same generalized episode share features not accounted for by that classification. In that case, a new concept described by the shared features is created. This concept is a generalization of the cases and a specialization of the original classification. Thus, if a set of patients who are diagnosed for Major Depression and also have heart problems respond to the same treatment, then a generalization can be made that this medication is good for treating Major Depressives with heart problems. These generalizations are indexed off of generalized episodes already in memory by those features that the individual cases used to create the generalization have in common (e.g., see Fig. 6.2 and the paragraph following it). They, in fact, take the place of the individual episodes that were indexed at that point. Those individual episodes are then indexed off of the new generalization by the features that differentiate them.

Of course, the process of making generalizations is much more difficult than just choosing the features a set of cases have in common. In particular, important features may be left out, some coincidental correspondences might be made part of the generalization, or some attributes may be too specific or too general. Such generalizations must be followed up and refined as later similar cases are encountered. An explanation of one way of taking care of this problem can be found in Kolodner (1983, 1984).

Learning also happens as a result of failure, which signals a need for explanation (Kolodner & Kolodner, 1983; Schank, 1982). When a hypothesis is violated, or a piece of knowledge (e.g., a rule) fails to work as expected, an explanation for the failure must be found, and the failed piece of knowledge must be modified. The previous psychiatric example points out some of the knowledge modifications that must happen as a result of that failure. In general, tracking down a failure and explaining it are difficult problems, especially in open domains such as medical diagnosis, where all the relevant information may not be available. We do not explain here how to track down failures, but rather point out that it must be done if learning is to occur. We do need to consider the results in memory once an error has been encountered and explained. If blame can be assigned (i.e., an explanation found) for a failure, the case is indexed by those features that caused the failure. When a second, similar situation is encountered, the marker serves as an index to a failed episode. If a solution was found in the first instance, it can be applied to the second case so that the failure won't happen again. When blame has not been assigned, the usual markers denoting the differences between the failed episode and others remain, again serving as an index when a similar situation is encountered. In this case, a procedure to be avoided will be found.

The combination of these two learning methods and the requirement for retrieval of previous similar cases necessitates indexing cases by two types of features: those describing the problem-solving case itself, and those describing any previous attempts to resolve the problem. Features that describe previous attempts include the plan that was tried; the results of trying it (as full a description of the resulting environment as possible); and, in case of failure, an explanation of why the original solution did not work (i.e., what was it about the environment surrounding this problem that made the original solution fail). During problem solving, this will allow recall of cases that are similar with respect to problem features or with respect to attempted plans. Figures 6.2 and 6.3 show both types of indices.

EXPERIENCE CONTRIBUTES EXEMPLARS FOR ANALOGY

The learning processes just described provide the generalized knowledge and previous cases that are used to evaluate later cases. The process by which knowledge is transferred from a previous to a current case is called similarity-triggered analogical reasoning. It is a type of case-based reasoning. When a new case is reminiscent of previous cases (either individual or generic), the previous cases are used as exemplars to aid in evaluation of the new case. Previous cases can be useful during any of the problem-solving steps. Using cases in problem solving depends on a reasoner's being able to: (a) locate previous similar cases from a potentially large long-term memory of problem-solving episodes; (b) integrate new cases into memory so that they can be located when necessary; (c) determine the applicability of an old case to a new one, and choose from among a number of potentially applicable previous situations; and (d) transfer knowledge from a previous case to a current one.

As described in the foregoing, a previous episode can be recalled if it is classified similarly to the current one and has similar features not predicted by that classification. This happens as a direct result of understanding the problem to be solved. To understand something, we must find the knowledge structures in memory (i.e., schemas) that describe it. The best schemas in memory are those that are most specific with respect to the problem we are trying to understand. To find them in the memory structure described, it is necessary first to choose an applicable memory structure (i.e., generalized episode), and then to traverse the hierarchical structure organized by that generalized episode, using the features of the current problem as indices. In the process of doing this, both previous similar cases and applicable generalized episodes in the hierarchy will be found.

During problem solving, we start with an initial problem description, which in the process of solving the problem becomes better understood and more detailed. As more detail is uncovered, better fitting structures can be found by traversing memory with the new information. Previous similar cases become available each time new features of a current case are discovered. As more is learned about a problem, better structures are found for it. The byproduct of this, of course, is that the problem solver is constantly being reminded of previous cases.

We must imagine, therefore, that there is a memory integration and reminding process running concurrently with problem-solving processes. Each time the memory traversal process encounters a relevant memory structure or previous case, it makes it available for processing. In the following sections, we discuss the use of previous cases in problem solving. We do not make a clear distinction between an individual previous case and a generic case (i.e., one which is a generalization of previous cases) because the memory processes may make either available, and both hold the same types of information.

In general, analogy to a previous case or set of cases serves many purposes in problem solving. A previous experience called to mind by a current problem can be useful in any of the following problem solving tasks:

- It can aid in problem *classification* by predicting additional features to be investigated or by pointing out alternative classifications.
- It can help in *planning* by suggesting procedures or courses of action to be followed or avoided, or by suggesting a means of implementing a plan.
- It can suggest an *explanation and means of recovery* for a failure.

These are the steps identified in Fig. 6.1 in presenting the problem-solving model. The following sections explain the role of case-based reasoning in each of those problem-solving steps.

Case-based Reasoning in Classification

Classification is an understanding process. In medical reasoning, it means choosing a diagnostic category into which a patient fits (APA, 1980; Kolodner & Kolodner, 1983). In general understanding, classification refers to finding the most applicable schemas in memory that describe the item being understood. Schemas chosen during understanding provide predictions to use in further understanding or other processing (Dyer, 1983; Schank, 1982; Schank & Abelson, 1977). Choosing a diagnostic category, for example, allows an appropriate treatment to be prescribed in medicine (APA, 1980). Choosing a schema in natural language understanding allows later ambiguous words to be understood correctly and references to be resolved (Birnbaum & Selfridge, 1981). In general problem solving, appropriate schemas (generalized episodes in our formulation) make predictions about possible strategies for problem resolution, difficulties that may be encountered along the way, and problem features to be especially careful about, to name just a few of a schema's uses.

We are purposely mysterious about how to choose a candidate schema. Several general triggering mechanisms have been proposed elsewhere (e.g., Charniak, 1982; Dyer, 1983), and some tasks have particular schemas for classification (e.g., differential diagnosis in medicine). We are dealing with the role of analogy once a candidate schema is chosen. Recall the memory process we assume: Once a classification is chosen, unaccounted-for features of the current case are used to traverse its episodic structure. More specific schemas and particular cases are encountered.

A case one is reminded of may confirm that the current case fits the current classification, but may also have other features salient to the problem to be solved. These features act as predictors. If the current case also has the predicted features, then a hypothesis is made that the present case can be treated like the previous one in later processing. If the current case does not have the features but they can consistently be assumed, then the predicted features provide additional detail to the current case; and the assumption is made that the present case can be treated like the previous one in later processing. If salient predicted features are not true of the current case or are not consistent with it, then using the previous case for any further predictions is ruled out.

A case one is reminded of may also suggest alternate or additional classifications. The previous case, for example, may have initially been classified like the current case, but on later evaluation (perhaps after failing to resolve it), it may have been classified differently and been resolved successfully using the plans of the alternate classification. In this circumstance, the previous case suggests an alternate classification or understanding of the problem, which must then be confirmed. After the alternate classification is suggested, processing using that classification proceeds as for the original one.

We saw experience functioning as an aid in classification earlier, when Dr. X diagnosed his second case of Major Depression combined with unexplained physical problems. Although the first time he had to wait for the treatment to fail before he could make the secondary diagnosis of Somatization Disorder, the second time he sees such a patient, he has an exemplar to base his diagnosis on. The additional diagnosis of Somatization Disorder in the first patient suggests an additional classification and should cause him to check the second patient for symptoms common to that disorder.

A previous case can thus serve two functions in the classification or understanding process:

- It can predict additional features to be investigated.
- It can suggest an alternate or additional classification.

Case-based Reasoning in Plan Selection

When a problem is understood as well as possible, a plan for its resolution must be formulated. This involves a number of steps: initial selection of a set of skeletal plans, evaluating them and choosing between the alternatives, and implementing the plan in an appropriate way. Experience can be useful during any of these steps. At the beginning of plan selection, plans associated with cases remembered during classification are available. As additional details about the current case and its applicable plans are inferred, other previous cases and their plans become available.

The first way experience is useful in plan selection is in suggesting a plan for problem resolution that should be used or avoided (e.g., a previous treatment that worked or did not work in a similar case). Suppose, for example, that a mediator of the Sinai dispute were reminded of the Korean conflict. In both cases, two different political entities want control of a piece of land, and, in both, military means had been attempted previous to the negotiations. Based on the Korean conflict, which had been resolved by splitting the land in half and giving half to each side, a suggested solution to the Sinai dispute is to divide the land equally between Egypt and Israel.

Analogical reasoning is also useful in evaluating the utility of a potential plan in order to choose between alternatives. Analogy's role is in predicting the outcome of a course of action. Plan evaluation involves simulating the results of alternative courses of action and evaluating them in light of previous experience. Simulation of alternatives provides hypothetical situations similar to previous ones. The success or failure of previous attempts at implementing the same plan under similar conditions provides a metric for evaluation of a potential course of action. We see this use of analogy quite often in medicine when treatment must be prescribed. Often, there are multiple treatments appropraite to patients fitting a particular diagnosis. Previous experiences serve as exemplars in evaluating the utility of an alternative. They may also provide additional information leading to a better strategy than could have been constructed with no experience. Patients in a manic state, for example, cannot be treated with drugs unless they are hospitalized. Otherwise, they will not take their medication. Consideration of drug treatment for a manic patient should remind a doctor of previous instances when he treated a manic patient with drugs. This, in turn, allows recall that those treatments were unsuccessful and became successful after the patients were hospitalized. This process is related to Schank's (1982) intentional reminding and Wilensky's (1983) Projector.

Experience can also be helpful in choosing the means for implementing a selected plan (similar to Mostow's, 1983, operationalization). Any particular plan that is selected for resolution of a problem might be applied in several ways. A suitable plan implementation can be derived by either considering how it was effected in a previous case or simulating alternative ways of carrying it out. Application of the common-sense plan "one cuts, the other chooses," for example, requires differentiating between the party who will do the cutting and the one who will do the choosing.

To summarize, a previous experience can help during planning in any of the following ways:

- It can suggest procedures to be followed.
- It can suggest procedures to be avoided.

- It can suggest a means of implementing a plan.
- It can help predict the outcome of a selected plan.

Case-based Reasoning in Error Recovery

Experience, as part of follow up, also aids with explanation of and recovery from failures (Simpson 1984). Plan failures can occur for a number of reasons, and in general, tracking down the reason for a failure can be arbitrarily difficult. If previous experience contains a failure similar to a current one, however, it may provide a clue to tracking down the error in the current case. The procedure is as follows: On failure recognition, the reasoner attempts to recall a similar previous error. Features available for such recall include the features that describe the problem plus the features that describe the failure. If a similar failure has occurred previously, the explanation from that failure can act as a guide to construct a hypothesis of why the failure happened. This reminding may also include suggested plans for error recovery.

This is exactly what we see happening in the portion of the Sinai dispute example given earlier. The memory of the orange dispute is a negative exemplar for the "divide equally" plan. The analogical transfer from that case to the Sinai dispute is as follows: Perhaps the goals of the disputants have been inferred incorrectly. Perhaps their real goals are concordant rather than competitive. If so, use *agreeable division* based on their real goals. In this case, an alternatative classification is suggested (one based on concordant rather than competitive goals), an explanation for the failure is suggested (the wrong goals were being considered), and a plan for recovery is suggested (find the real goals and then apply the plan *agreeable division* to that).

We summarize the roles a previous case can play in error recovery as follows:

- It can suggest a plausible new classification.
- It can suggest an explanation for the error or failure.
- It can suggest a plan for recovery.

A Complex Example

We continue to develop the Sinai dispute scenario to show multiple uses of analogy to previous cases in solving a complex problem. Our common-sense reasoner is reading in the paper about the dispute between Egypt and Israel over possession of the Sinai. She knows something about the Korean War and the recent dispute between the U.S. and Panama that resulted in the U.S. giving back economic and political but not military control of the canal to Panama. Initial consideration of the Sinai dispute causes reminding of the Korean War, because both involve disputes over land, both are competitive disputes between polities, both have previous histories of military conflicts, and in neither can the conflict be resolved completely for both sides. Based on this reminding, she predicts that Israel and Egypt will divide the Sinai equally.

She later reads that this advice was given and rejected by both sides. Considering that "divide equally" failed, she is reminded of the time her daughters were quarrelling over an orange (explained earlier). This reminding suggests that failures sometimes occur because the goals of the disputants are misunderstood. She therefore attempts an alternative understanding of Israel and Egypt's goals. Considering that Israel wants the Sinai as a military buffer zone in support of national security and Egypt wants the land for national integrity, she can now reconsider the conflict as a political dispute with concordant goals.

With this reclassification of the dispute, she is reminded of the Panama Canal dispute, which is also a political dispute over land with a concordant goal relationship. Further reasoning from this exemplar suggests that agreeable division based on the real goals of the disputants is an appropriate plan. The Panama dispute is also used to predict how agreeable division will be implemented. The U.S. is replaced by Israel (the party currently in control of the disputed object) and Panama is replaced by Egypt (the party who used to own it and wants it back). The prediction is made that, as was the case in the Panama Canal agreement, Egypt will get economic and political control of the Sinai, while its normal right of military control will be denied and given to Israel.

PROGRAMS

The processes and memory structures presented in this chapter are implemented in two computer programs: SHRINK (Kolodner & Kolodner, 1983) diagnoses cases of Major Depression; NEGOTIATOR (Simpson, 1984) suggests plans for resolution of disputes. The disputes NEGOTIATOR handles range from those encountered in taking care of children to the common-sense sorts of predictions we make about world events while reading the paper.

NEGOTIATOR has three major parts. First, its memory organization and indexing strategies allow previous similar cases to be recalled when appropriate. Second, it has rules for determining the most appropriate analogy when its memory returns more than one analogous past case. Third, its knowledge of where it is in the problem-solving process is a guide in selecting those features of a past case that should be transferred to the current one. Its analogical processes help NEGOTIATOR in classifying cases, choosing applicable mediation tactics, predicting the results of a tactic, and recovering from failure. The sample memory structure and all of the mediation examples in this chapter are taken from that program.

SHRINK's domain is psychiatric diagnosis. It currently has two major parts: a diagnostic module, which uses a slightly modified version of the rules given in the Diagnostic and Statistical Manual—III (APA, 1980) to diagnose (i.e., classify) cases of Major Depression, and a memory incorporation module that integrates new cases into the memory structures, causing remindings of previous cases along the way. Our next step is to integrate the memory incorporation and diagnostic processes to make better use of past experience. When complete, SHRINK will do both diagnosis and treatment of affective (mood) disorders based on analogy to previous cases and will also track down and explain its failures, correcting the knowledge that was at fault. We are currently working out the details of some experiments whose results will tell us more about the natural process of case-based reasoning in diagnosis.

WHERE DO WE GO FROM HERE?

In this chapter, we have attempted to provide a framework for experience's role in problem solving. We have named processes that use experience and have suggested a memory organization in support of those processes. We have not, however, stated exactly how each of the experiential processes work, nor have we pointed out potential bottlenecks in the processing framework. We are currently investigating these processes in the two domains cited, concentrating on explictly defining both the domain-specific (e.g., diagnostic) and domain-independent (e.g., analogic, learning) processes and on refining the memory structures. In particular, we must specify the types of features appropriate for indexing and the allowable types of classification structures. We must also specify what happens when the reasoner is reminded of multiple conflicting cases. In continuing this research, we have two aims: to discover in detail the processes by which experience can be used in problem solving and to explore the utility of having our expert computer programs use experience to do their tasks.

ACKNOWLEDGMENTS

This material is based upon work supported in part by NSF Grant No. IST-8116892, in part by NSF Grant No. IST-8317711, and in part by the Air Force Institute of Technology. The views expressed are solely those of the authors. Thanks to Dr. Robert M. Kolodner, Dana Eckart, and Katia Sycara-Cyranski.

REFERENCES

American Psychiatric Association. (1980). *Diagnostic and statistical manual of mental disorders* (3rd ed.). Washington, DC: Author.
Birnbaum, L., & Selfridge, M. (1981). Conceptual analysis of natural language. In R. C. Schank & C. K. Riesbeck (Eds.), *Inside computer understanding*. Hillsdale, NJ: Lawrence Erlbaum Associates.

Charniak, E. (1982). Context recognition in language comprehension. In W. G. Lehnert & M. Ringle (Eds.), *Strategies for natural language processing*. Hillsdale, NJ: Lawrence Erlbaum Associates.

Dyer, M. G. (1983). *In-depth understanding*. Cambridge, MA: MIT Press.

Hayes-Roth, B. (1980). *Human planning processes*. (Tech. Rep. R-2870-ONR). Santa Monica, CA: Rand Corp.

Kolodner, J. L. (1983). Maintaining memory organization in a dynamic long term memory. *Cognitive Science, 7*(4), 243–280.

Kolodner, J. L. (1984). *Retrieval and organizational strategies in conceptual memory*. Hillsdale, NJ: Lawrence Erlbaum Associates.

Kolodner, J. L., & Kolodner, R. M. (1983). An algorithm for diagnosis based on analysis of previous cases. In *Proceedings of MEDCOMP 83. Second IEEE Computer Society International Conference on Medical Computer Science/Computers in Medicine. Glouster, OH*.

Mostow, D. J. (1983). Machine transformation of advice into a heuristic search procedure. In R. Michalski, J. Carbonell, & T. Mitchell (Eds.), *Machine learning*. Palo Alto, CA: Tioga Press.

Newell, A., & Simon, H. (1972). *Human problem solving*. Englewood Cliffs, NJ: Prentice-Hall.

Reiser, B. J., Black, J. B., & Abelson, R. P. (1985). Knowledge structures in the organization and retrieval of autobiographical memories. *Cognitive Psychology, 17,* 89–137.

Ross, B. H. (1984). Remindings and their effects in learning a cognitive skill. *Cognitive Psychology, 16,* 371–416.

Sacerdoti, E. (1977). *A structure for plans and behavior*. Amsterdam: Elsevier North-Holland.

Schank, R., & Abelson, R. (1977) *Scripts, plans, goals, and understanding*. Hillsdale, NJ: Lawrence Erlbaum Associates.

Schank, R. C. (1981). Language and memory. In D. A. Norman (Ed.), *Perspectives on cognitive science*. Hillsdale, NJ: Lawrence Erlbaum Associates.

Schank, R. C. (1982). *Dynamic memory: A theory of learning in computers and people*. New York: Cambridge University Press.

Simpson, R. (1984). *Strategies for retrieval and prediction in an advisory system: A research proposal*. (Tech. Rep. GIT-ICS-84/03). Georgia Institute of Technology, School of Information and Computer Science, Atlanta.

Spitzer, R., Skodol, A., Gibbon, M., & Williams, J. (1980). *DSM-III case Book*. Washington, DC: American Psychiatric Association.

Wilensky, R. (1983). *Planning and understanding: A computational approach to human reasoning*. Reading, MA.: Addison-Wesley.

7

Learning How to Argue: Using Hypotheticals

Edwina L. Rissland
Department of Computer and Information Science
University of Massachusetts

ABSTRACT

We survey various uses of hypotheticals in legal reasoning, in particular in learning how to argue, and provide examples of each usage from standard first-year law courses such as contracts and torts. We also discuss several argument strategies that use sets or sequences of hypotheticals.

INTRODUCTION

Learning how to argue is one of the most difficult lessons for a student new to a field like law or mathematics, which has a rich structure and its own specialized modes of reasoning. Not only must the student be in command of a large body of material, but must also be adept at structuring what is said in acceptable rhetorical and inferential styles. For instance, in high school geometry, one must learn to cite theorems (e.g., side-angle-side) as justification for certain conclusions (e.g., triangle congruence) and learn not to rely too heavily on overly suggestive diagrams or special cases. In the Anglo-American legal system, one learns to argue according to the mode of *stare decisis,* the doctrine of precedent, which includes citing and arguing from precedents, for instance, by establishing analogies with those precedents favorable to one's position and by differentiating it from unfavorable ones.

One important ingredient of expert legal knowledge is hypothetical cases, or *hypos.* A hypothetical is "make-believe" in the sense that it has not actually been litigated. Often it is a skeletal or slightly modified version of a case that has been litigated. The generation of hypos is a rich and interesting process, which we have discussed elsewhere (Rissland, 1982, 1983). In current work, we are continuing with our research on hypo generation, particularly on the generation of "constraints" for hypos and the use of "dimensional" analysis to generate hypos that strengthen or weaken a party's case along a given doctrinal aspect (like consideration or reliance, in contracts).

Knowing how to use hypos is an important ingredient of legal expertise. For instance, teachers use hypotheticals to isolate issues in teaching their classes, and practitioners use them to sharpen their arguments by considering worst and best cases for their clients or their adversaries. In this chapter, we survey various roles hypotheticals serve in legal reasoning and learning how to argue. Our remarks here are based on observations and notes from actual classroom episodes (particularly from standard "1L" classes such as contracts, torts and property).[1] Although based on the experience typical to law school, they are relevant to other legal contexts, such as legal research and advocacy.

USES OF HYPOTHETICALS

In this section we list some of the ways hypos are used and give illustrative episodes. These usages are particularly concerned with hypotheticals; other usages of examples in general are discussed briefly in the next section. Background material and details on the relevant case law can be found in standard casebooks (e.g., Fuller & Eisenberg, 1981, for contracts; Gregory, Kalven, & Epstein, 1977, for torts; Haar & Liebman, 1977, for property).

Hypos Remake Experience

Hypotheticals allow one either to redefine the fact situation of a given case and then reargue it or to enter a new case into the body of common law, thus remaking the legal knowledge base and thereby allowing reargument of the case at bar in light of the new "precedent".

> EXAMPLE: The case of *Dougherty v. Salt* (New York Court of Appeals, 1919) involves the issue of the enforceability of donative promises. Here the plaintiff, a boy 8 years old, was promised $3,000 by his aunt payable at her death (the defendant is the aunt's executrix). The case was decided against the plaintiff on the grounds that there was no "consideration" for the aunt's promise.

---

[1]In particular these observations were made by the author in connection with her appointment as a Fellow of Law and Computer Science at the Harvard Law School in 1982–83.

Now consider the situation where the only case in the case base is the following hypo: The aunt promises $10,000 to her nephew; her assets are in ruin; keeping her promise means her own children starve; her nephew sues and loses. The exercise in legal reasoning[2] is to reargue *Dougherty v. Salt* for Dougherty in spite of the hypo. One way to do this is to "distinguish" the hypo from the the real case by saying the hypo involves extenuating circumstances that are not present in the real case (and appealing to the common-sense heuristic[3] that "promise plus extenuating circumstances $===\Rightarrow$ not enforceable"). Another way is to embellish the hypo with facts that support an "injurious-reliance" or "benefit-restitution" argument. (For such hypos, see Rissland, 1982.)

This exercise involves hypos in two ways: (a) the remaking of the "real" case by generation of a hypo through modifications to the fact situation (here to the state of the defendant, the value of the item promised, etc.); and (b) using the hypo as a new precedent for the case at bar. By such reargument, both pro and con the parties, under tougher and easier circumstances, one learns to "distinguish" (i.e., show how the case at bar is different), or "harmonize" (i.e., show how an apparent inconsistency can be explained and shown not to exist).

Hypos Create Experience

The law can respond only to cases actually brought before it. Thus, there can be a paucity of experiences to learn from (even for the law, which itself can be thought of as an evolving learning system). One convenient way to remedy this deficiency, especially in law school, is to add more examples to the stream of experience by making them up. In learning about a legal idea, one cannot afford to wait for the "right" case to come along, so one creates it hypothetically.[4] Another source of cases that provide new experience are those currently in litigation. Even though current cases will eventually become real, as long as they are undecided they remain only hypothetical, as far as the doctrine of precedent is concerned. There is no problem using these in class as hypos, and they sometimes make good additions to the class's body of case law, but they are not bona fide legal precedents.

EXAMPLE: In the law of property, the subarea of time-shared real estate has not been of concern to society long enough to have spawned

---

[2]Posed by Professor G. Frug in his contracts course, HLS 1981–82.

[3]I use the word *heuristic*, as opposed to *rule*, because it is more a statement of what generally does obtain than what should obtain.

[4]One does not have this difficulty in mathematics, where any example is as real as it is hypothetical.

many cases that have been litigated, certainly not all the way through the system (i.e., through trial and appeals to a Supreme Court decision). Therefore, to gain experience with the relevant issues and connect this new area with other more developed areas like rent control and condominiums, one considers a hypo like the following: Suppose you buy 1 week per year in a time-shared beach house in Malibu, and it subsequently falls into the sea. Just what do you own? What are your rights vis-á-vis the rights of the mortgagee? Is *fee simple* thinking appropriate here? What about analogies to cases concerning condos?

Hypos Are Tools to Explore Concepts, Propositions, and Rules

As in other fields like mathematics and medicine, examples provide a way to test the limits and reasonableness of concepts, propositions, and rules and to help generate and refine them. (For classic examples of this, see Lakatos, 1976, for the mathematics of polyhedra and Levi, 1949, for the law of products liability.) Many law school discussions are such explorations; some classic "master" questions for discussion are:

- In contracts, What promises should the law enforce?—with hypos spawned by cases like *Dougherty* discussed earlier;
- In property, What are mechanics of the *Rule against Perpetuities?*—with hypos related to the famous *Jee v. Audley* case of the "fertile octogenarian" and his will;
- In torts, What constitutes *intention?*—with hypos involving physical harm such as those derived from *Vosburg v. Putney.*

   EXAMPLE: The following hypo[5] can be dissected from many points of view: Each day you walk across the owner's field to the area you have been working. You say, "Morning; chance of rain." He nods his head. From the point of view of contracts, is there assent or implied contract? Is there an element of bargain? Should there be restitution damages for your services? From the point of view of torts, is this trespass? Suppose you spread dioxin contaminated top soil on the plot. Who pays for the clean up? Suppose the dioxin contaminates an abutter's property? From the point of view of property, are there issues of adverse possession or rights of way? What if you build a fence, a house? This has been going on for a week, a year, 20 years?

---

[5]From Frug's class on Contracts.

Hypos Refocus Cases (Especially by Excluding Issues)

Hypos can be used to exclude distracting or troublesome issues from later or earlier cases or in the context of the case at bar. This is especially useful when such issues would be likely to arise in the legal analysis. This refocusing involves mechanisms such as deletion or modification (e.g., by generalization to abstract actors A and B) or by rhetorical restructuring (instead of saying "X was promised to B by A . . .," shift the emphsis to the actors by saying "A promised B . . .").

> EXAMPLE: Refocus *Dougherty* by eliminating possible side issues such as the minority of Dougherty, the mental capacity of his aunt, the rights of women, the complexities of wills and trusts, by saying simply: The plaintiff Dougherty was promised $3,000 by the defendant.[6]

Hypos are Counter-examples in the "Realist Number"

The *realist number* refers to an argument to refute a mechanical or purely positivist concept of the law in favor of one of the legal realist school. For instance, if the law is posited to be rule-like, one can argue that either: (a) rules are ill formed, for instance, the exceptions "swallow up" the rule, or (b) the "predicates" in the rules are ill defined. In hypos used for this purpose, one demonstrates the open texture of legal concepts. By generating hypos one can cause trouble for just about any rule or concept.

> EXAMPLE: If one posits that a formal mechanism like a "wax and seal" rule will eliminate problems in contracts by providing a necessary or sufficient condition for enforceability, one can offer the hypothetical scenario where the rule is "The litigant with the longest name wins."[7] This rule seems straightforward enough. However, if this were the case, people would simply lengthen their names and cases would center around issues like what constitutes a "legal" name (e.g., Are hypenated names allowed and if so, is there any limit on them?), when can you change your name, and is this a "good" rule (people in the know will make sure they have long names), and so forth.
>
> The following is an example of a rule (full disclosure) being eaten up by an exception (distraught patient). It was used to explore the analogy,[8]

---

[6]The hypo we gave refocussed (through embellishment) the case from consideration to injurious-reliance doctrine.

[7]Posed by Frug.

[8]From Professor M. Horwitz's class on Torts, HLS 1982–83.

"Good medical practice is to full disclosure as objective standard is to subjective standard." The distraught patient says, "Doc, don't tell me; I trust you." Just what is left of objective or subjective standards after such a case?

Hypos Organize and Cluster Cases

This use of hypos is akin to that of a generalization or abstraction: the hypo captures the essence of a diversity of cases. It can bring together many scattered cases that seem to be just more cases of nothing in particular and can make them into a conceptual cluster with a retrievable token (thus allowing one to forget details since the gist is captured in the hypo).

> EXAMPLE: The hypo of the "nagging" case is used to tie together many cases that involve the issue of whether or not certain types of forbearance like "bargaining away" a "right" constitute consideration: I promise to stop nagging you (or asking you questions in class), if you pay me $5,000.[9]

> EXAMPLE: The case of *Hamer v. Sidway* (1891) revolves around a promise of an uncle to his nephew that if the nephew would "refrain from drinking, using tobacco, swearing, and playing cards or billiards for money until he became 21 years of age," he would pay him $5,000. The nephew arrived at the age of 21 years and had performed his part of the agreement, but the uncle did not pay.

> EXAMPLE: *Miller v. Miller* (1887) deals with a contract made between the parties, husband and wife, that said, among other things, "Each party agrees to refrain from scolding, fault-finding and anger . . . "

> EXAMPLE: In *White v. Bluett* (1853), a son made complaints to his father that he was being discriminated against and had not received as many favors as the other children. The father agreed that if the son would promise to cease complaining, he would absolve him from repaying a loan. After the father died, suit was brought against the son on the debt. During the course of argument, one of the barristers asked, "Is an agreement by a father in consideration that his son will not bore him a binding contract?" (Fuller & Eisenberg, 1981, p. 80).

Hypos Provide Argument Exercises

A hypo, especially one together with a set of alternative modifications or "endings," provides an opportunity to make an argument under varying degrees of

---

[9]Posed by Frug.

difficulty for either side. Many law book problems are of this nature, for instance the following problem in ''draftsmanship'':

> EXAMPLE: ''A father dies leaving two sons, Fairchild and Loser. The father's will leaves his entire estate, valued at about $200,000, to Fairchild. Though Loser makes no complaint, Fairchild feels that his brother was treated unjustly. He expresses his willingness to enter into a binding legal obligation to pay $20,000 to Loser. . . . (A) Which of the following devices should be avoided as doing more harm than good: (1) a seal; (2) a recital of $1 paid by Loser to Fairchild; (3) a recital that the agreement is 'in consideration of $1 by each to the other in hand paid'; (4) a recital that the promise was 'for value received'; (5) a recital that the promise was made in return 'for other good and sufficient consideration'; (6) a recital that the promise was made 'from love and affection'; (7) a recital that the promise was intended to rectify the injustice of the father's will; (8) a recital that the promise was made for Loser's stamp album; (10) a recital that it was Fairchild's intention to bind himself legally; (11) a promise by Loser to use the money wisely; (12) a promise by Loser not to contest his father's will.[10] (B) Instead of having Fairchild make a simple promise, would it be better to have him declare himself trustee of a portion of the estate for the benefit of Loser.'' (Fuller & Eisenberg, 1981, p. 19)

Hypos Tease Out Hidden Assumptions

By adding an explicit characterization of an element of a case, one creates a hypo which teases out one's default assumptions, for instance, that widows are nice, banks and big business are not nice, and the like.

> EXAMPLE: In the case of *Newman & Snell's State Bank v. Hunter,* (1928), the bank brought action against Zennetta H. Hunter, widow of Lee C. Hunter, who had died intestate with insufficient estate to pay his funeral expenses. At the time of Mr. Hunter's death, plaintiff bank held his note for $3,700. After his death, his wife exchanged the old note for a new note, the consideration being the return of old note plus interest payments, and the bank tried to compel payment of the new note. The court held that this bargain lacked consideration; that is, the widow won. What if Zennetta was craftily trying to get out of a debt?

> EXAMPLE: In the case of *Peevyhouse v. Garland Coal & Mining Co.* (1962), the jury awarded damages to Willie and Lucille Peevyhouse for breach of Garland's contract to restore their farmland after strip mining. Is the ''The Little House on the Prairie'' model accurate? What if the Pee-

---

[10]Option (12) is a ''nagging'' case, cf., *White v. Bluett* (1853).

vyhouses entered the contract knowing that the mine company would probably breach and that they could make a bundle in damages?

GENERAL ROLES PLAYED BY EXAMPLES

Of course, all the usual roles played by examples are played by hypotheticals. Here we briefly go through some of our previously discussed taxonomy for examples (Rissland, 1978, 1984).

Hypos Introduce Issues and Concepts

That is, hypos can function as start-up examples. This is especially so when one wants a class to generate a ''commonsense'' result that is then seen to be the foundation of a legal doctrine or rule.

> EXAMPLE: The very first lecture in my contracts course[11] began with the professor setting up a hypo by saying, ''Mr. Cramer, I promise you $10,000.'' This led immediately into the issues of consideration, reliance, the case of *Dougherty,* and many other hypos (see Rissland, 1982).

Hypos Bound Concepts and Issues

Hypos function as counter-examples, to limit and refute. One distinction between this usage in mathematics and in law is that in mathematics one counter-example has all the needed power for refutation, but in law things are not so clear cut. Nevertheless, by considering a group of hypos, one can effectively bound an issue or concept or refine a rule.

> EXAMPLE: To bound the notion of intent (e.g., willful and wanton, malicious, strong vs. weak, intention to act, intention to harm), consider the hypos:[12] (1) I punch you in the nose; (2) While putting on my jacket, I have difficulty with the sleeve, and punch you in the nose; (3) While waiting at a crowded bus stop, I get bumped violently from behind and hit you in the nose; (4) While waiting in line at the bank, an armed robber grabs me and shoves me in front of him like a shield and you are knocked down.

Hypos Provide Templates

Hypos act as models describing the general situation.

---

[11]With G. Frug, HLS 1981–82.
[12]From Horwitz's class in Torts.

EXAMPLE: In contracts, *A promises B X in return for Y* is a very simple template for a contract.

Hypos Provide Standard Cases

Hypos function as reference examples. The "Mr. Cramer" hypo became a case as standard as any in the case-book. Certain hypos can assume a life of their own: they can acquire names and the status of real cases.

STRATEGIES OF USING HYPOS

Certain strategies for arguing or teaching argument involve using a set or sequence of hypotheticals. For instance, in using a hypo to refocus a case away from distracting issues, one can either: (a) frame a hypo to exclude the distractions; or (b) collect the distractions into a hypo, analyze and dismiss it, and move on to a hypo without distractions.

Sometimes the hypos are presented as a set, that is, their order is unimportant; other times, they are presented in sequence, which is often derived by incremental modifications (for examples, see Rissland, 1983).

Hypo Sensitivity Sets

A set of hypotheticals, all of which cluster about (i.e., are modified from) a particular case, form a set of cases to explore issues. For examples, see the reference *Restatement, Second, Contracts,* a compendia of "rules" and principles illustrated by short hypotheticals and synopses of cases. Such a set of hypos allows one to see the extreme, or *reductio,* case from the beginning (cf. slippery slope sequences) and to develop reasons why it has, and ought to have, a different outcome. Then one can deal with the hypos "in the middle" and explore how rationales governing the polar cases apply. Note that in generating such sets, one does not generate cases by modifying every aspect; one practices economy. This is related to the idea of generating along "dimensions" and the art of hypo generation.

EXAMPLE: The following are illustrations from the Section 71 on The Requirement of Exchange from the *Restatement, Second, Contracts:*

- A offers to buy a book owned by B and to pay B $10 in exchange therefor. B accepts the offer and delivers the book to A. The transfer and delivery of the book constitute a performance and are consideration for A's promise . . . . This is so even though A, at the time he makes the offer, secretly intends to pay B $10 whether or not he gets the book, or even though B at the time he accepts secretly intends not to collect the $10.

- A receives from B a gift of a book worth $10. Subsequently A promises to pay B the value of the book. There is no consideration for A's promise. This is so even though B, at the time he makes the gift, secretly hopes that A will pay him for it . . .
- A promises to make a gift of $10 to B. In reliance on the promise, B buys a book from C and promises to pay C $10 for it. There is no consideration for A's promise.

Slippery Slope Sequences

In one type of sequence of hypotheticals, each successor hypo is a "small" modification of its predecessor. The sequence concludes with a case that refutes the principle supposedly "proved" by the initial case. Metaphorically, it is an example of getting into trouble with piled up epsilons. It has the pedagogical disadvantage of making students overly wary, suspicious of a "trap."

> EXAMPLE: The issue of what constitutes mutuality in an agreement arises in the case of *Laclede Gas Co. v. Amoco Oil Co.* (1975) in which Amoco contended that its agreement with Laclede was void because Laclede was the only one given a right to cancel it (with 30 days notice), and thus the contract lacked mutuality. The case was decided for Laclede.
>
> - The sequence of hypos[13] started with a remade case with 90 days written notice, which seemed acceptable to the class.
> - 30 days (the original case)—still acceptable.
> - 1 week—uncomfortable.
> - 30 seconds—clearly too little time.
> - "Any time I feel like it"—the final *reductio* case.
> - with written notice—no good.
> - 90 days with written notice—no longer so clearly acceptable.

This is an example of what I call a *reductio loop,* in which not only does one refute the original proposition (here, 90 days written notice is acceptable), but also the analysis of the original case no longer stands. Schematically, one has:

$$P \to H_1 \to H_2 \to H_3 \to \ldots \to H_n \to \neg P$$

(where P is a proposition and H_i are hypos)

An example of the slippery slope manuever denied is the following exchange involving Williston (the famous consideration theorist), reported from the debates during the writing of the *Restatement, First, Contracts.* He refuses to take the bait and slide down the slippery slope (Fuller & Eisenberg, 1981):

---

[13]From Frug's class.

"Williston: . . . Johnny says, "I want to buy a Buick car." Uncle says, "Well, I will give you $1,000." . . . [Uncle] knows that the $1,000 is going to be relied on by the nephew for the purchase of the car. . . .

"Questioner 1: . . . Suppose the car had been a Ford instead of a Buick, costing $600 . . . Johnny says, "I want to buy a Ford" and . . . . not being familiar with the market price of a Ford, the uncle says, "I will give you $1,000." Now, is the uncle obligated for the $1,000 or for the price of the Ford?

"Williston: I think he might be bound for the $1,000.

"Questioner 2: . . . Say, he goes out and buys the car for $500—would uncle be liable for $1000 or would he be liable for $500?

"Williston: . . . I think the uncle would be liable for the $1,000 . . ." (pp. 24–25).

In the opinion for *White v. Bluett* (1853) mentioned earlier, the chief barrister wrote, "By the argument, a principle is pressed to an absurdity, as a bubble is blown until it bursts."

SUMMARY

In this chapter, we have surveyed, through examples harvested from actual law school classes, roles played by hypotheticals in legal reasoning and in learning how to argue. Hypos are used to:

1. remake experience
2. create experience
3. explore concepts and rules
4. refocus cases
5. make "realist" arguments
6. organize cases
7. provide argument exercises
8. tease out hidden assumptions

These are in addition to the usual functions served by start-up, reference, anomalous, model and counter-examples. We concluded with some examples illustrating strategies involving the use of clusters of hypos, in particular, the use of sensitivity sets and slippery slope sequences. In these usages, we saw hypos used in two principle contexts: (a) stand-alone: as the case at bar; and (b) case-law: as another case in the legal data base of case law.

Hypotheticals are an important component of expertise in legal reasoning and, no doubt, in other domains that use case-based reasoning. They are an important adjunct to the body of "real" experiences and make important contributions to development and learning not only of individuals but also of the system itself.

ACKNOWLEDGMENT

This work supported in part by Grant IST-8212238 of the National Science Foundation.

REFERENCES

Dougherty v. Salt, 227 N.Y. 200, 125 N.E. 94 (N.Y. Crt of Appeals, 1919).
Fuller, L. L., & Eisenberg, M. A. (1981). *Basic contract law*. Minneapolis, MN: West Publishing.
Gregory, C. O., Kalven, H., & Epstein, R. A. (1977). *Cases and materials on torts*. Boston: Little, Brown.
Haar, C. M., & Liebman, L. (1977). *Property and law*. Boston: Little, Brown.
Hamer v. Sidway, 124 N.Y. 538, 27 N.E. 256, (N.Y. Crt of Appeals, 1891).
Jee v. Audley, 1 Cox 324, 29 Eng. Rep 1186 (Ch. 1787).
Laclede Gas Co. v. Amoco Oil Co., 522 F. 2d 33 (U.S. Crt of Appeals, Eighth Circuit, 1975).
Lakatos, I. (1976). *Proofs and refutations*. London: Cambridge University Press.
Levi, E. H. (1949). *An introduction to legal reasoning*. Chicago: University of Chicago Press.
Miller v. Miller, 78 Iowa 177, 35 N.W. 464, 42 N.W. 641 (Sup. Crt of Iowa, 1887).
Newman & Snell's State Bank v. Hunter, 243 Mich. 331, 220 N.W. 665 (Sup. Crt of Mich., 1928).
Peevyhouse v. Garland Coal Mining Co., 382 p. 2d 109 (Okla, 1962), cert denied, 375 U.S. 906.
Rissland, E. (1982). Examples in the legal domain: Hypotheticals in contract law. *Proceedings of the Fourth Annual Cognitive Science Society Conference,* 96–99, Ann Arbor, MI.
Rissland, E. L. (1978). Understanding understanding mathematics. *Cognitive Science, 2*(4), 361–383.
Rissland, E. L. (1983). Examples in legal reasoning: Legal hypotheticals. *Proceedings of the Eighth International Joint Conference on Artificial Intelligence* 90–93, Karlsruhe, Germany.
Rissland, E. L. (1984). Examples and learning systems. In O. Selfridge, E. L. Rissland, & M. Arbib (Eds.), *Adaptive control of ill-defined systems*. New York: Plenum Press.
Vosburg v. Putney, 80 Wis. 523, 50 N.W. 403 (1891).
White v. Bluett, 23 L.J. Ex. (N.S.) 36 (1853).

8 Assignment of Responsibility in Ethical Judgments

William M. Bain
Department of Computer Science
Yale University

ABSTRACT

When a judge determines a sentence for a criminal case, he must sift through facts about the crime and the criminal, arguments from the opposing lawyers, reactions from the victims, and the relevant sentencing statutes. The aim of the JUDGE project is to describe the content of this kind of common-sense ethical reasoning and implement it in a computer program. JUDGE uses about 15 *justification units* simultaneously to flesh out a causal account of a crime and determine whose actions were and were not justified. To constrain the search space of possible causal completions, explanations that fall at the extremes of justificational severity become the best candidates for the opposing lawyers to adopt, and for the judge to anticipate.

INTRODUCTION

When a judge determines a sentence for a criminal case, he must sift through a great deal of information. Quite likely, he has been bombarded with facts about the crime, reports and testimony about the criminal, reactions from victims, and he has considered the relevant sentencing statutes. One of the more important abilities he uses to interpret and organize all of this data stems from his sense of ethics. A judge knows, for instance, why an offender's intentions and actions were wrong. A person, or a program, that is to assess the bad and the good in criminal cases as a judge does must have some basic sense of ethics to direct the reactions to the intentions and actions of the people involved in the case (Delin, 1978; Kempe & Kempe, 1978).

127

Judges can decide initially how harshly to deal with an offender when they are told only about the circumstances of a crime. The facts of a case are the most significant portion of the material that a judge considers in determining a sentence, although other information, such as a prior record or a psychological assessment of the offender, can have a strong bearing as well. The aim here is to describe the content of common-sense ethical reasoning that centers primarily on the facts of criminal cases. In addition, a system for representing that information is presented, along with a process model using the representation to make initial decisions about punishment severity. This process is being implemented in a computer program called JUDGE.

It is because many different explanations can be constructed for the same given set of actions that legal and moral disputes arise. These explanations differ in the perceptions, motivations, and intentions (henceforth referred to collectively as *motives*) they incorporate. Each set of explanatory motives supports a different interpretation of what actions were justified and, therefore, who was responsible and to what degree.[1]

BACKGROUND: THE TASK OF THE JUDGE

In sentencing an offender, the judge must take into account the likelihood that the offender will repeat the crime, the extent of harm caused, and the degree to which the offender was justified in acting. To make a prediction about the offender's future behavior, the judge considers any prior record, as well as the causes of the current crime. Thus, the judge must understand *why* the offender violated the law and to do this, either constructs or accepts some explanation for the crime.

After we presented a judge in Connecticut with the facts of a child molestation case, he made the following comments describing his own explanation for the case:

> If he (the child molester, who was 16 years old] were treated as a youthful offender, then I would probably . . . if he were presented for determination [of youthful offender status], I would feel very strongly against it, because basically, I'd have to . . . it's very hard to judge, I mean, some people just goof up sexually as they're that age or so, and it's hard to tell with no prior record, I would tend to want to give someone the benefit of the doubt, especially since there is no severe trauma to the victims.

That the offender might have "goofed up" satisfies the judge as a reasonable explanation for the crime; furthermore, it predicts that he won't do it again.

---

[1]Similar argumentation strategies about justification can be found in (Birnbaum, 1982).

The amount of harm caused by an offender suggests the degree of punishment due. However, an offender whose actions were somewhat justified will not be held completely responsible for the outcome. With grave consequences typically at stake for an offender, it is incumbent on the judge to thoughtfully consider alternative explanations for a crime.

Two ways that the judge faces this task suggest processes that use essentially the same knowledge. First, the judge can anticipate the arguments of both attorneys after hearing the facts. To model this, we take the given facts of the case as input, as well as the high-level goal of the side under consideration. The goal is to suggest an explanation of the facts favorable to that side. For example, say that "Sam hit John" and "John hit Sam" are the facts and that the high-level goal is to show that John was justified. An interpretation of self-defense would explain the facts causally and satisfy the specified goal. Considering the same facts with the opposite goal should suggest interpretations favorable to the other side of the case. John could have been retaliating against Sam, for instance, which is not justified in the law.

The other means that a judge has for assigning responsibility to an offender is to consider explanations actually offered by the attorney for each side. Each has taken on one of the opposing high-level goals. The judge needs merely to listen to the accounts of motives suggested by their interpretations to verify that they are consistent with the facts and that the differing views of justification correspond to their high-level goals.[2]

The content of these inverse processes is discussed further with respect to the case presented in the following section.

A MOCK PLEA BARGAINING SESSION

The following is what the participants (a Connecticut Superior Court judge, a defense attorney, and a prosecutor) were told in a mock plea bargaining session:

> Here's the client that you're defending. His name is John. What happened was that John was standing on the street outside of a bar, and a man named Sam came up and attacked John. He began throwing punches at John. John responded to this by throwing one punch at Sam. Sam fell over backwards, fell on the ground, and hit his head on the ground, and suffered from a swelling of the brain from that one punch, and he died. John did not hit Sam any more after that, but he was charged with one count of manslaughter. Those are essentially the facts of the case.

---

[2]This more passive approach is related to the understanding of goal-based stories, as in (Wilensky, 1978).

On hearing this, the lawyers developed competing interpretations about what happened, and each tried to convince the judge that his version was the more sound. To make their points clear, they made up facts when they needed them, especially in situations that called for plausible explanations about the actors' intentions. The debate began between the two attorneys:

Prosecution: I can see a self-defense coming.

Defense: Yes, and I would certainly urge self-defense on behalf of my client.

Prosecution: But your client was no longer at the time suffering from the assault. The assault was over, ruling out your self-defense claim.

Defense: Well, I would certainly contest that, because, how did my client know, how would any reasonable person in those circumstances know, that the perpetrator of this assault was through throwing his punches?

Prosecution: Well, because the perpetrator had turned his back and was entering his car at the time. (laughs) Beat that one.

The prosecutor immediately anticipated an effective interpretation that was available to the defense attorney. The resulting argument concerned the most central interpretation issue of the case: whether the act committed by John was intended for self-defense, or whether it was simply retaliatory. A self-defensive act requires a valid explanation that the victim be in imminent danger of being hurt; it is therefore justifiable. Retaliation, on the other hand, occurs when the victim is no longer in immediate danger; it is not justified in the law. In a retaliation, the victim's action would not directly serve to prevent further harm, as would a self-defensive action, but instead would be designed to get even with the attacker.

The judge next sought to determine the initial cause of the events of the case:

Judge: What was the motivation for the original assault? Either one of you know that?

Prosecution: I'll answer, since I'm the prosecutor. It seems, your Honor, that the two participants were fighting over the favors of a young lady.

The judge's point in asking this question stemmed from his need to see that all of the known facts were accounted for. This is necessary to form an accurate explanation of what happened. Ultimately, the judge needs to know more than simply *what* specific criminal or violative events happened, such as that somebody killed somebody else; it is more important for him to know *why* they occurred. For example, if John had just mass-murdered Sam's family and blown up his house, we could understand why Sam attacked John, and we might even consider his attack justified. These facts could in turn lead us, and the judge, to the conclusion that John actually might have intended to kill Sam. An alternative explanation for the motives of the crime might arise from a fact such as that Sam was a junkie who attacked John during a drug-induced mania. This would be interpreted to mean that the attack was completely unprovoked by John, that John was justified in defending himself; the resulting motives would not likely indicate that John intended to kill Sam.

The judge turned the discussion again to issues of interpretation:

> Judge (to Prosecuting Attorney): Would you claim that the accused used more force than was reasonably necessary under the circumstances?

> Prosecution: It is our claim a) that more force was used than was required, and it's also our claim that the assault had already terminated and that the blow that was struck was in retaliation to the assault.

> Judge (to Defense Attorney): Are you claiming that there is not enough here to warrant a trial, that it should be negotiated, is negotiable?

> Defense: Absolutely, your Honor. I'm claiming more than that this is negotiable. I'm claiming that there is no basis for a trial in this case, that there's a prima facie . . . that this case should be dismissed, because I do not feel that the state can prove a case, and . . . he used nothing but his fists . . . and one blow, one blow in response to being attacked by this individual with a fist and no other weapon, in my humble opinion, does not make out a case for manslaughter.

With the attorneys holding widely disparate explanations about the intentions of the offender, the stage was set for the case to go to trial. In the next sections, we examine the knowledge necessary for extracting biased explanations of a crime, such as those proffered by the attorneys.

Representing the Case

When they discussed the case, the lawyers and the judge used terms such as *self-defense, excessive amount of force,* and *retaliation* to describe the actions that had occurred. The interpretations of the case that included those phrases suggested descriptions of John's and Sam's motives; they also imposed determinations of justification on the actors.

Any representation for this particular case must not only include data from the original input, but it must also demonstrate the causal connections between intentions and actions from one event to the next. In addition, we should be able to relate features of the representation to various interpretations, such as that actions were self-defensive or retaliatory.

The following representation of the case conforms to the first of these requirements, showing the input data and some of the causal connections between the actions:

EVENT 1

Sam's Intention: *?*

Sam's Action: Hit John (multiple incidents).

>Result: John physically harmed
>(Violated P-PHYSICAL-INTEGRITY
>(serious/reversible) of John by Sam).

John's Perception: Violation of P-PHYSICAL-INTEGRITY
(serious/reversible) of John by Sam).

(result)

John's Emotion: *?*

(result) . . .

EVENT 2

John's Intention: *?*

John's Action: Hit Sam (single incident).

>Result: Sam physically harmed
>(Violated P-PHYSICAL-INTEGRITY
>(serious/reversible) of Sam by John).

(result)

Event: Sam falls.

(result)

Event: Sam hits head on ground.

(result)

Event: Sam dies (Violated P-LIFE of Sam).

The Preservation goals (P-goals) (Schank & Abelson, 1977) included here indicate the degrees of harm caused by the actions. The foregoing representation shows the facts of the case organized into two main events; Sam hit John several times, and then John responded by hitting Sam once, followed by degenerate events where the injuries sustained by Sam resulted indirectly from John's blow. The representation expresses the causal connections between the actors' intentions, actions, results, perceptions and emotions that comprise each full event. For example, intentions motivate actions, and result themselves from perceptions of previous events, emotions, or both. Because the input for the case did not mention the intentions, perceptions, and emotions of the actors, they must be inferred to complete this representation, thus forming an explanation of the facts.

Justification Units

The process of inferring motives with this representation requires paying attention to both structural and semantic features. Of particular structural interest in this case is the lack of any known events before the first violative action when Sam struck John. A number of interpretations can support this feature, including that the first event was entirely unprovoked, that it stemmed from some thematic structure (e.g., Sam was insane), that it was responsive to some other event not represented (leading one to an expectation that something did in fact precede Sam's attack), or that it was unintended (unsupported by the semantic feature that striking another person is an intentional act).

Semantic features concern mainly the violative levels of actions. We represent these in a hierarchy of Preservation goals (P-goals), which indicates the relative badness of violative actions. A very general version of this hierarchy includes the following goals (Schank & Abelson, 1977):

- P-LIFE (most important goal class)
- P-PSYCHOSEXUAL-INTEGRITY
- P-PHYSICAL-INTEGRITY
- P-PHYSICAL-FREEDOM
- P-PROPERTY
- P-SOCIAL-INTEGRITY (least important goal class)

With respect to this hierarchy, the semantic features of interest in the case include the fact that John's response to Sam's attack did not exceed the goal class of Sam's attack, and that the ultimate result of John's action far exceeded the extent of Sam's violation against him.

To infer the missing motives in the case, we use a set of about 15 justification units. These processing structures are so named because they impose particular interpretive rules about who was justified and who was not, in addition to completing a causal account of the crime. The use of any one unit depends on structural and/or semantic features of the input representation (the facts).

For example, we can apply the justification unit of Self-defense to the manslaughter case at the point where John hit Sam in response to Sam's attack. If the representation explicitly noted that Sam's original attack had ceased before John responded, then this unit would be ruled out. Such a situation would be explained instead with a Retaliation justification unit. Self-defense provides representable inferences that John perceived a continued threat from Sam, that John had an emotion of fear about further harm, and that he intended to hurt Sam only to prevent Sam from hurting him more. In addition, justification units include rules that impose justification assessments on actions in the case, assigning responsibility to one of the participants. For example:

Self-defense Rule 1—If a threat is currently active against him, the *defender* in a crime or conflict situation is justified in intending to threaten or violate the *intimidator* at the same level of P-goal threats or violations made by the *intimidator* against the *defender*.

The roles of *defender* and *intimidator* specify the attacker and the attackee, indicating who has more justificational leeway. This rule stipulates that the person being attacked may defend himself or herself; a companion rule states that the *intimidator* may not. In the course of a fight these roles can change; they are assigned and altered by various justification rules.

Other justification units relevant to this case include parity retaliation (applies if Sam had ceased his attack before John struck back; this unit makes John unjustified), escalation (if John intended to harm Sam to a greater degree than he had been harmed—whether in the service of defending himself or not—he would be unjustified), and accident (the result of John's action exceeded his intended result).

Forming Disparate Explanations

Because several justification units can impose their own inferences about each missing piece of the representation (e.g., intentions), they can generate a large number of possible explanations for a case. Explanations that fall at the extremes of justificational severity become the best candidates for the opposing lawyers to adopt, and for the judge to anticipate.

Several possibilities for interpreting Sam's attack against John already have been discussed. These include that Sam's action was unprovoked or that it was responsive to an action of John's. In the latter case, several assignments of justification units show John and Sam as being alternatively unjustified and justified. Then, in the subsequent event, where John hits Sam back, we know of at least six different justification unit assignments; these are outlined below with corresponding explanations (justification assessments are shown in brief in parentheses):

1. Self-defense/Accident: John struck Sam out of self-defense, intending only to stop the attack, but accidentally caused Sam to die (Justified intent to protect, unintended but unjustified permanent result).

2. Self-defense/Escalation/Accident: John struck Sam out of self-defense, but felt that the only way to stop the attack was to use a great deal of force; he did not, however, intend to kill Sam (Justified intent to protect, unjustified intent to act at excessive level, unintended but unjustified permanent result).

3. Self-defense/Escalation: John struck Sam out of self-defense, but felt that the only way to stop the attack was to imperil Sam's life (Justified intent to protect, unjustified intent to act at extremely excessive level, intended and unjustified permanent result).

4. Parity Retaliation/Accident: Because he was angry, John struck Sam after Sam had stopped attacking; however, he intended only to hurt Sam to the same degree (Unjustified intent at parity level, unintended but unjustified permanent result).

5. Escalation/Accident: John struck Sam out of anger, not protectiveness, and wanted to be harsh to teach Sam a lesson (Unjustified intent at excessive level, unintended but unjustified permanent result).

6. Escalation: John struck Sam intending to kill him (Unjustified intent at extremely excessive level, intended and unjustified permanent result).

Because several justification unit assignments can satisfy the constraints given by the action for each event, the number of whole-case explanations runs into a combinatorial explosion. We therefore use a strategy for reducing the possibilities to only the extreme opposing positions held by the attorneys. To do this, the program will bias its selection of justification unit assignments. For the defense, for example, the goal will be to show that John was justified in his actions and that his adversary, Sam, was not. Thus, the Unprovoked violation unit is selected over others to interpret Sam's attack, because it optimizes the achievement of this goal. For John's response, self-defense casts him in the most justified light, and escalation the least; parity retaliation lies somewhere in between. As a result, the defense attorney chooses self-defense for his interpretation. The prosecutor, who has the opposite goals, selects escalation. Their resulting interpretations are as follows:

For the prosecution:
John started the fight (Unmentioned antecedent event—Unprovoked violation).
Sam attacked John (Self-defense).
John struck Sam intending to kill him (Escalation).
Sam died (intended by Escalation).
For the defense:
Sam attacked John (Unprovoked violation).

John struck Sam to protect himself (Self-defense).
Sam died (Accident).

Usually, some part of an extreme explanation is found to be implausible; in that case, the next most optimal justification unit should be considered.

Plausibility Constraints

There are four strategies for pointing out when it is necessary to modify an explanation in this process. First, an explanation can be found implausible owing to an immediately available clarification of the original facts. For example, the prosecutor asserted in this model that John actually started the altercation and that Sam, the eventual victim, responded in self-defense. However, a clarification of the facts would indicate that Sam initiated the fight. The prosecutor would have to abandon his assertion and adopt a less extreme interpretation, such as that Sam's actions arose from some thematic cause that made him angry, or that Sam had hit John accidentally.

The second strategy for determining plausibility would rule out the latter replacement possibility. Hitting a person is an intentional act, a fact which cannot support using the Unintended provocation justification unit. Structurally, this unit would apply; however, it violates semantic constraints concerning the intentionality and foreseeability of actions. Also violated is the contention by the prosecutor that John intended to kill Sam. As the defense attorney stated:

> Defense: Well, is it foreseeable . . . could you argue that it's reasonably foreseeable that a man receiving one punch to the jaw is going to die?

The prosecutor could not argue with this and adopted the next strongest position, as we saw, contending that John had used an unreasonable amount of force (constituting an Escalated retaliation followed by an Accident).

Third, inferences can be contradicted with additional facts. For example, the central issue in the case concerned whether Sam's assault on John had terminated before John hit back. This controversy is reflected in the competing interpretations of self-defense, held by the defense attorney, and retaliation (escalated), held by the prosecution. It is generally hoped by the court that witness testimony will help to resolve such interpretation conflicts.

Fourth, additional facts can also suggest contradictions to or support for an inference without providing direct evidence. For example, the assertion that John hit Sam out of retaliation can give rise both to a general expectation that John has been violent in this manner previously, and to a prediction that he will behave in the same way under similar circumstances in the future. However, the determination later in this case that John had no prior record violated the expectation. It suggested that there was no reason to believe that he was a violent person, nor that he had acted to retaliate against Sam; instead, lacking other information, it tended more to support the interpretation of his actions as self-defense.

CONCLUSIONS

The causal connections between intentions and actions are generally of great consequence to situational ethics. Any process that argues for the justification of actions must not only describe what an actor intended, but why he intended it. What results comprises a causal explanation of the events.

The kind of causal explanations that a judge seeks reflects the extremes of what could have happened in the crime. He must take great pains to feel assured that the interests of both the offender and the victim are considered in the criminal process. The effort of the JUDGE program is to use justification units to infer intentions and motivations from actions, and to ascribe measures of justification to intentions and actions for the purpose of exploring extreme interpretations.

Remaining problems include specifying clearly the connections between represented causal chains and the interpretations that support them. In addition, the process of mapping between a candidate interpretation and the inference of specific corresponding perceptions, motivations and intentions, as well as the processes of checking for plausibility constraints, must be further specified and implemented.

In domains other than criminal jaw, justification units would be able to make the same types of inferences, relating them instead to domain-dependent goal hierarchies. In addition, specific justification rules are flexible across and within domains. For example, although the common citizen in our society is not justified in retaliating against an attacker, the judicial system asserts justification in punishing criminals for their crimes, as well as in removing them for the protection of society.

ACKNOWLEDGMENTS

This work was supported in part by the Air Force Office of Scientific Research under contract F49620-82-K-0010.

I wish to thank Larry Birnbaum and Steve Lytinen for their extensive comments and advice, and Jeff Grossman for his implementation efforts.

REFERENCES

Birnbaum, L. (1982). Argument molecules: A functional representation of argument structure. *Proceedings of the American Association for Artifical Intelligence-82* (pp. 63–65). Pittsburgh, PA.

Delin, B. (1978). *The sex offender*. Boston: Beacon Press.

Kempe, R. S., & Kempe, C. H. (1978). *Child abuse*. Cambridge, MA: Harvard University Press.

Schank, R., & Abelson, R. (1977). *Scripts, plans, goals, and understanding*. Hillsdale, NJ: Lawrence Erlbaum Associates.

Wilensky, R. (1978). *Understanding goal-based stories* (Research Rep. No. 140). Unpublished doctoral dissertation, Yale University.

9
Explanation: A First Pass

Roger C. Schank
Yale University

ABSTRACT

Explanation is one of the most common things people do. Why? What are explanations useful for? In our previous writings, we have looked at how explanations of events index memories of similar past events, causing various kinds of remindings to occur. But we should really look at the nature of explanation itself. Here we present a number of examples of explanations, classify the kind of question each seeks to explain, and classify the kinds of answers that can be given to each question.

INTRODUCTION

People explain their actions to others, and to themselves, every day. Why do we need to send and receive these explanations? What is their value? After we explain a thing to ourselves or accept the explanation of another, what becomes of it? What is the point of these explanations? What is their role in the learning process? What do they tell us about what it means to be intelligent?

For some people, explanations are not important. Many people can observe events that would disturb others, and attribute these events to "inexplicable circumstances"; they may not even wonder about them at all. What is the difference between people who search for explanations for everything and those who do not need them? What are they doing differently? Is mere curiosity the major factor, with hardly more significant than the entertainment value of the explanation? Is there some emotional satisfaction in knowing why things have happened the way they did, or is something more significant afoot?

THE ROLE OF REMINDING

When we first began to study reminding (Schank 1981, 1982), it seemed clear that explanations held the key to reminding. Whenever two phenomena were related in a reminding experience, we found that the events shared an explanation. More specifically, both events usually had in common the explanation of some expectation failure. The explanation of the failure was the link between them. Thus, explanation appeared to play an important role in how new information was added to memory, that is, in learning. To make sense of, and correct, an expectation failure, explanations were made. These explanations were indices to the events they explained and, as such, could cause remindings. The result of all this was a "corrected expectation" or in some cases, a reorganized set of expectations. The steps we proposed were:

--- expectation-failure
--- reminding
--- generalization
--- learning (modification of the expectation that failed).

My favorite example of this was "The Steak and the Haircut" story:

The Steak and the Haircut
X described how his wife would never cook his steak as rare as he liked it. When X told this to Y, Y was reminded of a time, 30 years earlier, when he tried to get his hair cut in England and the barber just wouldn't cut it as short as he wanted it.

The argument that I made with respect to this reminding ran as follows: In order for Y, the understander of the steak story, to be reminded of the haircut situation, he must have been using a knowledge structure that was general enough to cover both stories. This structure must have contained expectations about what actors commonly do in situations such as this. For our purposes here we can call this structure PROVIDE-SERVICE. The assumption here is that in processing the story about the rare steak, the understander would have used a structure like PROVIDE-SERVICE as a source of predictions about the actions that are likely to come next in the story.

Because the predictions contained in a structure such as PROVIDE-SERVICE are about the behavior of the participants in the situation governed by that structure, the understander can be assumed to have predicted here that when someone has voluntarily assumed the SERVER role in that structure, he or she will do what is asked, assuming that the request is doable and within the domain of the area in which he or she normally provides service.

In the steak story, cooking steak rare is certainly within the range of abilities of the SERVER, yet she has failed to do so. This is an expectation failure. Such failures must be explained. So, the understander has to explain, "Why didn't the server do what she was asked?"

There are many possible avenues of explanation here. The SERVER could be feeling hostile, recalcitrant, petulant, or whatever. The issue is not what the correct explanation is, if one even exists. The issue is the explanation Y created, which led to Y's being reminded of the barber story. There are many possible explanations, but Y seems to have used: "SERVER must not believe that SERVEE wants what he said he wants; he must want something less extreme."

In constructing that explanation, an index to memory was also created. That is, 30 years earlier, Y must have explained the haircut story with the same rule. That rule has been waiting all this time to be used as an index to that story if it were ever needed. That is, Y had decided (subconsciously, we assume) to remember that story as an instance of a correction to an expectation he had.

The premise of our earlier work on reminding was that learning occurs as we gather failed expectations and correct them. Explanations, we hypothesized, are used as indices to prior experiences that have failed in similar ways. Comparing two such stories can lead to learning.

Now, as we have progressed in our work on reminding and memory organization, it's becoming clearer that we missed the mark somewhat. The aforementioned chain is correct enough; learning does seem to occur in this way. But the focus is wrong. Previously we focused on the value of reminding and the correction of expectation failure, whereas we should have been focusing on the explanations themselves. Here's why:

Intelligent human beings like to understand the people with whom they interact—people like to know what others may do and why they may do it. They seek to understand the institutions that they deal with; they want to know how to treat the rules that these institutions set up and how the institutions will treat them. They also want to know how the physical world behaves; they seek to understand why machines behave the way they do and how physical objects and forces can best be dealt with. People want to understand the world—personally, socially, and physically. They do this by constantly creating and modifying explanations and indexing memories by the explanations they caused to be formed.

MAKING EXPLANATIONS

A great deal of this attempt to explain the world is tied up with the concept of generalization. We don't just seek to know why a given person does what he does, although we may accept an explanation that pertains only to him if that's the best we can do. We also want to know how this new rule that we have just learned can apply to other, similar situations. We seek to generalize the behavior of others in such a way as to create rules that will hold in circumstances other than those we have encountered. If we are successful at a stock purchase, for example, we wish to know if our success was due to our keen insight, our broker, the day of the week, the industry our stock belongs to, the nature of the market, the weather. If we are to replicate successful behavior, then we must know what that behavior was. Behavior is so complex that just because the result was successful, it does not follow that we can easily repeat what we did. We may have done a great many things, most of which were probably irrelevant. (For example, my uncle, who was a successful football coach, always wore the same brown suit to the games. I assume that he knew in some sense that this suit was not the reason that he was successful, but he replicated everything that he could.) We need to know which aspects of an event are significant and which are relevant with respect to what we can learn from the event for the future.

If we wish to account for failures, then we must explain failures in such a way as to be able to modify the aspect of our behavior that was in error. Finding the most significant aspect can result in a serious problem, however. We must know how to generalize correctly. Thus, we must come up with an explanation that correctly covers the range of behaviors where it will be most useful. Our explanations must be *inclusive and instructive*. They must include more behavior than we just saw, and they must instruct us in how to behave in future situations of a like kind. Establishing what kinds of situations are similar is one of the main problems of generalization. In some sense, it is the purpose of explanation.

Not every explanation is instructive or inclusive. Sometimes we explain things to make sure that they are not of interest. This is one reason that the explanation process must be more critically examined than the reminding process. We are not reminded every time we attempt to explain something; not all explanations are so significant as to cause a reminding.

We do a great deal of explaining without learning anything of interest. Explanation is going on all the time. It is a much more pervasive phenomenon than either reminding or learning; and we must examine what starts it, how it is accomplished, when the result is pursued to the extent that it is generalized and causes learning to occur, and when a resultant explanation causes us to drop a line of inquiry as a target of further learning. Most important, of course, is to establish when and how it is pursued so that the explainer is satisfied that an anomalous situation is no longer anomalous.

Explanation is different from other processes in that we know the kind of explanation that we seek before we start the process. With reminding and learning, we often are surprised with what comes out; we don't begin by knowing where we are going. On the other hand, we know an explanation when we see one. Therefore, what constitutes an explanation is of key importance in discussing the nature of explanation. We must know the nature of satisfactory explanations beforehand in order to be able to be sure that we have one. In other words, a sense of the coherency of what we have processed is critical to the explanation process.

THE EXPLANATION PROCESS

Roughly, the explanation process involves the following:

* Find an anomaly.
* Establish the kind of explanation that will make it less anomalous.
* Formulate the explanation pattern that will suffice.
* Explain.
* Take explanation and establish whether:
  −it makes clear the anomaly but does no more than that, or
  −it must be generalized beyond the current case.
* If we must generalize, then find the right item for generalization.
* Write the new rule that has just been formulated.
* Find the breadth of its application.
* Verify (often by reminding).
* Reorganize at a greater level of generality.

REMINDING AS VERIFICATION

Clear from this list is the role of reminding in the process. If reminding occurs, it is one method by which the generalization of an explanation can be justified and through which the new explanation can be used at a high level to reorganize some rules in memory.

As an example of this, consider the following:

EXAMPLE 1

I was walking along the beach in Puerto Rico and noticed signs saying that it was unsafe to swim yet everyone was swimming and it was clearly safe.

After seeing a second sign of a different sort, warning about the dangers of walking in a given place, I explained this to myself by assuming that the hotel that put up these signs was just trying to cover itself legally in case of an accident.

At this point, that is, *after* the explanation, I was reminded of signs in Connecticut that say ''road legally closed'' on roads that are in daily use. I had previously explained these signs to myself in the same way.

Here we see a classic case of the real role of reminding. First an anomaly is discovered. Next an explanation is concocted. The role of reminding here is verification. The reminding convinces the mind that the explanation is reliable. It also gives potential for scoping the generalization that will be formed from the explanation. Here we see that both a state (Connecticut) and an institution (a hotel) can make the same rules for the same reason. Thus, our new rule has to be generalized high enough to cover "institutions who could have liability under certain circumstances." The trick here is to avoid overgeneralizing. We learn from these examples that some signs should be ignored—but which signs and under what circumstances? We want to learn to ignore signs some of the time but not all the time. Should we ignore stop signs, or signs asking us to register at a hotel? Clearly not. Honing the rule so that it applies correctly is an important part of the explanation process.

The role of explanation-by-example is thus crucial in reminding. It is well known that people learn better by the use of examples. The reason for this has eluded us, but reminding makes it clear that we construct our own examples to help in learning a new rule in memory. What seems obvious is that the rules we know are grounded in sets of examples.

FINDING ANOMALIES

The next question is how does explanation work? Why do we choose to explain something, and what do we do with the explanation? It is clear that remindings will be available as verification in only a small proportion of the explanations that we do. In unverified cases (that is, unverified by reminding), we may look for other types of verification, such as seeing if our explanation meets certain standards of coherency for explanation. Thus, *the partner of reminding is coherency,* or making sense of a new explanation.

What situations need to be explained? People have powerful models of the world. Through these models, which are based on the accumulated set of experiences that a person has had, new experiences are interpreted. When the new experiences that a person perceives fit nicely into the framework of expectations that have been derived from experience, an understander has little problem understanding. However, often a new experience is anomalous in some way; it doesn't correspond to what we expect. In that case, we must reevaluate what is going on. We must attempt to explain why we were wrong in our expectations. We must do this, or we will fail to grow as a result of our experiences. Learning requires expectation failure and the explanation of expectation failure.

But expectation failure is not a simple process. When we have only a few expectations and they turn out to be incorrect, indentifying the one that failed is not that complex a process. In the real world, however, at any given moment we have a tremendously large number of expectations. If we did not, we would find very little worthy of note in what we observe. In fact, people are constantly questioning themselves and each other, to find out why people have done what they have done and what the consequences of those actions are likely to be. Thus, in order to find out how we learn, we must find out how we know that we need to learn. In other words, we need to know how we discover anomalies. How do we know that something did not fit?

The premise here is that whenever an action takes place, in order to discover what might be anomalous about it, we have to have been asking ourselves questions about the nature of that action. In other words, during the course of processing, we are constantly asking questions about that event in order to understand it fully. Anomalies occur when the answers to one or more of those questions are unknown. It is then that we seek to explain what was going on. And it is then that we learn.

To get a handle on this process, we must sort out the kinds of anomalies that there are. Knowing the kinds of anomalies there are gives us two advantages. To know something to be anomalous we must have been unable to answer a question about some circumstance. Therefore, first we must discover the questions that are routinely asked as a part of the understanding process. Second, in finding out what anomalies there are, we also have the basis for the kinds of explanations that are created to take care of those anomalies. Thus, we understand what can be learned.

Because we learn from everything, by the foregoing reasoning it follows that everything can be anomalous. But what is "everything"? The "things" we seek are the types of events that there are in the world. For example, we observe the actions of others in the world around us. To find anomalies (or more directly, to understand what they are doing), we ask questions of ourselves about their actions. For actions by individuals, I propose the following set of questions, which are asked, in some sense, every time an action is observed:

- PATTERNS: Is this an action that this person ordinarily does? Have I seen him do it before? Is it an action that a member of a group that I classify him in ordinarily does? If not, then . . .
- REFERENCE TO SELF: Is this an action that I would do? If not, then . . .
- RESULTS: Is this an action that will yield a result that is clearly and directly beneficial to the actor? If not, then . . .
- PLANS: Is this action part of a plan that I know to be a plan of the actor's. If not, then is this an action that is part of an overall plan that I was previously unaware of that will, in the long run, be beneficial to the actor? If not, then . . .
- GOALS: Is this an action that might be determined to be effective in achieving a goal that I know this actor has? If not, then is this action helpful in achieving a goal that I did not know he had but might plausibly assume that he might have? If not, then . . .

- BELIEFS: Is there a belief that I know that the actor holds that explains this action? If not, is there a belief that I can assume he might hold that would explain this action?

In the end, the result of this process is either a new fact, (a plan, goal, or belief that one did not know that a given actor had), or else the action is unexplainable.

The theory is that every time someone does something, an observer, in the attempt to interpret the action being observed, checks to see if that action "makes sense." But actions do not make sense absolutely. That is, we cannot determine if actions make sense except by comparing them to some standard. Thus, we must propose a standard.

The standard that we believe to be in use in these circumstances corresponds to three issues we believe to underlie most observations. These are:

- PATTERNS
- CONSEQUENCES
- REASONS

In other words, as observers of actions, we are satisfied when the action we observe fits into a known pattern, has known consequences we can determine to be beneficial to the actor, or is part of an overall plan or view of the world that we can ascribe to the actor. To put this another way, when we see that something has done something, we try to find the pattern to which the act belongs. If no pattern presents itself, the consequences that result become an issue. If those consequences are beneficial to the actor, then nothing needs to be explained because there is no anomaly. If those consequences are not obviously beneficial, then we need to find out why the action has been attempted in the first place. This requires ascertaining what goals an actor has, what plans he believes will effect those goals, or what beliefs he has from which a goal may have been generated.

The premise here is not that people are trying to find out whether something is anomalous and needs explaining. In fact, quite the opposite is the case. An understander is trying to determine the place for an action that he observes. His goal is to find a place for the representation of the action within the context of the other representations that he has in memory. To do this, he must find a place in memory that was expecting this new action. Of course, he may not find one— not everything in life can be anticipated.

Therefore, an understander asks himself, "What structure in my memory would have been expecting this action had I reason to believe that that structure was active?" It is at this point that the issues just mentioned arise. In other words, we are always asking ourselves why things have happened the way they have. Most of the time we can approximate the answer because what we are observing is fairly usual. When things are unusual and must be explained, it is because some of the usual questions have gotten some unusual answers.

WHAT MUST BE EXPLAINED

We will not attempt to provide a complete list of questions that people ask themselves about the world around them. In general, there seem to be three classes of things that people explain:

- the physical world
- the social world
- individual patterns of behavior

The kinds of explanations we expect constrain the explanation process by giving us a hint of what to look for. Things are just not anomalous or coherent. We understand that there are limits to our knowledge, and we seek to explain what it is that we don't know. The first broad class of things that we examine here are physical explanations. We don't know all there is to know about how the physical world works and we occasionally find anomalies in our daily lives that we seek to explain. In the next section are some examples that I gathered from students at the Yale AI lab. They are intended to illustrate the types of physical anomalies that people find in their daily lives and the explanations that they concoct and accept, which are then added to their memories:

Physical Explanations

EXAMPLE 2 (The Ice Storm)

During the ice storm last night, Suzie and I were in my apartment. Neither of us realized that the snow had turned to freezing rain. We heard a long series of crackles and whooshing sounds. I said that it sounded like trees falling. During the ice storm of '79 (my first real winter) I was nearly killed by a falling limb, and I suppose I am now sensitized to that noise. Suzie was sure it wasn't trees because there were so many similar noises. When we awoke, it turned out to be dozens of fallen trees.

EXAMPLE 3 (Car Doors)

I've been spending more time in Alex's little Honda these days, and I never seem to be able to close the door completely. Whenever I get in or out of the thing, the dome light stays on to tell me that I haven't managed to close the door tight. Alex, on the other hand, never seems to have this problem. Last week, for the first time, I slammed the door hard enough to close it, but Alex didn't close his all the way. It struck me then that the problem wasn't me, but the second person to close a door can't do it. After pondering a moment, I decided that it must be air pressure—when the car is sealed save one door, the pressure in the car keeps the last door from closing all the way. When another door is opened, the air has another place to go.

EXAMPLE 4 (Snow Patterns)

Up around Kline Biology Tower this morning I noticed the following phenomenon. Along the causeway there are a number of large, round brick columns. Around these columns there was snow, as everywhere else. However, for about 1 foot outward from the base of each column, all the way around, there was no snow. In other words, the wind had cleared away the snow for some reason all the way around the column, even though it was 8 inches deep at the edge of the clearing.

The reason this needs an explanation is that the same phenomenon is not observed at a plain flat wall. The first explanation we came up with was that the wind hits the column and then blows up, down, and around it. The wind that is blown down blows the snow away from the column. If the wind comes from different directions at different times, the ground will be clear all the way around the column.

However, I was unhappy with this explanation, because it does not use the feature of columns that makes them different from walls. If this explanation were correct, one would expect to see clear spaces along the bases of walls, too, but this is not the case. I then came up with another explanation, which we agreed was more likely (although we still don't know if it is correct). Wind hits the column, and because of the circular shape, is more likely to blow to either side than up or down. The wind blowing along the side of the column adds its force to the wind that was already blowing there, giving you stronger winds along the sides of the column. These strong winds clear out the snow for a small area along the sides of the column parallel to wind direction. Given shifting winds, we would expect to see the snow cleared all the way around the column.

EXAMPLE 5 (Slipping on Snow)

This morning, as I stepped out the door into the snow, I expected it to be slippery but found instead that the snow was nice and crunchy—better than average traction. Walking to my bus stop, I became aware that it was a bit late and I had better hustle if I wanted to make the bus. I started to speed up to a jog and went into a skid, almost falling. I wondered what had happened to my nice crunchy traction. I thought that it might be that the weather was changing. This didn't seem likely since it had only been 3 minutes. I then thought that maybe the snow on this block was different. I have noticed in the past surprising differences in this few-block-area in how early flowers bloom, how soon snow melts, etc. This reminded me of ice I had noticed in that part of route previous day. While most of the way was clear, I had detoured around a bad-looking patch. Then I decided that the snow itself was still high traction. What was slippery was the ice underneath. I was slipping on old ice, which I had easily avoided when I could see it, but which now looked the same as where there was concrete under the snow.

EXAMPLE 6 (Lightbulbs)

The lightbulb in the hall blew for the second time in a month. Diane said that we must have put in an old bulb. I decided that it was 100 watt bulb in a closed container and that heat blew it. I put in a 60 watter and decided to give more strength to my belief that light bulbs in a closed space cause too much heat to accumulate, which causes them to blow out.

What do these examples have in common? They all are attempts by an understander to better understand the world around him. Clearly, there is a survival mechanism at work here. We cannot function effectively if we don't understand the world we live in. In three of the examples, for instance, we need to know about how to deal with winter. We are constantly learning about winter (the more experienced we are, the better we survive). So, we make hypotheses. The explanation process is thus critical to survival in the physical world. From our examples, we can glean some of the questions about the physical world that people seem to ask:

From Example 2 (The Ice Storm): We seek to identify strange noises. Roughly, the questions we ask are What was that strange noise? What caused it? Is there danger to me?

From Example 3 (Car Doors): We seek to learn how to make the objects around us work correctly. In this example, the question was how to get a car door to close. The general question is: Why won't this object do what it is supposed to do? The kinds of answers we seek to this type of question are either functionally specific (that is, facts gleaned about this particular object) or general physics (such as the principles of air pressure that the teller of this story concluded were active in this case.)

From Example 4 (Snow Patterns): In observing the world around us, we sometimes wonder why things turn out the way they do. Some people more than others concern themselves with the problems of general physics. This is an example of the continuing attempt of a person to determine the physics of the world.

From Example 5 (Slipping on Snow): As we saw with the strange noise example, people are, naturally, concerned for their physical well being. One problem is to avoid dangers the next time around. Roughly, the question is, how can I make sure that I don't do a second time that caused me pain the first time? Again, explanations can be specific or general. A simple explanation in this example might be that it is always icy in one spot so that spot should be avoided. But obviously there is no general utility in such an explanation. So, we seek to identify how a danger can be hidden from view. The question we ask, therefore, is what dangerous situation might we be able to avoid by understanding how and why a danger can be hidden from view?

From Example 6 (Lightbulbs): Here we want to preserve the physical status of objects. We also wish to prevent dangerous circumstances from occurring. The questions arising here are: How can I change the circumstances that have been endangering an object I value so that it will not be harmed? Also, how can I prevent danger by attempting to understand better the physics of the world in general?

Physical Questions.   To summarize, then, the following are a representative class of the types of things that people care about with respect to the physical world around them. People feel a need to explain any event for which there is no straightforward answer to these questions. The questions are:

- Is there something that caused a strange noise that might be of danger?
- Why doesn't an object do what it is supposed to do?
- What general principles of physics can explain why things are happening the way they are?
- How can I avoid a previously encountered dangerous situation? What might cause a dangerous situation to be hidden from view?
- How can I change the circumstances that have been endangering an object I value so that it will not be harmed?
- How can I prevent danger in general by a better understanding of the physics of the world?

Social Explanations

It is also critical that we understand the society in which we live. We want to know why the institutions we deal with behave as they do, so that we can better interact with them. Following are some examples of attempts at social explanations:

EXAMPLE 7 (Hairdressers and Credit Cards)

Diane was trying to figure out why hairdressers won't take credit cards. She thought that maybe they had a poor clientele but realized it was also true in Westport, a well-to-do area. She never found an answer.

EXAMPLE 8 (IBM Policies)

The conflict:
- IBM sells foreign-language versions of their word-processing software in foreign countries, but refuses to sell them in the US.
- There are people in the U.S. who would buy the foreign-language programs.

Explanation: Since IBM has a vast and sophisticated marketing department, they must have determined that it's not cost-effective to distribute the foreign-language software in the U.S.

EXAMPLE 9 (Reporter in Lebanon)

This morning, on the Reuters newswire on TV, one of the headlines at the beginning read "American TV network reporter feared kidnapped in Beirut." Immediately, Jerry Levin, CNN's reporter in Beirut, came to mind, not as a conscious prediction, but just sort of idly. When I first noticed that he had been posted as Beirut bureau chief for CNN, I remember thinking that it was a bit risky for a Jew to take that assignment. Sure enough, it turns out that it's Jerry Levin who is missing and believed kidnapped.

EXAMPLE 10 (Campaign Predictions)

I noticed all the news people yesterday were saying that "that's what Hart's been predicting for two years," as though he had such a sage understanding in advance of how the campaign was going to work. That's how they explain the situation, or at least provide background.

I got very annoyed as different news shows repeated this and I wondered why NONE of them were swift enough to look at other predictions made by other candidates of how THEY would do and blow the whole notion away. I explain this anomaly by positing they just want something to say to fill up air time and are too dumb to think about what is really going on.

EXAMPLE 11 (Yale and Tenure)

At dinner last night, we were talking about the woman who was denied tenure at Yale in the History Department and sued the university. Yale settled out of court.
- The woman claimed that she was denied tenure because she is female and that they gave her position to someone less qualified.
- For academic reasons, the woman did not deserve tenure (opinion of the history faculty). Her position was given to another woman. Courts cannot decide academic qualifications. One would have thought that

Yale would have fought it out in court, defending principles. Why didn't they?

Explanations:

- It's cheaper to settle out of court than to let the case drag through the courts.
- Yale settled out of court precisely BECAUSE courts can't decide academic qualifications, so Yale gets to say (implicitly) that the woman was a poor scholar, although they chose to pay her off.

We try hard to understand and predict the actions of the social institutions that make up the world in which we live. Here again, there are questions we ask in our attempt to deal with the events we witness. When the questions have satisfactory answers, we are unaware that we ever asked them. However, when answering the questions is in some way complicated, we are forced to seek an explanation. This complication usually arises when no preformed answer exists.

Here, then, are some of the questions, derived from the foregoing examples:

From Example 7 (Hairdressers and Credit Cards): When the goal of an institution is clear—for instance, businesses want to make money—any impediment to the achievement of that goal needs explanation. Also, the rough form of a solution to any quandary about a business can usually be assumed to be that, whatever the business decision, it probably was made in the attempt to make money. Therefore, the operating question whenever a business is the institution involved is: How can the decision that a business made be seen as a way of making more money in the long run? We will return to this later.

From Example 8 (IBM Policies): Given the explanation in Example 7, whatever policy of IBM's is at issue, the real question is how that policy makes them more money.

From Example 9 (Reporter in Lebanon): In an attempt to understand an event, we are wont to predict future events that may derive from an event we observe. Thus, questions we ask all the time are: What will the consequences of an action be? Are those consequences in conflict with known goals? In this case, the danger to the reporter was predicted by the predictable actions of a well-known political institution (the Shi'ite Muslims). The question that the explainer in this example was asking was how anyone could be so stupid, but he was not really expecting an answer, human stupidity being a common enough commodity.

From Example 10 (Campaign Predictions): There is a general question of why networks behave as they do. Here again, since institutions have known goals pursuant to their purpose as institutions, we can assume that the networks perform according to those roles. Thus, we assume that the networks in general wish to inform about the news and make money in so doing. Given a certain amount of air time to fill, and a lack of available expertise at given times of the day, they frequently must fill up air time with material that has only secondary importance. Thus, the underlying question here is: What is the order of priority for an institution with a complex set of (possibly conflicting) goals?

From Example 11 (Yale and Tenure): Yale of course, is an institution whose goals are known but are different from those of most other private institutions. On the assumption that Yale's goals are different enough for it to defend its principles every now and then, this observer wondered why Yale hadn't acted in usual fashion. His explanation was based on known principles of Yale's behavior. The question he asked was: Why would an institution that has a set of well-established principles not choose to defend them?

Social Questions.   To summarize again, we have derived the following general issues that people track in dealing with social institutions:

- What is the expected behavior of a social institution?
- When is it in violation of that behavior?
- What will the consequences of an action of an individual be when it interrelates with those of an institution?
- Are those consequences of the action of an institution in conflict with its known goals?
- How can a decision that a business makes be seen as a way of making more money in the long run?
- What is the order of priority for an institution given a complex set of (possibly conflicting) goals?
- Under what circumstances do institutions abandon their established patterns of behavior?

Patterns of Behavior

Most explanations deal with our attempts to understand the specifics of the world around us. These specifics include both the objects and the people we deal with. We expect certain patterns of behavior and spend time trying to find out which people belong to which groups in their behavior patterns, and what those patterns are. Here are some examples:

EXAMPLE 12 (Holding the Pillow)

I was spending a quiet evening with Suzie, who is in the midst of an internship in midwifery. She had had a difficult day (delivered her first dead baby) and was finally relaxing a little. We were sitting on the bed and she was hugging a pillow to her breast. It was not a focus of her attention, she was just holding it there as we talked. This reminded me that I had seen someone holding a pillow like that before; I didn't remember the particular scene, but I did remember that the other person had also been a woman. I asked her why women do that—she was surprised and said she hadn't even noticed she was holding it, but that it somehow made her more comfortable. The feeling was quite palpable, and changed when the pillow was held differently, My explanation, which she agreed with, was that it affected the level of some hormone associated with nursing; that would make holding things in that position feel good. The pillow is roughly baby-sized, and the phenomenon only worked in a narrow range of positions. There should be some sort of biological mechanism for making nursing attractive. Suzie's might have been activated by her work (or it might be always present in women of that age), and she could have been sensitized to the feeling by her stressed, emotional condition. We had no other explanation for why that sensation should be so strong or why neither of us could think of ever seeing a man in a similar position.

EXAMPLE 13 (Shoeless Students)

Yesterday I walked into a graduate student office and saw David sitting down with no shoes on, reading the paper. I chalked it up to idiosyncratic behavior. Ten minutes later, I was walking down the hall and saw Jonathan walking toward me barefoot. At that point I decided that there must be an explanation. I realized that it had been raining very hard that day and that David and Jonathan must have gotten their shoes and socks soaked. They had taken them off to let them dry. Jonathan confirmed my hypothesis.

EXAMPLE 14 (New Hampshire Primaries)

Political postmorteming over the Gary Hart win in New Hampshire provided a rich source of reminding, for example, to McCarthy's win in 1968. One explanation for the win is that in February in New Hampshire not much is happening other than waiting for the sap to rise in the maples, so voters are receptive to the energy and youth of young campaign workers. Moreover, since it was snowing, the candidate with the most supporters owning 4-wheel drive vehicles was likely to win.

EXAMPLE 15 (The Parking Lot Gate)

Yesterday, walking to my car, I approached the automatic gate to my parking lot. In order to enter, you insert a plastic card to open the gate. When you are ready to leave, the gate automatically opens when you approach it in your car.

At a distance of about 50 feet I noticed that the gate rose about half way up and went back down again. I also noticed that there were no cars moving in the vicinity. The spontaneous spasm of the gate was highly unusual. I have approached this same gate on foot countless times and this never happened before.

I tried to explain why the gate behaved in this way. The first thing I did was to check again that I had not missed a car approaching the gate. I saw no car, but I did see a government police car parked in the distance where cars do not usually park. I wondered if the police car had something to do with the gate's behavior. Did they have some device that triggered the gate? Were they watching the gate? I decided that this was unlikely and paranoid.

I then wondered if I had not in some way triggered the gate by approaching it. I was reminded of the times that I passed through airport metal detector gates and triggered the alarm because of something I was carrying. This seemed to make more sense, so I pursued it further. Was the parking gate triggered by some sort of metal detector? This seemed plausible, but cars have a great deal of metal in them and I did not. Was I carrying something with metal in it? Yes, but no more than I usually carry and the gate had never mysteriously moved before when I passed it. Furthermore, if a car were the distance I was from the gate, it would not have triggered the gate. I rejected the metal detection explanation as well.

I decided that the gate was acting unusually because it might be broken. I hoped that the gate would work when I tried to get my car out of the lot. Fortunately, the gate did work.

I told my wife the story of the gate, and she came up with two explanations that I hadn't thought of. One was that someone had left their card in the device that reads the cards and this was causing the aberrant behavior. The second was that it had been raining heavily that day, and perhaps the rain had caused some electrical problem in the gate.

EXAMPLE 16 (Barking Dog)

Walking home, I was deep in thought when I heard the sound of a dog barking fiercely and saw it coming at me. Without stopping to think, I slipped my hands into the pockets of my coat and, without breaking my stride, made eye contact with the dog and asked: "Just what to you think you're doing? Hunh? HUNH?! Just WHAT do you think you're doing?!" Startled by the sound of my own voice, I suddenly felt quite foolish. What was I doing speaking out loud (asking silly questions, no less!) to strange, hostile dogs in public places? Discretely glancing around, I was relieved not to detect any witnesses. Then I realized that "it had worked"—the dog had shut up, backed out of my way, and was looking totally cowed and confused.

What was it I had just done that deflected the dog crisis? Why did it work? How did I know to do it, given I was still first realizing what the threat situation *was?*

- My initial explanation was that I had *confused* the dog.
- My second explanation was that *I hadn't acted frightened.* A rule I had been taught as a child about dealing with hostile dogs is: Don't let

them know you're afraid; they'll only bite you if they think you're afraid of them. I had done just what I was supposed to do, just as I had been told. And it worked, just as they said it would.

- I had refused to go along with the dog's suggestion that I play the frightened-victim role and instead had selected the dominating-human role. That forced *him* into the subordinate-dog role, eliminating his aggressive options. (I had had a problem with a bothersome dog when I was a kid, and out of desperation to protect my own dog, whom I had already scooped up and was trying to hold out of reach, frustratedly told it to SIT! And it suddenly became all meek and apologetic—and sat! Warning it to "Stay, staaay. Bad dog! sit! Sit! Good dog! Now stay!" we made our exit. What I had learned from this is: Dogs with collars are already trained to obey SOMEone, already have the concept of human authority.)

EXAMPLE 17 (Simultaneous Primaries)

Jim questioned why the primaries dragged on so long. He complained that they dominated the news, making it harder to find out what else was happening in the world. He advocated a much shorter primary season, suggesting that best of all would be if they were all the same day.

My explanation: The primaries issue skeleton is under the control of each political party. It's in the interest of the political parties to drag this on as long as possible, because it is a way of getting free press coverage. The candidates don't have to pay for advertisement; they need only hold another debate, and the media will compete over who can cover it most thoroughly.

Here again are some questions that may have been operating that would produce the kind of explanation behavior exhibited in those examples:

From Example 12 (Holding the Pillow): Men often ask why women behave the way they do, and women often ask why men do what they do. The same is true of Catholics and Protestants, the English and the French, and any other groups that could be put in opposition. What we have in this example is an attempt at a serious explanation, but the basic question is: Why does someone from the group that I am not in, do what no one from my group would do?

From Example 13 (Shoeless Students): Often we can come up with better explanations by placing people into behavior-prediction groups. The two people concerned were computer-types of course, so it is easy to say that computer-types are likely to go shoeless in an office (which they are). But finding a cause is better. The question here, then, has to do with the individuals in question, namely: Why would someone do something odd when I have not noticed that odd behavior? And why is an odd thing happening more than once (for which chance seems a poor explanation)?

From Example 14 (New Hampshire Primaries): The pattern of behavior of groups is often interesting where an outcome is known but the group is not. Thus, when there is an election upset, we often here explanations based on how various groups behaved and why. In this case the question is: Why was a particular outcome beneficial to a given group. And what random factors might have caused a given group not to try as hard or not to be able to perform as well as might have been expected?

From Example 15 (The Parking Lot Gate): Not only do people exhibit patterns of behavior; objects do as well. When an object fails to perform as expected, we seek to find out why. The question is: what could be causing something to behave in a completely unexpected and unusual way, especially when the object is presumed to have no will of its own?

From Example 16 (The Barking Dog): All this is true of animals, as well as people and machines. We expect one dog to be like another, but we have, at best, a poor model of why animals do what they do. Occasionally it can be very important to know what an animal will do, however. The questions are: What can I do to control a wild animal? Why does an animal behave the way it does? What patterns of behavior are operating for given classes of animals?

From Example 17 (Simultaneous Primaries): Often we find that an annoyance keeps re-occurring regardless of how absurd it may seem. Often the explanation is that circumstances have combined to make it almost impossible to prevent the occurrence. In other words, there is no rational person in charge who can call a halt to the absurdities. (I am reminded of gas price wars here, an oddity that has faded into the past.) Questions that bring such circumstances to mind are: Why do people or institutions seem to be doing what is not in their best interests? How are circumstances able to control a situation?

Patterns of Behavior Questions. To summarize, we have derived the following general issues that people track in dealing with patterns of behavior:

- What behavior can be predicted by the knowledge that an individual belongs to a given group?
- Why does a given group behave the way it does?
- Why does another group fail to behave that way?
- What causes new odd behavior to appear?
- When odd behavior comes in pairs, what is the common explanation?
- How can given groups effect beneficial outcomes with their behavior?
- Why was a particular outcome beneficial to a given group?
- What factors might prevent a given group from achieving its desires?
- Why does a given object stop doing what it has previously done?
- Why do animals behave the way they do?
- How can animals be controlled?
- What patterns of behavior are operating for given classes of animals?

- Why does a person or institution seem to be doing what is not in their best interests?
- How are circumstances able to control a situation?

TYPES OF EXPLANATIONS

We are concerned with both what to explain and what constitutes an explanation. The aforementioned classes and their associated questions indicate the types of things that need explaining. The following are broad classifications of explanations that tend to satisfy us when we hear them. That is, once given one of these explanations, we tend to accept them.

1. Excuses. When people fail to do what we want them to do, we complain. They explain by citing a fact that contributed in some way to their behavior. This fact is an excuse. In fact, we know that it will be an excuse before it is said. What makes it an excuse is that an excuse is needed. We don't have to analyze it to see if it's an excuse. We do analyze it to see if it's a VALID excuse. Invalid excuses are likely to be collected as anomalies for reminding purposes.

2. Alternative Beliefs. When someone does something we had no reason to expect they would do, we try to find out why, by trying to simulate their reasoning to see what they might have been thinking. This type of explanation tells us to modify the belief that we thought the individual held. All predicted behavior stems from what we believe another person believes. We are constantly constructing and modifying models of why people do what they do. Since we realize that we do not know everything that another person believes, we accept explanations that inform us with respect to our incomplete knowledge.

3. Laws of Physics. Because we do not know all the physical laws of the universe, we often find ourselves speculating about why something physical has happened. We change our rules to correspond with experience. Hearing a new law of physics therefore can often satisfy us as an explanation. We expect that the physical rules we know will change over time, not because the world is changing, but because our knowledge of the world is incomplete.

4. Institutionalized Rules. When we know that someone is playing according to externally defined rules, we can look for explanations of the person's behavior in those rules. We assume that we don't know exactly what all those rules are; therefore we constantly update them. This kind of explanation is analogous to #3, except that the rules are defined by people, not the physical world. Here again, our understanding of these rules is likely to be incomplete.

5. Rules of Thumb.   There are "tricks" for living that get people where they want to go. "Ask for advice," or "Never date the boss' daughter" are examples. We try to pick these up as we go. Thus, in success or failure explanations, we try to validate or add to our rules of thumb. Here we are dealing not with expectation failures, but with actual successes and failures in achieving goals. We want to know why Joe always does well or why Sam always fails. We look for a rule-of-thumb explanation when we want a simple heuristic rather than an operating principle. It is not necessary to know why a given rule works in order to use it.

6. New Facts.   We want to learn about things in the world as well as people. We need to know about cats, dogs, cars, computers. Again, we learn by explanation. Here, classification is important. When we find a new rule, we try to put it in the right class. When an automatic teller machine catches fire, our explanation seeks reasons. We could look at the physics involved, but simpler explanations about new-fangled machinery seem to many people to be quite adequate. By putting an explanation into a class of objects, we make it more usable.

7. Appearances.   People do some things because of how they imagine it will make them look. They buy cars, dress, even marry because those actions evoke an image of themselves in their own or others minds that they would like to maintain. Since people do things for this reason, we can often explain their actions in these terms as well. The learning that takes place in these instances relates only to the objects we are particularly concerned with. We learn about particular actors in our memories and are thus able to make better predictions about what they will do next time.

8. Plans.   We can explain the actions of others by understanding where the particular action that we do not understand fits within a broader plan. Saying that an action is a step on a coherent plan towards a goal explains that action. Two kinds of learning take place using this type of explanation: we can learn how a plan is constructed in general; and we can learn about the kinds of plans that a particular individual is likely to use in a given circumstance.

9. Goals.   An action can be explained by connecting it to the goal it was intended to achieve. Knowing what someone wants is an important part of understanding. Accordingly, explaining how an action makes sense in terms of what someone wants is the plan explanation, explaining how it tells us what he wants is the goal explanation.

10. Role Themes.   Knowing what role theme a person is acting under reveals much about why he is doing what he is doing. Thus pointing out a role theme can be an explanation. For instance, saying that a man is a doctor and that a particular type of behavior is what doctors do, will serve as an explanation.

11. Scripts.   Scripts are fossilized plans; script explanations are just simpler versions of plans.

12. Delta Agency.   Doing something for someone else does not require a coherent plan of action. It merely requires that one believe that someone whom you want to please wants something. Thus an action can be explained by saying that the real explanation is to be found in someone else's plan.

13. Lack of Alternative Plan.   Sometimes people do things because they can't think of anything better to do. Usually there is a goal in mind, but its achievement may not come easily from the action that was taken. This is a kind of "explain it away" explanation—it's not very coherent, but sometimes it is the best we can do.

14. Mystical Laws.   Not everyone shares the same belief system. Those who are religious or mystical may hold beliefs that are deemed spurious by others. Understanding alternative beliefs is part of the explanation process, as we saw in No. 2. The difference between alternative beliefs and mystical laws depends largely on whether or not one agrees with the plausibility of the explanation. The major difference between them is whether this explanation is part of a pattern of belief that would allow one to predict other beliefs that are also likely to be held by this individual.

15. Coordination of Anomalous Facts.   If two anomalies occur together in time or space, we automatically assume that there must be some causal connection. For example, if we hear a loud strange noise, and then the power goes out in our house a few minutes later, we guess that whatever caused the noise also caused the power failure.

An Example of Explanation Classes in Use

To see how these classes might be used, consider the situation where a professor asks his advisee why he has not been working on his thesis lately. It is possible, using the foregoing classes of explanation, to concoct many different types of explanations. Each of these explanations would cause his professor to update his model of this student in some way, that is, in a small sense, to learn something:

WHY AREN'T YOU WORKING ON YOUR THESIS?

1. Excuses—Because I had to celebrate my wife's birthday last night.
2. Alternative Beliefs—Because I don't think it needs work.

3. Laws of Physics—It was so hot that the paper kept melting.
4. Institutionalized Rules—Yale doesn't require one any more.
5. Rules of Thumb—I have discovered that not writing it gets your professor to the point where he will sign anything.
6. New Facts—It's finished.
7. Appearances—I didn't want to appear stupid in front of the other students.
8. Plans—Not writing it every other week is the best way to stay sane while writing.
9. Goals—Oh, you thought I wanted a PhD!
10. Role Themes—I've quit school.
11. Scripts —I just don't do that sort of thing.
12. Delta Agency—My wife is writing it for me.
13. Lack of Alternative Plan—Not working seemed the best thing to do at the time.
14. Mystical Laws—Lama Dama says that that which is not approached directly is first finished.
15. Coordination of Anomalous Facts—If you don't work on Sunday, it rains on Monday, thus preventing any distractions from thesis writing.

KNOWING WHEN AN EXPLANATION IS RIGHT

The next critical question is how do we know that the explanation that we have received from another or concocted for ourselves is valid? Clearly, verifying an explanation is closely linked to being able to create an explanation. If we have the ability to recognize a good explanation when we hear it, that is, if we know when we are satisfied, then the knowledge that we have used in that case can be relied on in constructing our own explanations.

To clarify what I am referring to here, let us consider some more explanation stories, this time without the explanations. (You can peek at the end for them if you cannot wait to find out.)

EXAMPLE 18 (Vermont store)

In a store in Vermont, there is a sign saying that they will close tomorrow for inventory. This seems anomalous as it is the middle of their busy season.

EXAMPLE 19 (Hotel)

At a hotel they ask my name as well as my room number when I request a wake-up call. Why?

EXAMPLE 20 (Navy)

The Navy was very apologetic about one of the people they scheduled me to see, a man who turned out not to be with the Navy. Why were they apologetic? What did they do that was bad to me and why?

EXAMPLE 21 (Subway)

FROM the *New York Times:*
After dashing down the long flight of stairs to the subway, a woman just missed her train and was exasperated. A guard informed her that she shouldn't worry as he felt a local coming soon. How could he "feel" that?

The explanation process focuses on the available data. In Example 18 (Vermont store), the anomaly is that businesses want to make money and this one seems to be counterproductive. Now the question is what kind of explanation will be satisfying, that is, as if something (though not necessarily something cosmic) had been learned?

The available data here is sparse. But suppose I told you that this store was part of a national chain. That information helps because it changes one of the available data items—who made this bizarre decision. Now we find that the maker was someone other than who we thought it was. The decision is still odd, but now we believe that other factors may have entered into the decision.

I shall call this the INCOMPLETE INFORMATION RULE. If something that needs to explained can be seen as something different, maybe that different thing can be more easily explained, or perhaps it needs no explanation at all. So, one step in trying to make an explanation is to try and change the variables, one at a time, to see if some hypothetical event comes out that is easily explainable.

The actual explanation of Example 18 was that the store was part of a national chain headquartered in Ohio, where it was most certainly not the busy season. All the stores do inventory at the same time. Why this had to be the case I never found out. I assumed that it had to do with taxes. In any case, the basic principle behind the anomaly was unchanged. This business did indeed care about making money, but this was how it had to cope. Nothing crucial is learned when the explanation simply involves picking up uninteresting new facts.

Now let's consider Example 19 (Hotel). One possibility here is that the hotel asked my name simply as a way of making sure that they did not wake up the wrong person. However, what we have here is a script violation. When a script is violated, it is usually for a reason. Scripts tend to be unchanging. People do things in a given way because they have always done them that way. In any case, I wondered why they had done that, but as it wasn't a particularly fascinating problem, I soon forgot about it.

Explanation of Example 19: I assumed that it was just a check to make sure I was the right person. Later, my wife told me she had called, and they said I hadn't yet registered. I then realized they probably had no record of anyone being in that room.

Here we have a case of a new fact constituting an explanation of an event that had been almost forgotten. Obviously, it had not been completely forgotten; I could retrieve the relevant information and connect it with the new information.

The question here is how I knew that this new information constituted an explanation of the earlier minor mystery. One method of explanation is COORDINATION OF ANOMALIES. Sometimes when two events occur that both seem anomalous, we assume, without any hard evidence, that they are related. These two events were certainly candidates for application of that rule. But, it was also important that the EXPLANATION CLASS be correct. For a script to be violated, usually some other aspect of the script had to be violated first. For example, there isn't a free-for-all on airplane seating unless some problem occurred that causes the airplane seating script to go awry. The same is true of hotels. Presumably, the explanation type that I sought was from SCRIPT VIOLATION RULE, which says to look for an explanation for a script violation in some other preceding condition in the script. In other words, something must have gone awry somewhere, and I was looking out for it.

Now consider Example 20 (Navy). Why would this organization be apologetic to me? The first part of this reasoning chain is simple: they must have done something bad to me. That is why people apologize. But why would this organization have done something bad to me, since my visit there was entirely one of good will? This is also easy to answer: someone must have made them do it.

Here we have two rules of explanation. The first I call the STATE-EVENT CORRESPONDENCE rule. When there is an extant state (e.g., being apologetic, in this case), look for a causal event (i.e., something to apologize for). This an obvious and simple rule. For example, if the dog is cowering in the corner, he must have done something bad and his owner will look around for what.

The second rule is one of a category of rules that relate to people's behavior. A common rule of this sort is QUID PRO QUO. If you want to know why someone has done something, one possibility is that he has done it because he perceives it as an equal response to something you did earlier to (or for) him. Though this rule might be considered, it is rejected in this case. Another rule is a variant of the DELTA AGENCY rule (Schank & Abelson, 1977), known as SOMEONE MADE ME DO IT. If you cannot find an equivalent action that caused the event that needs explaining, then look for a second actor who made the first actor do what he did. In a large organization, this might be someone further up in the hierarchy.

In other words, the STATE-EVENT CORRESPONDENCE rule was triggered by the Navy's apologetic state and set me to looking for an event that would be unpleasant for me. The SOMEONE MADE ME DO IT rule started me looking for a reason for that event that had something to do with the fact that the man I was meeting had some power over the people I was visiting.

Explanation of Example 20: Both rules turned out to be true. This man was someone who knew very little about what he was talking about and was quite annoying. He turned out to be a personal friend of the head of the organization.

Now consider Example 21. Here we have an example of a phenomenon that seems quite out of the ordinary. We need an explanation because most people do not have the belief that you can feel a train coming, particularly a given type of train. What will satisfy us as an explanation?

Earlier, we listed some questions that we claimed are ordinarily asked about the actions of persons and that, among other things, help us find anomalous behavior. In this case, we have an instance of a belief-based anomaly. That is, clearly this guard has a belief that we do not share. The explanation is either that there is a fact missing from our belief systems or that his belief system is peculiar in some way. Thus, the explanation we seek is either a fact about trains that makes them "feelable" or a fact about this person that enables him to feel things that others cannot. Failing that, we seek a fact about this person that makes it clear exactly what kind of craziness he has. (However, given that this human interest story appeared in the *New York Times,* it seems obvious that the latter type of explanation will not be forthcoming.)

Explanation of Example 21: The guard said, "You can always tell which train is coming by the strength of the breeze down the platform. The local gives off a weak breeze, the express a strong one."

As we stated earlier, a new fact will always serve as an explanation. However, in this case the new fact is not enough. We are forced to make sure that this new fact makes sense. We must ask ourselves why a train would give off a breeze. Answering this requires knowing something about the effects of objects going through enclosed spaces and the effects of the variant speed of those objects. In other words, an understander, in order to believe the statement of the guard, would have to know, or be able to figure out, that expresses travel faster than locals in the New York subway system.

CONCLUSIONS

We have looked at the role of explanation in the overall learning and understanding process. We have considered how we know that an explanation is needed, how we come up with explanations, and how we judge explanations to be valid or not. Most important, we have looked at a number of typical explanations. It is too easy to overlook the richness of the explanation process, explaining it away as just a matter of deductive inferences chained together. The examples given show that it is much more than this. The explanation process:

- often has to deal with very incomplete knowledge,
- is often based on idiosyncratic personal knowledge,
- usually generates multiple hypotheses, and
- is willing to leave some things unexplained.

Our work is just beginning on developing mechanisms capable of explaining how people come up with their many different kinds of explanations. With a promise of more to come, we close this first pass at understanding explanation.

REFERENCES

Schank, R. C. (1981). Language and memory. In D. A. Norman (Ed.), *Perspectives on cognitive science*. Hillsdale, NJ: Lawrence Erlbaum Associates.

Schank, R. C. (1982). *Dynamic memory: A theory of learning in computers and people*. New York: Cambridge University Press.

Schank, R., & Abelson, R. (1977). *Scripts, plans, goals, and understanding*. Hillsdale, NJ: Lawrence Erlbaum Associates.

10 Acquisition of Device Models in Instructionless Learning

Jeff Shrager
Carnegie-Mellon University

ABSTRACT

People often learn about complex devices by observation and experiment, instead of by reading instructions. The goal of our research is an analysis of what constitutes an understanding of complex devices and a model of the mechanisms underlying this sort of learning. A brief review of the present model of instructionless learning is presented, concentrating on the learners' use of experiments, expectation failure, and the activation and mapping of memory structures, in order to explain observations and construct hypotheses. This leads to an analysis of the representation of computer-controlled devices that will support learning and problem solving. Synchronous planning in the movement and device model domains is suggested to account for the meaning of "memory" in this understanding

INSTRUCTIONLESS LEARNING

The most direct way to learn is to have someone explain things to you personally or in writing. However, often there is no one around to provide advice, and there is no user's guide. People are sometimes able to learn about reasonably complex systems even in these information-sparse environments. The development of a model of how this can be done is the goal of our present research.

In our experimental work, college students are asked to learn about a Big-Trak™ computer-controlled toy tank without instruction or experimenter intervention. There are numerous interesting aspects of the model that has been developed to account for subjects' behavior. The topic most interesting here is

167

the representation of computerized systems and how reasoning takes place with that representation.

The next section introduces the BigTrak so that the examples of later sections are clear. The following section summarizes the behavior of subjects in the instructionless learning experiments. A more complete discussion of this can be found in Shrager and Klahr (1983; in preparation). Here we focus on subjects' explanations of unexpected behaviors as a key to noticing the need for, and subsequently constructing, a *device model* of the BigTrak. The last part of the chapter discusses a representation for this device model that captures crucial aspects of learning and performance, including the ability to represent correct and incorrect understandings of the device and the ability to support reasoning in both the domain of movements of the toy and the domain of changes in its internal state.

The BigTrak

Figure 10.1 shows a BigTrak and the keypad that is attached to its back. The toy is about a foot long. It can move forward (⇑) backward (⇓) and turn in place (⇐ and ⇒), as well as execute various other commands. Turns are in 6-degree units analogous to clock minutes. It is a programmable system. The user can enter up to 16 command+argument steps, and then press the GO key to cause the BigTrak to execute the specified movements. The RPT key is an iteration function that repeats the preceeding N steps once. The CLR key clears all memory. The CLS key clears only the last entered step. The CK key executes the most recently entered step.

The program: ⇑ 5 ⇐ 1 5 FIRE 2 ⇓ 5 ⇒ 3 0 HOLD 1 0 RPT 3 GO will cause the toy to move forward 5 feet, turn left 90 degrees, fire the ''cannon'' twice, back up 5 feet, turn 180 degrees clockwise, pause for 1 second, and then repeat

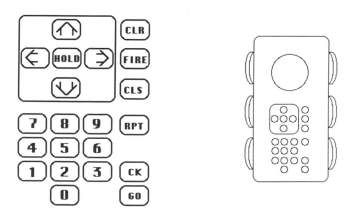

FIG. 10.1.   Schematic diagram of BigTrak and control panel.

the most recent three steps again: that is, back up 5 feet, turn around, and then pause for 1 second.

WHAT IS LEARNED IN INSTRUCTIONLESS LEARNING?

The instructionless learning paradigm is a sort of concept acquisition task. The instructions read something like: Figure this thing [the BigTrak] out. There is reasonably good agreement between subjects about what constitutes having obtained this goal. They try to learn *what the BigTrak does* and *how to obtain this behavior from the system*. Initially, is necessary to learn what constitutes the domain of action of the system. It isn't even clear at the outset that the BigTrak is meant to move around. Refinement of the domain of movement includes, for example, learning that turns are in place as opposed to moving to the left or right by a number of feet. In the process of learning about movement, subjects learn the operators necessary to obtain these behaviors from the device. For example, they learn that pressing the forward arrow followed by a number will make the tank move forward the specified number of feet and that pressing a turn arrow followed by a number will make it turn in the specified direction some number of units.

Movement operators and the movement description are not all that people learn. During the task, subjects use information about the system as a computer controlled device whose internal structure plays a role in its external behavior. This constitutes a different but related domain in which to reason, with separate terminology, structure, and operators. The acquisition and use of this *device model* knowledge is a primary focus of this research and is the principle concern of later sections.

The Structure of Instructionless Learning

We assume a goal-directed model of cognition. Learning begins with observation and hypothesis formation (if possible). If no hypotheses can be formed by observation then an exploration takes place; something like: Let's try X and see what happens. This then yields data that can be used to form hypotheses.

Once a hypothesis is formed, an experiment is constructed to confirm it. The construction and performance of experiments are interwoven in people's behavior. This construction yields a predicted result. If the predicted result is obtained, then the experiment is deemed successful and the hypothesis is accepted. If the experiment fails, an explanation process is invoked to try to analyze what went wrong. This leads to more hypotheses and experimental examinations. It is not necessarily the case that the goal which started off the initial experiment is satisfied in the course of a series of experiments. Often an experiment meant to confirm a particular hypothesis will fortuitously yield evidence relevant to a completely different part of the system.

When does learning stop? Because the target knowledge is problem-solving information, it makes sense that one can stop looking for more information when it is possible to set goals and obtain them with what one already knows. After something new is learned, people exercise it in the context of the other information they have accumulated by setting themselves "play" tasks, such as "Walk over to the lab door and shoot the camera then come back," and trying to solve them. Additionally, there is the desire to learn about obviously available operators. For example, a person will ask what the function of the RPT key is, after having figured out all the others. This goes the other way as well: if one has inferred the existence of an obtainable action (e.g., that the toy can turn left), then there must be some operation that will yield this result.

Experiments Confirm Hypotheses

Experiment construction is central to instructionless learning. It is viewed as a problem-solving process where the goal is to obtain evidence confirming a hypothesis. Experiments can address the syntax of correct interaction with the device, the semantics of the operators, or the structure of the movement or device model spaces. It is easy to see how the semantic structure of the hypotheses plays a role here. As a simple example, consider that if one's hypothesis about the meaning of the numerical argument to the FORWARD command were in terms of millimeters instead of feet, then the experiments to test this hypothesis would use numbers much larger than 1 and 2. Similarly, the most often used turn experiments are 90, 180, and 360 degree turns. In order to compute which experiments will obtain recognizable real-world movements, the learner must have semantics for the actions in the real world and some way of determining which of these are easily recognizable.

The relationship between device model state and real-word (surface) movements of the BigTrak (the "mapping" in Young's, 1983, terms) is a very subtle matter and is the focus of a great deal of current research (Collins, 1985; deKleer, 1979; de Kleer & Brown, 1983; Halasz & Moran, 1983; Williams, Hollan, & Stevens, 1983; Young, 1981; Young, 1983). They are, in some sense, synchronous descriptions of the same state of the BigTrak. For example, the correct theory of RPT-N is that it repeats the preceeding N steps. Entering ⇈ 1 ⇉ 1 5 ⇊ 1 RPT 2 GO will effectively do: ⇈ 1 ⇉ 1 5 ⇊ 1 ⇉ 1 5 ⇊ 1. To test this hypothesis, first arrange the preconditions for application of RPT: that is, memory has in it the required N steps; then enter RPT-N. (In order for this to be a good experiment, one needs to use controls such as differentiable steps. This sort of control is often ignored by real learners.) Setting up the state of memory in preparation for RPT can be computed from the semantics of the RPT operation along with the previously described operational knowledge about the rest of the device.

It is possible that this analysis of setting up memory for RPT does not require processing in the device model domain. RPT can just as easily be described as repeating the last N movements instead of the last N steps. Here is another similar example: Another subject hypothesizes that the CLS key switches between two memories, each of which maintains a separate program. Using CLS will switch back and forth, letting GO access one or the other program. To test this, she makes up two completely different programs (call them "A" and "B") and does this experiment: CLR . . . enter-A . . . CLS . . . enter-B . . . CLS GO . . . observe . . . CLS GO . . . observe. In the "correct" model, CLS just deletes the most recently entered step. Unless she is unnaturally lucky in selecting examples, the BigTrak's behavior will not satisfy her expectations. In this case, it is more certain that reference is being made to the state of some sort of switch in the user's device model of the machine.

HYPOTHESES AND EXPERIMENTAL FAILURE AND EXPLANATION

Hypotheses are formed directly from observation or by using observations to key stored structures that are then mapped into the current domain. An observation may be nothing more than an association between an operation and the resulting behavior of the system. So, for example, if you press FORWARD-1 and then the GO key, it is possible to learn merely by associating the resulting forward movement with pressing FORWARD-1-GO. Of course, more complex learning requires more machinery than that. In order to infer that FORWARD-2-GO will take the device forward 2 feet, one must have a set of reasonably rich heuristics, number concepts, and the notion of a foot as a unit of movement.

It is easy to imagine that a concept-free system might learn this entirely by search and rule compilation if the result of an experiment were merely a success or failure signal. This unfortunately is the case with much of the psychological concept acquisition research and AI machine learning that has been done to date. In instructionless learning with a sufficiently rich domain, a great deal of use is made of the result of an experiment. *Although the success of an experiment enables the learner to accept the hypothesis being tested, the analysis of the failure of an experiment leads to explanation and leads to new hypotheses.*

Teleological Indexing and Mapping Leads to Device Model Hypotheses

The BigTrak is a programmable system. When you enter commands without having cleared the device, it appends the commands together. This leads to failures of prediction and thus to explanation. However, the sort of explanation that takes place as a result of seeing that the system is behaving in a "programmable'' manner is quite different from simple association between input and output of the system.

A protocol example will illustrate this phenomenon: FC is exploring the meaning of the numerical argument to the FORWARD command. He presses ⇈ 1 GO and, as predicted, the toy moves forward 1 foot. Then he tries ⇈ 2 GO, which causes the BigTrak to move forward 3 feet because it appends the two commands. However, 3 feet is close to 2 feet as far as normal observation is concerned, so FC takes this to confirm his hypothesis. Then he hypothesizes that, like the forward arrow, the left arrow causes the toy to move left 1 foot. He presses: "⇐ 1 GO", the BigTrak moves forward the 3 feet, following the previous program, and then does a 6 degree left rotation (the action of ⇐ 1). We don't know whether he notices the left rotation, but he does notice that "it did the same thing [as before] even though I pushed different buttons." From this he infers that it "remembers things"—that it has a memory. From that point onward he always uses the CLR (clear) key before performing experiments.

FC makes much more of the experience than that. He constructs a model of the memory in which the numbers refer to line numbers, as in the BASIC programming language, and the arrows have implied 1 foot movement semantics of their own. This is consistent with his previous observations. He next does an experiment to confirm this analysis: CLR ⇒ 1 ⇈ 2 GO, which causes the tank to do a 6 degree right turn and then move forward 2 feet (Fig. 10.2). Note that his expectation is that it will go right 1 foot and forward 1 foot. It is almost as if the toy were doing vector addition and moving along the resultant vector. This is what his explanation of that unexpected behavior is. This mistaken modelling goes on for a short while until he tries to put a FIRE command in the fourth

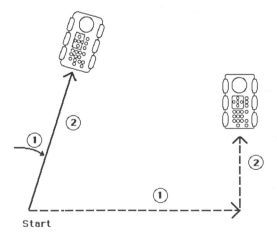

Start

FIG. 10.2.   The Result of Entering: "CLR ⇒ 1 ⇈ 2 GO" (Dotted lines approximate the subject's expectation. Solid lines show the actual behavior of the BigTrak.)

"line," and instead of firing once, the BigTrak fires four times. His belief that numbers are line numbers can't be made compatible with this, so he is forced to change it and ends up with something very close to the right model. Of course, he has to relearn the turns, which he does much later.

We postulate that structures in human memory are indexed by their function or purpose (teleology) and that these are selected and then mapped by a process similar to that proposed by Burstein (1983). A model similar to this one has been suggested by Collins (1985). Bott's (1979) model of complex learning by analogy is also very much in agreement with this model.

One difference between instructionless learning and completely reasoned explanation in the use of teleological indexing, explanation, and mapping is that although the function to be explained is a buggy model, the learner is constructing an explanation of the bug as correct behavior instead of trying to debug it. We see the building of new models of what goes on in the BigTrak rather than the debugging of a current one. These new models are often substantially different from the preceeding incarnations—as demonstrated earlier by the vector addition and BASIC memory examples. The apparent simplicity of this modelling mechanisms may be due to the role of experiments in instructionless learning. The ability to generate and easily test models probably alleviates the mental effort necessary to generate complex explanations. This is not to say that the models people construct are worse than they would otherwise be; their support is simply not necessarily as well worked out. (Of course, the structure mapping process is not a trivial matter.) There is other evidence that our subjects do not think very carefully about their task in instructionless learning. As pointed out earlier, they perform mainly hypothesis-confirmatory and not very well-controlled experiments, and thus often obtain confounded and confusing results.

THE STRUCTURE OF BIGTRAK KNOWLEDGE

What exactly is in a device model, and what is it that associates the device model with the surface behavior of the system? Both a declarative description of the model and a set of processes that work with that description are necessary to support instructionless learning.

The device model is composed of loosely coupled objects, each of which may have a structure of its own or may be a primitive; and of descriptions of processes that operate on the objects in the model. The objects may name one another, but are not necessarily physically or logically connected. Also, they possess state information either in themselves or as emergent from their structure and the information contained in their component objects.

In the "correct" model of the BigTrak, there is a memory constructed of "cells," each of which "contains" a virtual movement in the real-world planning space. In the CLS-switch model, discussed before in the section on experiments, there are two memories and a switch, which is set to "point to" (enable) one or the other. The semantics (a procedure that has side effects in the device model) associated with pressing the CLS key is to change the state of this switch. In both models, there is the notion of "entering" a "step" into memory—whose method is pressing a command and an argument—and in both models, pressing the GO key "runs off" the steps contained in memory. These important notions will be examined momentarily.

This model of thinking about complex systems does not follow from the actual structure of the device. Imagine describing the stacking operation of adding a step to memory. In the actual hardware implementation of this there are counters and tests for under- and overflow, and so forth. This is not like what one thinks of as the action of stacking: Put things on top of the stack until it's full; Take things off until it's empty. Note that the primitives used to construct the latter (natural) descriptions make reference to the "perceptual" state of the stack (full, empty, top) and actions that are, in a sense, real world: put on, take off, move.

The present theory makes a fundamental distinction between the manner in which people think about these complex systems and the way the systems actually function—according to, for example, the envisioning models of deKleer and his associates (deKleer & Brown, 1979; deKleer & Brown, 1981; deKleer & Brown, 1983). In the present theory, the systems are represented as if the person were doing the actions in real world, and as if the system itself were a physical system. Young (1981, 1983) concludes that this sort of seemingly vague description of a system may be exactly correct at a level useful to the problem solver. Also, Papert's (1980) notion of "transitional" knowledge, which imparts body-centered actions to complex systems, is very close to what is suggested here. Most important, this is predicated on the thesis that these objects are learned by mapping memory structures into the current domain in order to explain behavior. People typically have experience with physical systems, not with electronic/symbolic ones. (This does not preclude the possibility of learning and subsequently using electronically based structures.)

What's In a Cell?

Device model hypotheses refer to the contents of the device model, not the state of planned movements. Thus, in order to plan and execute experiments, there must be some mapping from device states to these movements. There is still the fundamental problem of what it means for memory to "contain" a "step," which refers to a virtual movement in the real world. This sort of model is not needed only when memory is consciously realized by the learner; the GO key, which people learn reasonably quickly, must be conceived of as a "releaser" of movements, and so the entire movement plan is being remembered by the tank from almost the very beginning of the learning session.

The essential question is: What does it mean to remember something? At first this seems to be asking for a solution of the persistent problem of what it means for something to be a symbol. However, we are here concerned with people's *conception* of what makes a symbolic system, not what *actually* makes something a symbolic system. (Whether or not these are different is a discussion for another time.) One might imagine adding an act for encoding something into a symbol and for decoding a symbol into its meaning. However, it is unlikely that people are capable of keeping straight a unique encoding and decoding scheme for each possible movement in each cell of the BigTrak's memory. Also, as soon as these are added, we need to enhance other complex action structures to account for special symbol processing primitives like "copy", which do not apply to physical objects.

One solution to this, at least for the BigTrak case, is to observe that the device state and movement plan are developed synchronously by the learner. When reference needs to be made to the state of memory, it can be computed from the contents of the movement plan in accordance with the learner's current model of their association. The memory cells, in effect, contain nothing. They are merely in correspondence with the contents of the movement plan via some mapping represented by the "running off" function. It isn't clear, in some cases, what this mapping function is. In the vector addition and BASIC line number model, the memory contains vectors that are added to form the sum. However, these vectors are a part of the movement plan, not the device state. When movement problem solving takes place, operators put vectors into the movement plan and thus, in a virtual sense, into the memory cells. The GO key then "computes" a vector sum and results in the actual behavior of the BigTrak.

CONCLUSION

Instructionless learning is a paradigm in which people learn about complex systems by rapidly forming hypotheses and trying experimentally to verify them. Hypotheses are formed by mapping memory structures (analogy and rule instantiation) and some representational search. Experiments to confirm hypotheses are constructed by solving the problem of obtaining a predictable behavior from the device. The analysis of the failure of predictions leads to theory change.

The choice of a programmable system as the learning target provides the interesting feature that it is necessary to learn a device model in order to understand the target system properly. The device model results from explanation and helps guide operator acquisition. In thinking about how the device model is represented and used, we discover that it is necessary to explain what constitutes an understanding of complex computer-controlled systems. We hypothesize that problem solving in two domains, synchronized by a mapping function, provides an answer to the difficult question of what it means for a system to "remember" without relying on special symbol processing primitives. This is also consistent with the hypothesis that the device model is developed from an analogous physical counterpart.

ACKNOWLEDGMENTS

This research was funded in part by NSF and an IBM graduate research fellowship. The BigTrak is manufactured and distributed by the Milton Bradley toy company. Frank Boyle and Brian Reiser reviewed this paper. John Anderson, David Klahr, Herb Simon, and numerous others have contributed greatly to this research.

REFERENCES

Bott, R. A. (1979). *A study of complex learning: Theories and methodologies.* (Processing Rep. No. 7901). University of California at San Diego, Center for Human Information.

Burstein, M. H. (1983, June). Concept formation by incremental analogical reasoning and debugging. In *Proceedings of the International Machine Learning Workshop* (pp. 19–25). Champaign-Urbana, IL.

Collins, G. C. (1985). Teleology + bugs = explanation. In *Proceedings of the 7th Cognitive/science Conference,* Irvine, CA.

deKleer, J. (1979). *Causal and teleological reasoning in circuit recognition.* Unpublished doctoral dissertation, Massachusetts Institute of Technology.

deKleer, J., & Brown, J. S. (1981). Towards a theory of qualitative reasoning about mechanisms. In J. R. Anderson (Ed.), *Cognitive skills and their acquisition.* Hillsdale, NJ: Lawrence Erlbaum Associates.

deKleer, J., & Brown, J. S. (1983). Assumptions and ambiguities in mechanistic mental models. In D. Gentner & A. L. Stevens (Eds.), *Mental models.* Hillsdale, NJ: Lawrence Erlbaum Associates.

Dietterich, T. G., & Buchanan, B. G. (1983, June). The role of experimentation in theory formation. In *Proceedings of the International Machine Learning Workshop* (pp. 147–155). Champaign-Urbana, IL.

Douglas, S. A., & Moran, T. P. (1983, August). Learning operator semantics by analogy. In *Proceedings of the National Conference on Artificial Intelligence.* Washington, DC.

Halasz, F., & Moran, T. P. (1983). Analogy considered harmful. In *Proceedings of the Conference on Human Factors in Computer Systems* (pp. 212–216). New York.

Papert, S. (1980). *Mindstorms.* New York: Basic Books.

Shrager, J., & Klahr, D. (1983, December). A model of learning in the instructionless environment. In *Proceedings of the Conference on Human Factors in Computing Systems* (pp. 226–229). New York.

Shrager, J., & Klahr, D. (in preparation). *Instructionless learning: Hypothesis generation and experimental performance.*

Williams, M. D., Hollan, J. D., & Stevens, A. L. (1983). Human reasoning about a simple physical system. In D. Gentner & A. L. Stevens (Eds.), *Mental models.* Hillsdale, NJ: Lawrence Erlbaum Associates.

Young, R. M. (1981). The machine inside the machine: User's models of pocket calculators. *International Journal of Man-Machine Studies, 15,* 51–85.

Young, R. M. (1983). Surrogates and mappings: Two kinds of conceptual models for interactive devices. In D. Gentner & A. L. Stevens (Eds.), *Mental models.* Hillsdale, NJ: Lawrence Erlbaum Associates

III
MEMORY-BASED NATURAL LANGUAGE UNDERSTANDING

Natural language understanding has long been one of the most internally controversial areas of research in AI. The task seems simple enough: given some scheme for representing knowledge, write a program that takes natural language texts, for example, stories written in English, and produces knowledge structures that represent what the texts mean. The importance of this task is also clear; with natural language abilities, a program could

- gain knowledge from non-computer programmers, and from everyday sources of information, such as newspapers and encyclopedias, and
- communicate what it knows back to non-programmers.

The basic conflicts arise over the roles played by syntax and semantics both during processing and in the final output of the language understander. Modern theoretical structural linguists have been concerned primarily with theories of grammatical judgments, theories accounting for why people call some word sequences grammatical and others ungrammatical. This has little direct bearing in AI, where the real concern is with semantic interpretation, but many feel that the grammatical judgment process is an essential part of the understanding process. In the extreme, this view posits the

177

model of understanding where a syntactic analyzer first reads a text and sends one or more parse trees to a semantic interpreter, which in turn reads the parse trees, chooses the one that makes the most sense, and sends the associated meaning structure to memory.

More commonly, the syntactic analyzer calls the semantic interpreter during processing to help choose between various possible grammatical constructions. For example, in parsing "I saw the Grand Canyon flying to New York," the syntactic analyzer would call the semantic interpreter after seeing "flying" and ask which was more likely to be flying, the speaker or the Grand Canyon. Assuming the semantic interpreter says that people fly, not canyons, the syntactic analyzer would then attach the phrase "flying to New York" to "I saw" and pass the resulting syntactic analysis to the interpreter for final comprehension.

Having a syntactic analyzer ask a semantic interpreter to understand "flying" in order to decide where the phrase "flying to New York" should be attached is like getting into a locked house by asking someone inside to pass a key out to you. There must be more direct ways to get there.

The authors in this section have a very different model of language understanding, in which semantic and syntactic sources of information are used in parallel. Furthermore, the semantics of these systems is not the minimal toy semantics often invoked to handle cases such as the Grand Canyon example. The semantics is everything an understander knows, the same knowledge that he or she uses to solve problems, make plans, write speeches.

Lytinen's MOPTRANS system is a multiple-language machine translation system. One of Lytinen's major design goals was to share as much parsing knowledge as possible, both semantic and syntactic, not only between words within one language, but between different languages. To do this, MOPTRANS uses a MOP-style abstraction hierarchy to generalize semantic and syntatic concepts and stores parsing rules at the most general level possible. Once a general conceptual structure is found, other parsing rules specialize it into the most specific conceptual structure possible. Thus, when MOPTRANS reads a story about an arrest, it starts with the conceptual structure for "take control," which contains rules for finding actors and objects. After filling these in, MOPTRANS then specializes the "take control" structure into the particular kind of "arrest" structure being referred to.

Lytinen's abstraction hierarchy is memory-like, but differs from dynamic memory in several ways. First, some of the nodes MOPTRANS uses do not appear to be conceptual nodes so much as useful gathering points for certain parsing generalizations. Second, MOPTRANS' memory does not change as stories are read. Third, MOPTRANS' memory contains general semantic knowledge, rather than particular episodic knowledge. It knows about arrests in general, such information as an encyclopedia might contain, but not about particular arrests that have happened.

Lebowitz' RESEARCHER program is more narrowly focused. RESEARCH-ERS's memory contains very specific knowledge about objects in the patent domain, such as that disk drive covers are made out of metal. Such knowledge is only one step removed from knowledge about a particular disk drive. Disambiguating the language of patent abstract texts depends more on specific details of the objects being talked about than on general syntactic or semantic rules, such as MOPTRANS has. Probably the best way to view these two systems working together is to see MOPTRANS as specializing general structures into specific ones, at which point RESEARCHER takes over.

Riesbeck's Direct Memory Access (DMAP) system has elements in common with both MOPTRANS and RESEARCHER. The DMAP system views parsing as a problem primarily of memory search, given cues from the input text. Using the particular implementation technique of marker passing, DMAP goes directly from words to domain-specific memory nodes, like RESEARCHER. DMAP's major goal is to get to the most specific nodes in memory, using specialization rules like those in MOPTRANS. DMAP currently has the modest, if unusual goal, of simply finding which pre-existing episodic knowledge an input text is referring to.

Granger's ATLAST system also uses marker passing to integrate parsing with memory. More attention is paid, however, to accounting for psychological data regarding lexical access to multiple word senses, and to incorporating pragmatic considerations into the parsing at an early stage. The marker passing processing model links ATLAST with DMAP, but the general semantic and syntactic knowledge employed links ATLAST with MOPTRANS.

We can summarize briefly, if not accurately, the four systems in this section with the following chart:

Kind of Knowledge

		Semantic	Episodic
	Build a form	MOPTRANS	RESEARCHER
Processing Model			
	Find a form	ATLAST	DMAP

11 Using Memory in Text Understanding

Michael Lebowitz
Department of Computer Science
Columbia University

ABSTRACT

Text processing undoubtedly takes place at many levels simultaneously. We discuss how the access of detailed long-term memory can be used in low-level text processing in the context of a computer system, RESEARCHER, that reads, generalizes, and remembers information from patent abstracts. We show specific points where memory can be applied during text processing, rather than just suggesting general principles. In particular, we focus on how linguistically ambiguous structures can be resolved using memory (and only using memory). A computer example of RESEARCHER applying our memory application principles is presented.

INTRODUCTION

It is clear that text processing proceeds at many levels simultaneously (Charniak, 1983; Marslen-Wilson, 1975; Schank, Lebowitz, & Birnbaum, 1980). Such processing presumably includes the access of detailed, long-term memory for the purpose of finding information relevant to a new text. It seems plausible that such high-level information should be useful in assisting low-level processing. We have suggested in our earlier work, as have others, that memory access may help determine resource allocation and in identifying the important parts of a text (Lebowitz, 1981; Schank et al., 1980). However, these are imprecise ideas, and difficult to apply. For example, IPP (Lebowitz, 1980; Lebowitz, 1983a), a program that reads, remembers, and generalizes from news stories about international terrorism, might know from accessing memory that the destination of a hijacking in a story that begins, "A United 727 en route to Miami was comman-deered. . ." is likely to be Cuba. However, it would not know how to use this information should the story continue "to Havana." Because of the inherent redundancy of language, it is easy to process this information bottom up. (Had no destination been mentioned, we would have used Cuba as a default.)

It is our feeling that the best way to use specific information in memory for text understanding in the context of current systems is to identify specific points during processing where memory can be applied. In this chapter, we present suggestions for using memory for low-level text processing in the context of RESEARCHER, a program that reads patent abstracts and builds up a gener-alized long-term memory (Lebowitz, 1983b). We illustrate this process with a version of RESEARCHER that simulates memory access by asking a user ques-tions at key points during the processing of an abstract. (Answering these ques-tions has been largely automated, but the memory search is not central to this paper.) Crucial to the development of RESEARCHER is that its text understand-ing process be robust enough to handle many patents without special preparation. We feel that memory application is necessary to achieve this ability.

We are talking here about using *memory* for understanding, not just general semantic information about words or concepts. Although such general informa-tion is crucial for our conceptually based understanding methods, to resolve many understanding questions it is necessary to look at very detailed information in memory—in our case, how the various parts of the objects described in a patent abstract are constructed and how their pieces relate to each other.

To illustrate why memory is needed, consider the following simple example:

EX1 — A read/write head touching a disc made of XXX. . .

In EX1, there is no way to determine whether XXX is the material used for the read/write head or the disc without knowing something about the objects involved. Indeed, depending on the context (the type of object being described), we might come up with different analyses.

The main area in which we feel memory will be immediately useful in under-standing (other than supplying default values) is in resolving linguistic ambigu-ities of the kind illustrated by EX1. Although it is probably possible to use memory to resolve lexical ambiguity, we are looking one structural level higher, as word ambiguity has not proven to be a major problem for RESEARCHER.

The idea of applying memory (or at least semantic information) to resolve ambiguity is not a new one (e.g., Riesbeck & Schank, 1976; Small, 1980). However, we show here exactly how detailed memory can be applied to resolve ambiguity, rather than just stating a general principle. We begin by outlining the understanding techniques used in RESEARCHER, indicating where memory application might be useful, and then look at specific memory application techniques.

BASIC *RESEARCHER* UNDERSTANDING TECHNIQUES

In this section, we show how RESEARCHER processes patent abstracts by using only very simple syntactic rules to identify "pieces" of the ultimate representation and then "putting the pieces together." EX2 shows a patent abstract typical of the sort read by RESEARCHER. We are concerned primarily with abstracts that describe the physical structures of objects. The goal of the text interpretation phase of RESEARCHER is to build up descriptions of objects, including the physical relations between various sub-parts of the objects, using a canonical, frame-based representation scheme (Wasserman & Lebowitz, 1983).

EX2   P41; U.S. Patent Abstract #4323939

A hard fixed head disc drive assembly having a rotating record disc with a transducer cooperating with the surface of the disc. The transducer is mounted on a
carriage which has three spaced, grooved bearings, two of which are received by a
fixed cylindrical track, the third bearing engages a spring-loaded cylindrical track
which urges said first two bearings against said fixed track, whereby the carriage is
centered on said tracks for movement therealong radially of said disc surface.

There are several important points about EX2 for text processing purposes. First, in traditional terms, the syntax of the abstract is very strange; for example, the first "sentence" has no main verb. Furthermore, very different syntactic structures can function quite similarly. For example, the phrases "a transducer cooperating with the surface of the disk" and "the third bearing engages a spring-loaded cylindrical track" describe very similar physical relations, but use different linguistic structures. While preliminary identification of the syntactic structure might aid in the building of a conceptual representation, patent abstracts seem like an ideal domain to test strongly semantic-based methods that build conceptual representations directly from text.

EX3 shows EX2 segmented in a manner that motivates RESEARCHER's text processing techniques. This text, and most other patent abstracts that provide physical descriptions, can be broken into two types of segments—those that describe physical objects, which we refer to as *memettes,* shown in italics in EX3, and those that relate various memettes to each other. The memette-describing segments are usually (though not always) simple noun phrases, but the relational segments are of many different forms, including verbs and preposi-
tions. The key point is that the functionality of the relational segments is largely independent of their syntactic form, so we can process them solely on the function they serve.

EX3 - (*A hard fixed head disc drive assembly*) (having) (*a rotating record disc*) (with) (*a transducer*) (*cooperating* with) (*the surface*) (of) (*the disc*). (*The transducer*) (is mounted on) (*a carriage*) (which has) (*three spaced, grooved bearings*), (*two*) (of which) (are received by) (*a fixed cylindrical track*), (*the third bearing*) (engages) (*a spring-loaded cylindrical track*) (which urges) (*said first two bearings*) (against) (*said fixed track*), (whereby) (*the carriage*) (is centered on) (*said tracks*) (for movement therealong radially of) (*said disc surface*).

The analysis shown in EX3 leads directly to RESEARCHER's text interpretation methods. These methods are based on the memory-based understanding techniques designed for IPP (Lebowitz, 1983a). The RESEARCHER interpretation phase consists largely of two subphases—memette identification and memette relation, or "identifying the pieces" and "putting the pieces together." Processing involves a top-down goal of recognizing conceptual structures integrated with simple, bottom-up syntactic techniques.

Because patents are not focused on events, as are the news stories IPP processed, the action-based methods of IPP (or other conceptual understanding systems [Birnbaum & Selfridge, 1981; Riesbeck & Schank, 1976; Wilks, 1973]) must be modified in a manner consistent with the analysis shown in EX3. RESEARCHER does careful processing of noun phrases to identify memettes, modifications to memettes, and reference to previous mentions of memettes. This processing is integrated with the application of relational words to create relations among memettes.

In broad terms, the structure of our processing is similar to the cascaded ATN methodology (Bobrow & Webber, 1980; Woods, 1980), where syntactic grammars frequently hand off syntactic components to a semantic analyzer, which builds semantic structures and eliminates impossible constructs. However, we use only a few different syntactic constructs, eliminating the need for a formal syntactic grammar by focusing on the roles of words in the conceptual representation. Furthermore, whereas the cascaded ATN methodology views the understanding process as a syntactic processor giving what it finds to the semantic analyzer, we look on the process as being primarily a conceptual analysis that requests linguistic information when needed (much as in DeJong, 1979).

The noun phrase recognition process involves the same "save and skip" strategy described in Lebowitz (1983a). Using a one-word look-ahead process, RESEARCHER saves noun phrase words in a stack until the head noun is found. Then the words in the stack are popped off and used to modify the memette indicated by the head noun. Analyzing how the parts of noun groups interrelate is one place where information from memory will be needed. For example, in the first noun phrase of EX2, *A hard fixed head disc drive assembly,* there is no way of knowing whether *hard* modifies *head, disc, disc drive* or *assembly,* without using information about the structure of disc drives. We discuss this further in the next section.

The final aspect to "finding the pieces" involves checking for previous references in the text. Here we take advantage of some of the arcane nature of patent abstracts. A very strict formalism is used to identify previous references, involving the word "said" and repetition of identifying modifiers. Without such formalism, the process would be very complicated, as abstracts frequently refer to many very similar objects. As it is, we can use a fairly simple, procedural reference process.

The second major subphase to RESEARCHER text processing involves putting together the pieces identified. This process occurs as soon as the objects involved are found. By and large, there are two different kinds of relations found that tie objects together—assembly/component relations and physical (or functional) relations between memettes. The basic RESEARCHER strategy for each is the same: maintain information from the relational segments of the text in short term memory; and then, when the following memette is identified, determine how the appropriate pieces relate to each other. This process, which is largely independent of the form of the relational text segments, immediately builds up a conceptual representation for later use.

The process of relating memettes to each other involves a number of ambiguous situations that we discuss in the next section. We initially used simple focus heuristics, including some related to Grosz (1977), Sidner (1979), and others based on the various relations involved. However, we believe that this is only part of the solution (perhaps a small part), and must be extensively augmented with the kind of memory access described in this paper.

The point here is not that it is impossible to develop heuristics to handle any *specific* problem. We have done so for a number of cases in RESEARCHER. However, these rules get increasingly clumsy as we add them. An approach that accesses long-term memory will give us a more general method.

USING MEMORY TO RESOLVE AMBIGUITY

In this section we show specifically how memory can be used to resolve certain classes of ambiguity. This process is a matter of the understanding process "asking questions" of memory. The questions ask which of several possible physical structures is most plausible. Our discussion is divided the same way as the processing: identifying "pieces" (processing noun groups) and then connecting the pieces. We are concerned here not only with the details of the cases we have identified, but also with illustrating the level at which we believe memory should be applied to parsing.

Noun phrases in English (phrases that describe objects) have very complex structure (see Gershman, 1977, for a conceptual analysis approach to noun phrase processing). In our earlier work, we concentrated on properly delineating such phrases. However, RESEARCHER's emphasis on object descriptions requires more attention to the internal structure of noun phrases, so that we can identify how the pieces of those phrases fit together. Memory application is crucial in doing this. EX4 shows the first case requiring memory.

EX4:

Form: modifier object-word1 object-word2
Example: A metal drive cover . . .
Question: Does the modifier (metal) apply better to object-word1 (drive) or object-word2 (cover)?

Noun-noun constructions in English introduce a multitude of problems. EX4 illustrates one problem—a modifier preceding such a combination can modify either of the objects mentioned. In EX4 either the drive or the cover could be made of metal. In more complex situations, that is, those containing more nouns or a series of modifiers, syntax can reduce the possible targets of a modifier. Only by asking memory which is more plausible in the context of the object being described can the right choice be made.

Notice that memory, not just general semantic properties, is needed here. Although for most disc drives it is more likely that the cover, rather than the disc, is metal, the contrary could be the case in another device. We might even find that the abstract refers to a special class of disc drives with metal discs and plastic covers.

EX5 illustrates a somewhat similar noun group problem.

EX5:

Form: object-word1 object-word2 object-word3
Example: A disc-drive transducer wire . . .
Question: Is object-word3 (wire) "related to" (one being a part of the other) object-word1 (disc-drive) or object-word2 (transducer)?

When multiple nouns appear in succession, it is not always easy to tell how they group together. In EX5, there is no way to tell whether the wire is a (direct) part of the disc drive or the transducer (or, more precisely, which it is functionally connected to). Again, an appeal to long-term memory of similar devices is the way to resolve this problem.

The "putting together the pieces" phase of RESEARCHER processing also involves ambiguities that must be resolved with memory. EX6 shows what happens when more than one relational word must be processed.

EX6:

Form: object-word1 relation-word1 object-word2 relation-word2 object-word3

Example: A transducer on top of a disc supported by a rod . . .
Question: Does relation-word 2 (supported by) connect object-word3 (rod) with object-word1 (transducer) or object-word2 (disc)?

In some sense, the problem shown in EX6 involves noun group problems, in that it deals with prepositional phrase attachment. However, in our scheme of understanding, it falls into a somewhat different category. As described in the previous section, relating various objects together is a separate part of processing. This allows us to handle many other structural manifestations of this problem with the same mechanism. The mechanism here is to query memory about which of the possible objects most appropriately takes part in the relation. In EX6, we need to appeal to memory to determine whether the rod is more likely supporting the transducer or the disc, either of which is syntactically appropriate.

EX7 illustrates a similar problem, this time with "part indicators" (words that introduce a list of a part's subparts).

EX7:

Form: object-word1 part-indicator1 object-word2 part-indicator2 object-word3
Example: A disc drive including a disc comprising a metal plate (and) . . .
Question: Is object-word3 (metal plate) a part of object-word1 (disc drive) or object-word2 (disc)?

In patent abstracts there are frequently descriptions of parts and then of the subparts. This often creates considerable ambiguity of the sort shown in EX7, which is structurally similar to EX6. We handle this case separately as the part/component relations are represented differently from other relations, since they are so crucial, and are expressed slightly differently in the abstracts. Once again, the only way to determine the correct analysis, in this case whether the metal plate is part of the disc drive or the disc, is to query memory, quite possibly looking at descriptions of specific objects or classes of objects.

The final class of structural ambiguity we deal with involves a combination of physical relations and part/component indicators, as shown in EX8.

EX8:

Form: object-word1 relation-word object-word2 part-of-indicator object-word3
(There are several related configurations.)
Example: A disc on a spindle for a disc drive . . .
Question: Is object-word1 (disc) or object-word2 (spindle) a part of object-word3 (disc drive)? (Directly a part, as both are parts indirectly.)

EX8 is used as an illustration of the many ways part and relational indicators can interact. As always, the simple syntactic processing outlined earlier limits the possibilities, but memory is required to evaluate the different choices, in this case whether the disc drive has as a part the spindle or the disc (or which is a direct functional part).

Integrating Memory Access With Text Processing

The disambiguation questions described in the previous section fit in easily with the overall RESEARCHER text processing algorithm. RESEARCHER's "save and skip" noun group strategy naturally accommodates memory-based disambiguation. As RESEARCHER is processing the items it has maintained in its short-term memory stack, it keeps track of the objects identified by the head noun and the most recent noun. Then, if there is more than one distinct object described in the noun group, as it continues to work back through the stack, memory can be queried to determine which object new words modify or relate to. Without performing the memory query, it is necessary to employ a set of complex and rather unsatisfying heuristics to determine how the parts of noun groups fit together.

Memory access fits in equally well in the "putting together the pieces" phase of RESEARCHER understanding. RESEARCHER maintains short-term memory buffers with the most recent object described and the last "base object" (usually identified as the head noun of a noun phrase being modified by a series of prepositional phrases, although there are other possibilities). Then, if these two objects are different and a new relation (physical or part/component) is being established, memory can be queried for the more plausible of the two objects with which to relate the new object. As with noun group processing, it is possible to develop heuristics that handle most cases, but they are complex and do not seem to be the right way to go for robust understanding.

Can Memory Answer the Questions?

We have shown here how certain ambiguities in language can be resolved with the answers to specified questions. Obviously, we must believe that our system can automatically answer these questions. The questions we are concerned with take the form of asking which of two memettes can more reasonably be modified in a certain way or relate to another memette in the context of the device being described. Phrased another way, the needed process is to determine which of two partial descriptions of a device is more plausible.

Indeed, we do believe that these questions will be answerable by RESEARCHER. At the moment, because we have only a modestly sized memory, we have tested the disambiguation process by allowing a user to answer the key questions. However, since the process of finding an object in memory that fits a specified partial description is crucial to generalization and question answering, the disambiguation process will need no information not needed for other purposes. In fact, we have been able to automate answers to all the questions used in this paper, including the example in the next section.

Our basic approach to memory in RESEARCHER is to store objects in terms of prototypes automatically generalized from earlier patent abstracts (Lebowitz, 1980, 1983b, 1983c). This approach was successful in answering similar sorts of questions for IPP and other Generalization-Based Memory systems. It allows us to take partial descriptions of objects and determine whether they are represented by objects or generalized objects in memory. We do not plan, at least at first, to answer questions of this sort which require more complex inferencing from information in memory; instead our concentration is on having as complete as possible a set of examples in memory.

An Example

We will complete this discussion of RESEARCHER's use of memory in text understanding by showing how the program processes the first sentence of the patent abstract we looked at in Section 2, using a version of the program that queries a user at the points where memory access is needed.[1] Figure 11.1 shows how the first noun group is processed. Queries to memory are preceded by ">>>" and each response follows an asterisk.

In Fig. 11.1 we can see how RESEARCHER first skips and saves the words *hard fixed head disc drive* (treating the phrase *disc drive* as a single word) until the head noun, *assembly,* is reached. It then works back through the noun group, establishing *disc drive* as part of the assembly. Then, when it processes *head,* RESEARCHER must decide whether the head relates directly to the assembly or the disc drive, by making a memory check. Either object is plausible here, but we will assume the assembly is the correct parent part of the head. Then, the modifiers *fixed* and *hard* are processed. In each case, RESEARCHER must decide whether the assembly or the head is being modified. (The disc drive is eliminated by linguistic considerations). Again, these questions can be answered only from memory, and we presume that the head is fixed (mobility = none, in our representation scheme) and hard.

Figure 11.2 shows the rest of the first sentence of the abstract being processed, illustrating additional disambiguation points.

RESEARCHER must determine whether the *transducer* is part of the *record disc* or the assembly and whether the *surface of the disc* is *cooperating with* (adjacent to) the assembly or the transducer. Each of these cases is ambiguous structurally, and can be disambiguated only with memory access.

---

[1]Since this paper was written, we have implemented automatic memory access to answer the questions described here. This work is described in Lebowitz, 1984.

Patent: P41

(A HARD FIXED HEAD DISC DRIVE ASSEMBLY HAVING A ROTATING RECORD DISC
WITH A TRANSDUCER COOPERATING WITH THE SURFACE OF THE DISC *PERIOD*
THE TRANSDUCER IS MOUNTED ON A CARRIAGE WHICH HAS THREE SPACED
COMMA GROOVED BEARINGS *COMMA* TWO OF WHICH ARE RECEIVED BY A
FIXED CYLINDRICAL TRACK *COMMA* THE THIRD BEARING ENGAGES A SPRING-
LOADED CYLINDRICAL TRACK WHICH URGES SAID FIRST TWO BEARINGS AGAINST
SAID FIXED TRACK *COMMA* WHEREBY THE CARRIAGE IS CENTERED ON SAID
TRACKS FOR MOVEMENT THEREALONG RADIALLY OF SAID DISC SURFACE *STOP*)

Processing:

A	:	New instance word—skip
HARD	:	Memette modifier; save and skip
FIXED	:	Memette modifier; save and skip
HEAD	:	Memette within NP; save and skip
DISC DRIVE	:	Phrase
→ DISC-DRIVE	:	Memette within NP; save and skip
ASSEMBLY	:	Memette word—memette UNKNOWN-ASSEMBLY#

New UNKNOWN-ASSEMBLY# instance (&MEM0)
New DISC-DRIVE# instance (&MEM1)
Assuming &MEM1 (DISC-DRIVE#) is part of &MEM0 (UNKNOWN-ASSEMBLY#—
'ASSEMBLY')

New HEAD# instance (&MEM2)

>>> Select memette to merge with &MEM2 (HEAD#) from &MEM0 ('ASSEMBLY')
&MEM1 (DISC-DRIVE#) * &mem0

Assuming &MEM2 (HEAD#) is part of &MEM0 (UNKNOWN-ASSEMBLY#—'ASSEM-
BLY')

>>> Select memette modified by MOBILITY/NONE from &MEM0 ('ASSEMBLY')
&MEM2 (HEAD#) * &mem2

Augmenting &MEM2 (HEAD#) with feature: MOBILITY = NONE

>>> Select memette modified by TEXTURE/HARD from &MEM0 ('ASSEMBLY')
&MEM2 (HEAD#) * &mem2

Augmenting &MEM2 (HEAD#) with feature: TEXTURE = HARD

FIG. 11.1.   RESEARCHER processing the first noun group of P41

Figure 11.3 shows the final representation constructed by RESEARCHER
after reading all of P41. It consists of a set of identified memettes, indications of
which memettes are parts of others, and a list of relations between memettes. The
relations prefixed with R- are physical, and those beginning with P- are functional (purposive). There is also a single "meta-relation," which indicates a

HAVING	:	Parts of &MEM0 (UNKNOWN-ASSEMBLY#—'ASSEMBLY') to follow
A	:	New instance word—skip
ROTATING	:	Memette modifier; save and skip
RECORD	:	Memette modifier; save and skip
DISC	:	Memette word—memette DISC#

New DISC# instance (&MEM3)
Augmenting &MEM3 (DISC#) with feature: DEV-PURPOSE - STORING
Augmenting &MEM3 (DISC#) with feature: DEV-PURPOSE = ROTATION
Assuming &MEM3 (DISC#) is part of &MEM0 (UNKNOWN-ASSEMBLY#—'ASSEM-BLY')

WITH (WITH1)	:	Parts of &MEM3 (DISC#) or &MEM0 (UNKNOWN ASSEM-BLY#—'ASSEMBLY') to follow
A	:	New instance word—skip
TRANSDUCER	:	Memette word—memette TRANSDUCER#

New TRANSDUCER# instance (&MEM4)

>>> Select assembly of &MEM4 (TRANSDUCER#) from &MEM3 (DISC#) &MEM0 ('ASSEMBLY') * &mem0

Assuming &MEM4 (TRANSDUCER#) is part of &MEM0 (UNKNOWN-ASSEMBLY#—'ASSEMBLY')

COOPERATING WITH

	:	Phrase
→ COOPERATING	:	Relation word—save and skip
THE	:	Antecedent word—skip
SURFACE	:	Memette word—memette SURFACE#

New SURFACE# instance (&MEM5)

>>> Refine roles for &REL5 [R-ADJACENT-TO]
SUBJECT &MEM4 (TRANSDUCER#) &MEM0 (UNKNOWN-ASSEMBLY#—'ASSEM-BLY')
OBJECT &MEM5 (SURFACE#)
Enter memette for SUBJECT slot * &mem4

Establishing R-ADJACENT-TO relation; SUBJECT: &MEM4 (TRANSDUCER#);
OBJECT: &MEM5 (SURFACE:) [&REL5]

OF	:	Par of indicator

Assuming &MEM5 (SURFACE#) is part of the following

THE	:	Antecedent word—skip
DISC	:	Memette word—memette DISC#

Reference for DISC#: &MEM3

>>> Select component of &MEM3 (DISC#) from &MEM5 (SURFACE#)
&MEM0 ('ASSEMBLY') * &mem5

Assuming &MEM5 (SURFACE#) is part of &MEM3 (DISC#)

PERIOD	:	Break word—skip end of sentence—resetting part flag

FIG. 11.2. RESEARCHER finishing the first sentence of P41

Text Representation:
** ACTIVE INSTANCES **
&MEM0 (UNKNOWN-ASSEMBLY#—'ASSEMBLY')
  Components: &MEM1 &MEM2 &MEM3 &MEM4
&MEM1 (DISC-DRIVE#)
&MEM2 (HEAD#) [Mods: TEXTURE/HARD MOBILITY/NONE]
&MEM3 (DISC#) [Mods: DEV-PURPOSE/ROTATION DEV-PURPOSE/STORING]
  Components: &MEM5
&MEM4 (TRANSDUCER#)
&MEM5 (SURFACE#)
&MEM6 (CARRIAGE#)
  Components: &MEM7
&MEM7 (BEARING#) [Mods: NUMBER/3 DISTANCE/SEPARATE TEXTURE/INCISED]
  Components: &MEM8 &MEM10
&MEM8 (BEARING#) [Mods: NUMBER/2 ORDINAL/1]
&MEM9 (TRACK#) [Mods: MOBILITY/NONE SHAPE/CYLINDRICAL]
&MEM10 (BEARING#) [Mods: ORDINAL/3]
&MEM11 (TRACK#) [Mods: TENSION/SPRING SHAPE/CYLINDRICAL]

A list of relations:

Subject:			Relation:	Object:	
[&REL5]	&MEM4	(TRANSDUCER#)	{R-ADJACENT-TO}	&MEM5	(SURFACE#)
[&REL6]	&MEM6	(CARRIAGE#)	{P-SUPPORTS}	&MEM4	(TRANSDUCER#)
[&REL7]	&MEM9	(TRACK#)	{P-RECEIVES}	&MEM8	(BEARING#)
[&REL8]	&MEM10	(BEARING#)	{P-ENGAGES}	&MEM11	(TRACK#)
[&REL9]	&MEM11	(TRACK#)	{P-IMPELS}	&MEM8	(BEARING#)
[&REL10]	&MEM8	(BEARING#)	{R-ADJACENT-TO}	&MEM9	(TRACK#)
[&REL11]	&MEM11	(TRACK#)	{R-SURROUNDED-BY}	&MEM6	(CARRIAGE#)
[&REL12]	&MEM11	(TRACK#)	{R-ALONG}	&MEM5	(SURFACE#)
			ORIENTATION/RADIAL		

A list of meta-relations:

Subject:	Meta-rel:	Object:
&REL10	{M-CAUSES}	&REL11

FIG. 11.3.   RESEARCHER Representation of P41

causal connection between its component relations. This representation captures all the information from P41 that is needed for the learning aspects of RE-SEARCHER. It was acquired using the memory-augmented ''putting pieces together'' strategy described in this chapter.

CONCLUSION

As we have seen, memory application is an absolute necessity in understanding. However, it is crucial to delineate exactly how memory should be used, as illustrated here. In the RESEARCHER framework, simple syntactic rules, driven by generic memory structures (semantics), limit the possible ways a representation can be constructed, and searching detailed memory resolves ambiguities. This allows each phase of the processing to be relatively simple, and lets the redundant nature of language help us obtain robust performance. While a different conceptual understanding scheme or a different domain would liekly require different points of memory access, this same framework should still be appropriate.

To date, we have run RESEARCHER without memory access on about 100 patent abstracts as complex as P41; about 20 texts were fully processed with good accuracy. However, even at this stage of development the heuristics needed to avoid memory use are rather complex. Hence we view the addition of the memory access methods described in this paper as crucial to the further progress of RESEARCHER as a robust understander.

ACKNOWLEDGMENTS

This research was supported in part by the United States Defense Advanced Research Projects Agency under contract N00039-84-C-0165. This paper also appeared in the Proceedings of ECAI-84, Pisa, Italy.

REFERENCES

Birnbaum, L., & Selfridge, M. (1981). Conceptual analysis of natural language. In R. C. Schank & C. K. Riesbeck (Eds.), *Inside computer understanding*. Hillsdale, NJ: Lawrence Erlbaum Associates.

Bobrow, R. J., & Webber, B. L. (1980). Knowledge representation for syntactic/semantic representation. *The First Annual National Conference on Artificial Intelligence* 316–323, Stanford, CA.

Charniak, E. (1983). Passing markers: A theory of contextual influence in language comprehension. *Cognitive Science, 7*(3), 171–190.

DeJong, G. F. (1979). Prediction and substantiation: A new approach to natural language processing. *Cognitive Science, 3*(3), 251–273.

Gershman, A. V. (1977). *Analyzing English noun groups for their conceptual content* (Tech. Rep. 110). Yale University, Department of Computer Science.

Grosz, B. J. (1977). Representation and use of focus in a system for understanding dialogs. *Proceedings of the Fifth International Joint Conference on Artificial Intelligence* (pp. 67–76). Cambridge, MA.

Lebowitz, M. (1980, October). *Generalization and memory in an integrated understanding system.* (Research Rep. No 186). Unpublished doctoral dissertation, Yale University.

Lebowitz, M. (1981). Cancelled due to lack of interest. *Proceedings of the Seventh International Joint Conference on Artificial Intelligence* (pp. 13–15). Vancouver, BC.

Lebowitz, M. (1983a). Memory-based parsing. *Artificial Intelligence, 21*(4), 363–404.

Lebowitz, M. (1983b). RESEARCHER: An overview. *Proceedings of the Third National Conference on Artificial Intelligence* (pp. 232–235). Washington, DC.

Lebowitz, M. (1983c). Concept learning in a rich input domain. *Proceedings of the 1983 International Machine Learning Workshop* (pp. 177–182). University of Illinois.

Lebowitz, M. (1984). *The use of memory in text processing.* (Tech. Rep.). Columbia University, Department of Computer Science.

Marslen-Wilson, W. D. (1975). Sentence perception as an interactive parallel process. *Science,* (189), 226–228.

Riesbeck, C. K., & Schank, R. C. (1976). Comprehension by computer: Expectation-based analysis of sentences in context. In W. J. M. Levelt & G. B. Flores d'Arcais, (Eds.), *Studies in the perception of language.* Chichester, England: Wiley.

Schank, R. C., Lebowitz, M., & Birnbaum, L. (1980). An integrated understander. *American Journal of Computational Linguistics, 6*(1), 13–30.

Sidner, C. L. (1979). *A computational model of co-reference comprehension in English.* Unpublished doctoral dissertation, Massachusetts Institute of Technology.

Small, S. (1980). *Word expert parsing: A theory of distributed word-based natural language understanding.* Unpublished doctoral dissertation, University of Maryland. TR-954.

Wasserman, K., & Lebowitz, M. (1983). Representing complex physical objects. *Cognition and Brain Theory, 6*(3), 333–352.

Wilks, Y. (1973). An artificial intelligence approach to machine translation. In R. C. Schank and K. M. Colby (Eds.), *Computer models of thought and language.* San Francisco: W. H. Freeman.

Woods, W. A. (1980). Cascaded ATN grammars. *American Journal of Computational Linguistics, 6*(1), 1–12.

12

A More General Approach to Word Disambiguation

Steven L. Lytinen
Department of Computer Science
Yale University

ABSTRACT

An approach to word disambiguation is presented that involves the use of a small number of general inference rules in conjunction with a hierarchically organized conceptual memory. This is in contrast to a commonly used method that relies primarily on disambiguation rules stored in the dictionary definitions of ambiguous words. The disambiguation of very vague or general words is problematical for the latter method because of its reliance on lexically based disambiguation rules. However, because of its more integrated organization, the disambiguation method presented here does not suffer from these problems.

INTRODUCTION

A common approach to the task of word disambiguation in conceptual parsers is to use lexically based disambiguation rules. Examples of parsers in which this approach has been taken are ELI (Riesbeck & Schank, 1976), the Conceptual Analyzer (Birnbaum & Selfridge, 1979), the Word Expert Parser (Small, 1980), and to some extent the Integrated Partial Parser (Lebowitz, 1980). In this approach, disambiguation rules take the form of requests or demons, stored as part of the dictonary definitions of ambiguous words. At least one request or demon is written for each possible meaning of an ambiguous word. A word is disambiguated when one of these requests or demons is executed, thereby choosing its word sense as the meaning of the word in the given context; or when a request activated by a previous word in the sentence is executed, choosing a word sense of the ambiguous word.

This paper demonstrates that very vague or general words which have many possible meanings are problematical for this approach to word disambiguation. This is because of the large number of requests or demons that would be necessary to perform the disambiguation of these words. An alternative is to not use lexically based disambiguation rules. Instead, use only a very few general-purpose disambiguation rules, in conjunction with a hierarchically organized conceptual memory. This approach does not suffer from the same rule explosion when used to disambiguate very vague or general words.

This word disambiguation method has been developed within a machine translation project at Yale called the MOPTRANS system (Lytinen & Schank, 1982). Word disambiguation is a crucial task in machine translation: ambiguous words can often be translated in any of several different ways because there is usually no equivalently ambiguous word in other languages. For one meaning of the ambiguous word, a particular word might be used in another language; but for another meaning of the original word, another word in the second language might be more appropriate. The MOPTRANS parser uses the disambiguation method discussed here to determine the proper translation for ambiguous or vague words.

PREVIOUS WORK IN SEMANTICS-BASED WORD DISAMBIGUATION

One of the initial attempts to deal with word disambiguation in a semantics-based parser was Riesbeck's (1975) analyzer in the MARGIE system (Schank, 1975), a story understanding and paraphrasing system. In Riesbeck's parser, and in a later version called ELI (Riesbeck & Schank, 1976), disambiguation of words was performed by requests. Requests were test-action pairs activated when the parser encountered a particular word, or when a particular representation was built. A request *fired,* (was executed) when necessary conditions were met by the state of active memory.

Requests disambiguated words in Riesbeck's parser in either of two ways, which more or less correspond to *bottom-up* and *top-down*. An ambiguous word typically had as part of its dictionary definition a group of requests, which were activated when the parser encountered the word. Usually there was at least one request for each possible meaning of the word. In the bottom-up method, a word was disambiguated when one of these requests fired, thereby choosing its word sense as the meaning of the word. In the top-down method, some request from a previous word in the sentence fired. This request was then responsible for building the appropriate representation of the ambiguous word, thus disambiguating it.

The bottom-up method performed the disambiguation of the word *wants* in the following two examples:

> John wants Mary.
> John wants the book.

The conceptual dependency parses for these two sentences are quite complicated and the details of how *wants* is represented are not relevant here, inasmuch
as it is represented the same way for both sentences. What is represented differently in these two examples is the object of John's wanting:

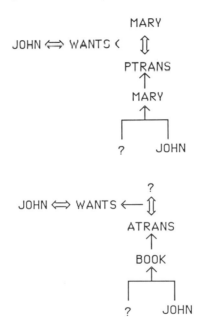

Thus, *John wants Mary* is parsed as meaning *John wants that Mary be near him,*
whereas *John wants the book* is parsed as *John wants possession of the book.*

In order to produce two different parses for these two sentences, Riesbeck's
dictionary definition of the word *wants* contained two requests (among others)
that would each produce one of the two conceptual dependency configurations
above. These requests, in a slightly simplified form, were as follows:

If *wants* is followed by a word that refers to an inanimate object, then the
OBJECT of *wants* is an ATRANS of the inanimate object to the ACTOR of
wants.
If *wants* is followed by a word that refers to a person, then the OBJECT of
wants is a PTRANS of the person to the ACTOR of *wants.*

Top-down disambiguation methods, on the other hand, performed the disambiguation of *beat* in the following example:

> John and Mary were racing. John beat Mary.

The dictionary definition of *beat* consisted of two senses, BEAT1 and BEAT2. BEAT1 corresponded to the *physical beating* sense of *beat,* whereas BEAT2 corresponded to the *victory* sense of *beat,* as in the preceding example. BEAT1, the sense corresponding to a physical beating, was the default sense of the word. Thus, if no requests fired when the parser encountered the word *beat,* it was taken to mean BEAT1. In the example, however, the context of *racing* activated a request, that, in turn, activated a *contextual cluster of conceptualizations.* This cluster contained information about other conceptualizations likely to appear in a racing story, as well as information about which senses of ambiguous words would be used in a racing context. One piece of information in the cluster pointed to by *racing* was that the BEAT2 sense, meaning *victory,* is the sense of *beat* used in racing stories. Thus, when the contextual cluster of conceptualizations was activated by the word *racing,* a request was activated that expected the sense BEAT2 of *beat.* When the parser encountered the word *beat,* this request fired, and BEAT2 was activated instead of BEAT1.

Similar lexically based disambiguation methods have been used in many parsers since Riesbeck's. In Birnbaum and Selfridge's (1979) Conceptual Analyzer (CA), similar requests were used to disambiguate the word *left* in the following examples:

> John left the restaurant.
> John left a tip.

In the first sentence, *left* should be represented by the conceptual dependency primitive PTRANS, but in the other sentence, ATRANS is the appropriate CD primitive. To handle this ambiguity, requests contained in the dictionary definition of *left* looked for something that could be a location, in which case PTRANS was chosen as the representation; or for a physical object, in which case ATRANS was used.

More recently, similar word disambiguation strategies have been used in *integrated parsers* (Schank, Lebowitz, & Birnbaum, 1980), that is, parsers in which the distinction between parsing and inferencing is made less strong. In earlier conceptual parsing systems, such as the MARGIE system, a strong distinction was made between two processes: parsing, or the process of building a conceptual representation from text; and inferencing, which involved further conceptual processing and the application of higher level knowledge structures. In an integrated parser, however, this distinction is weakened; high-level knowledge structures such as scripts (Schank & Abelson, 1977) are used directly in the parsing process. The motivation for integrated parsing is that more specific expectations can be provided by higher level structures, thus helping to solve problems such as word disambiguation encountered during parsing.

Although high-level structures have been used to some extent in the disambiguation of words in integrated parsers, many of the word disambiguation techniques used by these parsers are similar to the techniques used in Reisbeck's parser and in CA, often relying on lexically-based requests to perform word disambiguation. Lebowitz's (1980) Integrated Partial Parser (IPP) is an example of an integrated parser that used lexically based disambiguation rules. For instance, the word *attacked* in IPP was ambiguous, with senses corresponding to the several high-level structures that could be used to represent this word. Among the possible high-level structures in IPP used to represent *attacked* were $SHOOT-ATTACK, $EXPLODE-BOMB, and $ASSAULT. To resolve the ambiguity of this word, the possible structures to which *attacked* could refer were listed in its dictionary definition. Then, words strongly related to these various structures were responsible for loading requests that looked for the word *attacked,* or other such words, and disambiguated them. Thus, the word *gunman,* strongly related to the structure $SHOOT-ATTACK, loaded a request looking for ambiguous words that could possibly mean $SHOOT-ATTACK. If one was found, such as *attacked,* then this request performed the disambiguation of the word. This disambiguation technique is very similar to the top-down technique used in Riesbeck's parser.

Another parser that used a similar disambiguation method was the Word Expert Parser (Small, 1980). The Word Expert Parser used demons to disambiguate words, in much the same way as requests were used in the other parsers discussed. WEP disambiguated very vague or ambiguous words, using complex dictionary definitions that consisted, in part, of discrimination nets of possible concepts to which an ambiguous word could refer, as well as a group of demons used to determine under what conditions an ambiguous word referred to a particular concept.

An example of an ambiguous word that WEP disambiguated is *throw.* Small considered several possible meanings of the word, such as *to throw out garbage, to throw a party, to throw in the towel,* and *to throw a ball.* Part of the dictionary definition of throw consisted of a discrimination net of the concepts to which *throw* could refer, such as PERSON-THROW, THROW-OBJECT-TO-LOCA-TION, THROW-OUT-GARBAGE, and so on. Also included in the dictionary entry for *throw* were demons that determined which definition applied to a given context. Some of these demons were "If the agent of 'throw' is a person, then refine 'throw' to PERSON-THROW", and, "If the object of PERSON-THROW is garbage, then refine PERSON-THROW to THROW-OUT-GAR-BAGE," or, "If the object of PERSON-THROW is a small object, then refine PERSON-THROW to THROW-OBJECT-TO-LOCATION."

PROBLEMS WITH LEXICALLY BASED
DISAMBIGUATION RULES

There are problems with using lexically based rules to disambiguate highly ambiguous or vague words. First, since this method requires at least one request or demon for every sense of a word, very vague words require many rules for their disambiguation. Second, often the rules required for disambiguation of words are quite complex, checking for many combinations of concepts appearing in the context of the ambiguous word.

To demonstrate this, consider the following story, which was encountered by the MOPTRANS program[1]:

Spanish: La policía REALIZA INTENSAS DILIGENCIAS para capturar a un reo que dio muerte a una mujer.

English: The police ARE UNDERTAKING AN INTENSE INVESTIGA-TION in order to capture a criminal who killed a woman.

The Spanish phrase *realizar diligencias* is a very vague phrase that can mean many things. Literally, it means *to realize diligent actions*. Here, it means *to investigate*. However, it can mean many other things, and thus could be repre-sented in many different ways, depending on the context.

In many contexts, *realizar diligencias* means the equivalent of the English *to run errands,* as in the following[2]:

Spanish: María no puede ir a la reunión porque tiene que HACER MUCHAS DILIGENCIAS.

English: Mary cannot go to the gathering because she HAS TO RUN A LOT OF ERRANDS.

There are many contexts in which *hacer diligencias* takes on other meanings:

Spanish: Juanita salió a HACER UNAS DILIGENCIAS AL MERCADO.

English: Juanita went TO SHOP FOR GROCERIES.

Spanish: Va a pintar su apartamento? — Sí, pero antes tengo que HACER UNAS DILIGENCIAS PARA VER si consigo la pintura que quiero.

ENGLISH: Are you going to paint your apartment? — Yes, but first I have TO GO SEE if I can find the paint that I want.

From these examples, we see that many, many actions can be expressed in Spanish using *hacer diligencias,* and thus many different representations must be used to represent the phrase in different contexts. In the examples cited, repre-

---

[1]This example was encountered during work done on Spanish to English translation. Thus, the examples I discuss here are in Spanish, accompanied by English translations.

[2]Often, the verb *hacer* (to do or make) is used in place of *realizar*.

sentations like $GROCERY-STORE, $SHOP, and $POLICE-INVESTIGA-TION would be needed. There are contexts in which many other representations would have to be used.

How could a phrase like *realizar diligencias* be parsed using lexically based disambiguation techniques? It would be difficult, if not impossible, to write all the requests that would be needed to disambiguate *realizar diligencias*. This technique would require a request in the dictionary definition of *realizar diligencias* for each possible meaning of the phrase. Thus, first we would need an exhaustive list of the possible representations which could be used to represent *realizar diligencias*, so that we would know what requests would need to be written. For all practical purposes, this is an impossible task, since the phrase could conceivably refer to just about any action.

Even discounting this problem, though, writing lexically based disambiguation rules for "realizar diligencias" would be a difficult task. Consider the requests that would be required just for the sense of *realizar diligencias* meaning $POLICE-INVESTIGATION, as in the first example. On first glance, one might think that it would be sufficient to check for the appropriate conceptualization, namely, POLICE, appearing to the left of *realizar diligencias*. In other words, whenever POLICE is the ACTOR of *realizar diligencias*, the phrase means $POLICE-INVESTIGATION. However, this is not the case, as the following example illustrates:

Spanish: La reina Isabela va a visitar a la ciudad de Nueva York el lunes. La policía realiza diligencias para insurar su seguridad durante la visita.

English: Queen Elizabeth will visit New York city on Monday. The police are taking precautions to insure her safety during her visit.

In order to determine what representation of *realizar diligencias* is appropriate for a given sentence, other portions of the sentence must also be checked. To see which other parts of the sentence are relevant, consider the line of reasoning that a human reader might follow in order to infer that *realizar diligencias* means $POLICE-INVESTIGATION in the earlier example. First, since the prepositional phrase *para capturar* (in order to capture) follows *realizar diligencias*, a human reader knows that the action expressed by *realizar diligencias* somehow will lead to a capture, or that the capture is the goal of the *diligencias*. Capturing something involves getting control of it, and we know that before we can get control of an object, we have to know where it is and we have to find it. This indicates that perhaps *realizar diligencias* refers to some sort of finding. But when police are trying to find something in order to get control of it, they usually do a formal type of search, or an investigation. Therefore, we know that in this case, the word *diligencias* refers to a police investigation.

Requests that determine that *realizar diligencias* means $POLICE-INVESTIGATION in the example, then, must check for all of the conceptualizations mentioned in the above line of reasoning. First, the concept POLICE must appear before the verb. Next, a CAPTURE must appear after the verb, with the appropriate preposition (*in order to, so that,* etc.) appearing before it. Finally, the OBJECT of the CAPTURE must be a CRIMINAL. Thus, the requests which would be necessary to disambiguate *diligencias* to this meaning would be the following:

REQUEST 1: If a word meaning POLICE appears to the left of *diligencias,* then activate REQUEST 2.

REQUEST 2: If the preposition *para* (in order to) appears after *diligencias* and is followed by a word meaning $CAPTURE, then activate request 3.

REQUEST 3: If a word meaning CRIMINAL appears after the CAPTURE, then fill the OBJECT slot of the CAPTURE with CRIMINAL and build the representation $POLICE-INVESTIGATION for *diligencias.* Fill the ACTOR slot of the $POLICE-INVESTIGATION with POLICE.

This is a fairly complex set of requests just for the disambiguation of *realizar diligencias* to one of its meanings. But, even worse, it is so tailored to this particular example that it will not work for semantically similar sentences that are worded differently. For instance, consider the following sentence:

Spanish: Intensas diligencias por parte de la policía resultaron en la captura de un reo.

English: An intense police investigation resulted in the arrest of a criminal.

Here, the same line of reasoning applies as for the previous example. A human reader knows that *diligencias* means $POLICE-INVESTIGATION because it is being done by the police, in service of the capture of a criminal. However, these requests will not perform the disambiguation of *diligencias* in this sentence. Another set of requests would have to be written, looking for *por* (by) followed by a word meaning POLICE appearing after *diligencias,* then looking for the verb *resultar* (to result) followed by a word meaning CAPTURE, and finally looking for a word meaning CRIMINAL.

Judging from the number of requests needed to disambiguate *diligencias* in just these two examples, we can see that it is very difficult to use lexically based disambiguation rules for very vague words like *diligencias,* which have many possible meanings. First, the number of meanings of such words is very large. Second, even the number of rules for each possible meaning of a very vague word would have to be quite large, and each rule would have to be quite complex, owing to the number of possible items in the surrounding context that can play a role in the disambiguation of very vague words.

A DIFFERENT APPROACH TO WORD DISAMBIGUATION

This section discusses an approach to word disambiguation that uses much more general disambiguation rules, in conjunction with a hierarchically organized conceptual memory. Consider the line of inferencing I suggested a human reader might use in order to infer that *realizar diligencias* means $POLICE-INVESTI-GATION in the first example earlier. This line of reasoning consisted of several steps, each of which further limited the possible concepts to which realizar diligencias could refer. At first, *realizar diligencias* could have referred to any action. But then, since the *diligencias* were done in service of a CAPTURE, which is a type of GETTING-CONTROL, the action must be some sort of FIND because in order to get control of something, one must first find it. Thus, this step would enable a human reader to limit the action to which *realizar diligencias* referred to some sort of FIND. Next, since the police were the actors of this FIND and since police often perform investigations, which are a type of FIND, the FIND could be further refined, to a POLICE-INVESTIGATION. Thus, this chain of reasoning would allow a human reader to refine the original, vague conception of what action *realizar diligencias* referred to down to the more specific concept, POLICE-INVESTIGATION.

The disambiguation methods used in the MOPTRANS system parallel this line of inferencing, using general disambiguation rules that refine the representations of vague or general words. These representation refinements correspond to the steps in the line of inferencing mentioned earlier that limited further and further the possible concepts to which *realizar diligencias* could refer.

This general disambiguation method uses a hierarchically organized conceptual memory. The conceptual structures needed for the police investigations examples are the following:

GET = KNOW + FIND + GET-CONTROL

POLICE-CAPTURE = POLICE-INVESTIGATION + POLICE-SEARCH + ARREST

In this diagram, the dotted lines connecting the concepts ACTION, FIND, and so forth represent IS-A links. All of the concepts in this IS-A hierarchy have case frames specifying the prototypical fillers for various slots, such as ACTOR, OBJECT, and so forth. For example, the case frame for FIND indicates that its ACTOR should be a PERSON, its object should be a PHYSICAL OBJECT, and its RESULT should be a GET-CONTROL. The case frame for POLICE-SEARCH indicates that its ACTOR should be an AUTHORITY, its OBJECT should be a CRIMINAL, and its RESULT is an ARREST.

In addition to the hierarchical information, information is needed about stereotypical event sequences, similar to scripts (Schank & Abelson, 1977), and more recently MOPs (Schank, 1982). The two event sequences needed for this example are GET, which consists of the actions KNOW, FIND, and GET-CONTROL (note that this is the same event sequence that begins the named plan USE in Schank & Abelson, 1977); and POLICE-CAPTURE, which consists of a POLICE-INVESTIGATION, followed by a POLICE-SEARCH, and finally an ARREST.

With this hierarchical memory organization and stereotypical event sequence knowledge, very general rules can be used to perform the disambiguation of *realizar diligencias* along the same lines as a human reader would follow to infer the phrase's meaning. First, the word *capturar* refers to the concept GET-CONTROL. From the aforementioned event sequence GET, we know that GET-CONTROL is often preceded by the event FIND. Since the story says that some action, *diligencias,* precedes the GET-CONTROL, we can infer that the action is probably a FIND. This suggests the following general inference rule: If a scene of a script is mentioned in a story, then other scenes of the same script can be expected to be mentioned. Thus, if an abstraction of another scene of the script is mentioned, we can infer that the abstraction actually is the other scene. In more concrete terms, in this example, GET-CONTROL is a scene of the script GET. Another scene of GET is the scene FIND. *Realizar diligencias* refers to an abstraction of the concept FIND, namely, ACTION. Since GET-CONTROL was mentioned, indicating that other scenes of the script GET are likely to be encountered, we can infer that the ACTION is actually a FIND, since ACTION is an abstraction of FIND.

Put more precisely, this line of inferencing can be expressed in the following rules:

SCRIPT ACTIVATION RULE: If an action that is part of a stereotypical event sequence is activated, then activate the stereotypical event sequence and expect to find the other actions in that sequence.

EXPECTED EVENT SPECIALIZATION RULE: If a word refers to an action that is an abstraction of an expected action, and the slot-fillers of the action meet the prototypes of the slot-fillers of the more specific action, then change the representation of the word to the more specific expected action.

Next, consider how we can infer that the FIND is a $POLICE-INVESTIGA-TION. First, in the story the ACTOR of the FIND is the POLICE. One piece of knowledge that we have about POLICE is that often they are the ACTORs of $POLICE-INVESTIGATIONs, that being part of their job. Then, since the IS-A hierarchy tells us that $POLICE-INVESTIGATION is a refinement of the concept FIND, we can infer that in this story, the FIND is most likely a $POLICE-INVESTIGATION.

This suggests the following inference rule:

SLOT-FILLER SPECIALIZATION RULE: If a slot of concept A is filled by concept B, and B is the prototypical filler for that slot of concept C, and concept C IS-A concept A, then change the representation of concept A to concept C.

In this case, concept A is FIND, and concept B is the POLICE. The POLICE are the prototypical ACTORs of concept C, a $POLICE-INVESTIGATION. Because FIND is above $POLICE-INVESTIGATION in the IS-A hierarchy, we can conclude that FIND in this case refers to $POLICE-INVESTIGATION.

There are, then, three general inference rules—the script activation rule, the expected event specialization rule, and the slot-filler specialization rule—that can perform the disambiguation of *realizar dilgencias* in the previous examples. These rules require the organization of knowledge structures in a hierarchical fashion, so that they can use this hierarchy to guide the refinement of concepts. They also require the existence of event sequences (scripts) in memory, to provide expectations as to what actions are likely to occur together in stories.

Given these rules, the disambiguation of *realizar dilgencias* in the two police investigation examples would proceed as follows: first, a general representation would be built for *realizar dilgencias;* simply, the concept ACTION. Then, the ACTOR of ACTION would be filled in by an appropriate request (either one looking to the left of *realizar dilgencias* for its ACTOR, in the case of the first example, or one looking for the object of the preposition *por* in the case of the second example) with the concept AUTHORITY (the representation of *policia*). Next, the concept GET-CONTROL would be built from the word *captura*. This would also cause the event sequence GET to be activated, because of the script activation rule. This, in turn, would cause the concept ACTION to be changed to the concept FIND, owing to the expected event specialization rule above. Since the ACTOR slot of FIND is filled by AUTHORITY, and since the prototype of the ACTOR slot of POLICE-SEARCH is AUTHORITY, the concept FIND would be changed to be $POLICE-INVESTIGATION because of the slot-filler specialization rule above.

CONCLUSION

This chapter has presented three rather general inference rules—the script activation rule, the expected event specialization rule, and the slot-filler specialization rule—which can be used to disambiguate vague or general words. These rules draw on information from a hierarchically organized conceptual memory, which provides knowledge about abstractions of events and sequences of events.

This disambiguation method is in sharp contrast to the lexically based disambiguation methods that have predominated in previous conceptual parsers. In the lexically based method, at least one disambiguation rule is needed for each sense of an ambiguous word. Thus, using lexically based disambiguation rules to disambiguate very vague or general rules results in an explosion in the number of rules needed. On the other hand, the disambiguation method advocated here does not suffer from the same rule explosion, because only general inference rules are used to perform disambiguation.

In addition to the practical advantage of avoiding rule explosion, the psychological implications of disambiguation using general inference rules seem intuitively more plausible than the implications of the lexically based approach. The latter approach to disambiguation implies that all disambiguation knowledge is linguistic because it appears in the dictionary definitions of ambiguous words and therefore is not applicable to other cognitive tasks. However, intuitively it seems that much of the knowledge that enables people to disambiguate words would be applicable to other tasks. For example, in the Word Expert Parser, two of the rules appearing in the dictionary definition of *throw* were:

If the agent of *throw* is a person, then refine *throw* to PERSON-THROW.

If the object of PERSON-THROW is garbage, then refine PERSON-THROW to THROW-OUT-GARBAGE.

These rules should also be useful in a vision system, for example, observing someone throwing out garbage. If a vision system identified that a person was the agent of the action of throwing something, and if it also identified the object being thrown as garbage, we would want this system to be able to make the inference that the garbage was being disposed of, or thrown out, not just that the garbage was being transported from one place to another by means of throwing it. Therefore, we would like the same knowledge useful in word disambiguation to be available to a vision system also.

In the disambiguation method presented here, disambiguation knowledge is not stored in the dictionary entries of ambiguous words; instead, it is stored in terms of general inference rules and conceptual memory. This approach does not imply that disambiguation knowledge is exclusively linguistic and thus only applicable to linguistic tasks. On the contrary, it suggests that the majority of knowledge used in word disambiguation is not specifically linguistic, since it comes from conceptual memory. Thus, this approach suggests that much of the knowledge used to disambiguate words would also be applicable to other cognitive tasks.

ACKNOWLEDGMENTS

This research was supported in part by the Advanced Research Projects Agency of the Department of Defense and monitored by the Office of Naval Research under contract No. N00014-82K-0149.

REFERENCES

Birnbaum, L., & Selfridge, M. (1979, October). *Problems in conceptual analysis of natural language.* (Tech. Rep. 168). Yale University, Department of Computer Science.

Lebowitz, M. (1980, October). *Generalization and memory in an integrated understanding system* (Research Rep. No. 186). Unpublished doctoral dissertation, Yale University.

Lytinen, S., & Schank, R. C. (1982). Representation and translation. *Text, 2*(1/3), 83–112.

Riesbeck, C. K. (1975). Conceptual analysis. In R. C. Schank (Ed.), *Conceptual information processing.* Amsterdam: North Holland.

Riesback, C. K., & Schank, R. C. (1976). Comprehension by computer: Expectation-based analysis of sentences in context. In W. J. M. Levelt & G. B. Flores d'Arcais (Eds.), *Studies in the perception of language.* Chichester, England: Wiley.

Schank, R., & Abelson, R. (1977). *Scripts, plans, goals, and understanding.* Hillsdale, NJ: Lawrence Erlbaum Associates.

Schank, R. C. (1975). *Conceptual information processing.* Amsterdam: North Holland.

Schank, R. C. (1982). *Dynamic memory: A theory of learning in computers and people.* New York: Cambridge University Press.

Schank, R. C., Lebowitz, M., & Birnbaum, L. (1980). An integrated understander. *American Journal of Computational Linguistics, 6*(1), 13–30.

Small, S. (1980). *Word expert parsing: A theory of distributed word-based natural language understanding (TR-954).* Unpublished doctoral dissertation, University of Maryland.

13 Direct Memory Access Parsing

Christopher K. Riesbeck
Charles E. Martin
Department of Computer Science
Yale University

ABSTRACT

Direct Memory Access Parsing views conceptual language analysis as a problem of recognizing the structures in memory to which a text is referring, not as a problem of building a meaning structure for the text. That is, conceptual analysis is a memory search process very similar to other recently developed dynamic memory inference processes. Linguistic information in a DMAP parser is linked directly to concept nodes in memory, rather than to a separate parser lexicon.

PARSING INTO MEMORY

Claiming that even the most semantically oriented parsers of today are critically off the mark as cognitive models, we argue in this chapter for a radically new approach to the problem of natural language understanding.

Current parsers all share a common goal: to construct representations of the meanings of texts. In addition, some parsers are connected to a memory into which they place the meaning forms they build. This is the *Build and Store* model of understanding, where the *Store* is an important but optional component of the understanding process. This is the model that we claim is basically incorrect. Any system whose goal is to construct meaning representations for storage in memory is doing the wrong thing.

The proposed alternative model is just the opposite: Instead of building a structure and then finding a place for it in memory, the parser first finds the relevant place in memory and then records any differences between what the text says and what is already known. We will call this the *Recognize and Record* model.

One way to see the difference between the two kinds of models is to consider what kinds of sentences they are most appropriate for. The Build and Store model is most at home with sentences like "A boy kissed a girl." This is a classic example of an English sentence, with no connection to what the hearer knows beyond the ability to understand English. The primary task of a Build and Store model is to understand pieces of language put together in new ways. Less important is the ability to recognize that a phrase has been seen many times before or that it bears particular relevance to the hearer's personal experience or intentions.

A Recognize and Record model is best suited for texts like "Ready for lunch?" This is a canned phrase, of marginal grammaticality, referring to a specific upcoming event, probably uttered in a recurring context by the same speaker, at the same time of day, in the same place. The primary task of a Recognize and Record parser is to quickly connect such inputs to the hearer's own beliefs and goals. Less important is the ability to handle novel utterances, utterances unconnected to the things the hearer is most interested in.

Why propose Recognize and Record parsers if they have to be significantly extended to handle "A boy kissed a girl?" The productivity of language, that is, the ability to generate an infinite set of sentences from a finite grammar, is the keystone of modern linguistic theory. Why put this productive capacity on the back burner?—because we claim that the full productive nature of language (as opposed to the ability to understand minor variations) should not be our first concern in developing parsing systems. First, much of what we hear is highly familiar. This includes not only actual phrases, but conceptual combinations as well. We recognize invitations to dinner, excuses, greetings, and many other commonplaces. This special case nature of language has received far too little attention in AI (except for Becker, 1975). Second, the function of normal language use is to pass on information closely connected to our plans and interests. No one outside of language class says a sentence to someone just to see if he or she knows how to parse it.

AN EXAMPLE SYSTEM

Since virtually every modern parser is a Build and Store parser, there is no need to describe what it looks like. Most people, however, probably have little experience with Recognize and Record parsers. Fortunately, there is a classic language understanding system that is the inspiration for the model of parsing we are proposing: Quillian's (1969) Teachable Language Comprehender (TLC).

In TLC, English words point directly to *units* in a semantic memory. A unit has a pointer to a superset plus zero or more pointers to properties. A *property*

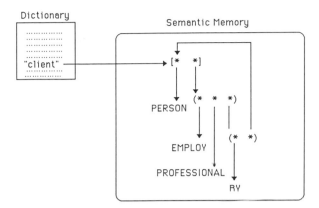

FIG. 13.1.   An example of TLC units (Quillian, 1969, p. 13).

has an *attribute,* a *value,* and zero or more sub-properties. Figure 13.1 shows a simple example. The word *client* points to a unit that says that a client is a PERSON, with one property. That property is EMPLOY PROFESSIONAL, with one subproperty, namely, that the professional is employed by the client.

When TLC reads an English phrase, it places markers on the units referred to. For example, when it reads *lawyer's client,* it puts markers on LAWYER and CLIENT. Then TLC spreads the markers from the marked units to their supersets and properties, then to those items supersets and properties, and so on until the markers meet somewhere in memory. With *lawyer's client,* CLIENT marks the property EMPLOY PROFESSIONAL, LAWYER marks the superset PROFES-SIONAL, and TLC finds the intersection at EMPLOY.

An intersection is only a candidate connection. To determine if a connection is actually expressed by the input, TLC uses *form tests.* Form tests are stored with memory units and look for certain features in the input. When a unit is a candidate connection, its form tests are applied to the input. If the input passes one of the tests, then the connection is accepted as a meaning of the input.

For example, EMPLOY has a form test that says that the word referring to the property value must have an *'s* attached and must be followed immediately by the word referring to the source word. In this case, *lawyer* refers to PROFES-SIONAL and *client* is the source of the marker that went to EMPLOY, so the form test checks for *lawyer's client* in the input.

TLC was far more semantically driven than any natural language analyzer that followed it. In TLC, semantic connections came first, and then syntactic filters were applied. The hope was that TLC could be "taught" new form tests in a fairly direct way. For example, if TLC had no form test under EMPLOY and it parsed *lawyer's client,* it would still find the connection through EMPLOY, but now no form test would verify the connection. At that point, TLC could ask a human user whether *lawyer's client* was a way to say *the person who employs a lawyer*. If the answer was yes, TLC could then add the form test to EMPLOY for future use.

Quillian (1969) made the following observations about TLC:

> TLC draws information from its memory to produce a representation of a piece of input text that is:
> 1. Encoded in the regular memory format.
> 2. Much richer and less ambiguous than the input text itself.
> 3. A highly intraconnected structure with the various concepts mentioned in the text linked in ways supplied from a memory of facts about the world.
> 4. Linked to the permanent memory by many pointers to established concepts (although its creation in no way changes the permanent memory, except for the addition of temporary tags used by the intersection routines).(p. 29)

TLC's model of memory became the foundation of semantic net research, both psychological (Collins & Quillian, 1969) and computational (Fahlman, 1979). However, until recently, there appears to have been no serious follow-up work on TLC's model of language analysis, even by Quillian. We would like to rectify this situation with a TLC-inspired parser called the Direct Memory Access Parser (DMAP-0).

DMAP-0 differs from TLC in many ways. The memory is organized quite differently, and DMAP-0's form tests are intimately connected with the marker passing algorithm. In exchange for the ability to parse more complex sentences directly into our memory model, we have given up, but only for the moment, the TLC ability to find connections in a purely semantic way.

THE DIRECT MEMORY ACCESS PARSER

Basics of DMAP[1]

DMAP has two basic elements: (a) an episodic memory, and (b) an activation-based recognition process.

Episodic Memory.   The episodic memory contains the elements to which input text elements refer. An episodic memory is different from a semantic memory in that the very act of using an episodic memory to understand an input is itself an episode to add to the memory. Hence, an episodic memory is a

---

[1]DMAP-0 is a very tentative step, and the description here should be taken primarily as an example of the kind of parser that fits well with the basic idea of "Recognize and Record" parsing. There are essential understanding tasks DMAP-0 cannot do. We have already made substantial changes to our algorithms and expect to make many more.

dynamic memory (Schank, 1982). A dynamic memory never reads a story or solves a problem without being permanently changed by the process.

The idea of dynamic memory raises serious problems for Build and Store parsers, especially those that keep knowledge structure building information in special lexicons, as in Riesbeck (1978), and Birnbaum and Selfridge (1981). If the memory changes, the lexicon has to be changed too; otherwise the parser will produce structures that "don't fit" in the changed memory. This could require fairly complex routines for updating the lexicon everytime the memory changes.

DMA parsing avoids all this by not having a separate lexicon and by not building intermediate meaning structures.

The MOP Model of Memory.   Although DMAP-0 has no processes that change memory (see later discussion of instantiation), the memory in DMAP-0 is based on the MOP (Memory Organization Packets) model of dynamic memory (Kolodner, 1984; Lebowitz, 1980; Schank, 1982) in preparation for the addition of such processes. For the purposes of this paper, all that needs to be said about MOPs is that they organize knowledge about event sequences into two hierarchies: (a) an abstraction hierarchy, and (b) a packaging hierarchy.

In the abstraction hierarchy, one MOP is above another MOP when the first MOP is an abstract version of the second MOP, that is, the second MOP is a specialization of the first MOP. For example, "a professional office visit" is a MOP that is an abstraction of the MOP "visit a doctor." A MOP can be an abstraction of more than one MOP and can be abstracted by more than one MOP.

In the packaging hierarchy, one MOP is above another MOP when the first MOP has the second MOP as a component. Packaging relationships are labelled with *roles*. MOP X has a role R filled by MOP Y. For example, "a professional office visit" has the role "waiting period," filled by the MOP "sit in waiting room." A MOP can package more than one MOP and can be packaged by more than one MOP. The same MOP may in fact be packaged more than once by some other MOP, as long as the roles are different. For example, "economic event" is packaged by "economic causation" twice, once to fill the "antecedent" role and once to fill the "consequent" role.

The abstraction and packaging relationships organize event types the same way that IS-A and PART-OF links organize objects (Fahlman, 1979).

DMAP-0 Extensions to the MOP Model.   DMAP-0 adds the following to the basic MOP model of memory:

- concept patterns, which participate in the abstraction hierarchy, and package together a root concept with a concept sequence
- concept to concept pattern links from root concepts to the concept patterns they belong to

• concept refinement or cref links that cross-connect the abstraction and packaging hierarchies

DMAP-0 is part of a larger project invovled in economic reasoning (Riesbeck, 1984), so the nodes in DMAP-0's memory correspond to conceptual items such as: [interest rates],[2] [economic variable], and [causal argument].

Concept Patterns.   Concept patterns encode DMAP-0's lexical knowledge. They cross TLC's form tests with a phrasal lexicon notion (Becker, 1975; Wilensky, 1981). A concept pattern associates a *root concept* with a *concept sequence*. A concept sequence can be a simple list of words, as in the pattern that associates the root concept [interest rates] with the sequence {"interest", "rates"}. This says that the phrase "interest rates" is one way to refer to the concept of interest rates.

A concept sequence can be more complex, specifying how various pieces of the root concept are filled in by concepts in the input, as in the concept pattern that associates the root concept MTRANS-EVENT[3] with the sequence {*actor*, MTRANS-word, *object*}. This sequence says to look in the text for an appropriate *actor* of an MTRANS event, followed by an MTRANS-word, for example, "say", "tell", "claim", or even ":", as in "Speaker: . . ," followed by an appropriate *object* of an MTRANS.

Some examples of other concept patterns in DMAP-0 are:

CONCEPT SEQUENCE	ROOT CONCEPT
{"interest", "rates"}	[interest rates]
{"will"}	[future]
{"rise"}	[state change up]
{*economic-variable, behavior*}	[economic state change]
{*time, event*}	[economic prediction]

Marker Passing.   The basic process in DMAP-0 is marker passing, using two kinds of markers: (a) activation markers, or *A-markers;* and (b) prediction markers, or *P-markers*. The *parse* or interpretation of a text is the set of memory nodes left with A-markers at the end of the text.

A DMAP-0 marker is a structured object, containing information about the source of the marker:

---

[2]The following notational conventions are used in the text that follows: "Item" is a word or the directly equivalent lexical concept node for that word; [item] is a concept node; *item* is a role name; {item, item, . . .} is a concept sequence; and <[item]> and <[item], *item*> are A- and P-markers (see Marker Passing).

[3]MTRANS is the primitive concept in Conceptual Dependency (Schank, 1973) representing a movement of information.

- An A-marker is a 1-tuple of the form <source node>. A node [N] would pass A-markers of the form <[N]> to its abstractions.
- A P-marker is a 2-tuple of the form <source node, packaging role>. If node [N] had a role *r,* it would pass a P-marker of the form <[N],*r*> to the node that filled *r.*

A-markers are passed in three situations:

A-1. When a word is read, an A-marker is sent to the associated lexical node.
A-2. When a node receives an A marker, it sends A-markers to its abstractions.
A-3. When the last element of a concept pattern sequence receives an A-marker, an A-marker is sent to the associated root concept.

All P-markers in DMAP-0 originate from concept pattern sequences. P-markers are passed around in three situations:

P-1. When a node with a P-marker P receives an A-marker, a cref-link (see Section 3.1.6) is used to send a P-marker P' to the source of the A-marker. The source of P' is a specialization of the source of P.
P-2. When a node with a P[marker receives an A-marker, a P-marker is sent to the next element of the associated concept sequence (if the sequence is done, Rule A-3 is triggered).
P-3. At startup time, the first elements of concept pattern sequences are given P-markers.

There are also several marker removal rules:

R-1. Any activation marker that does not meet a prediction is removed.
R-2. Any prediction that meets an activation is removed. Also removed are sibling predictions, i.e., if A is activated and the prediction had been for "A or B or C", then B and C are removed also.
R-3. Predictions passed down cref-links are removed from the higher-level nodes.

Concept Refinement Links.   Fast concept refinement is a primary goal of DMAP-0. We want the parser to find the *most specific node that packages the greatest number of activated nodes,* that is, we want to go down the abstraction hierarchy, but up the packaging hierarchy. But our default links go in the opposite direction, that is, up the abstraction hierarchy and down the packaging hierarchy, because:

- linking a node to its abstraction fits the intuition that it is easier to determine

the supertype of something ("What kind of thing is a dog?") than to determine its subtypes ("Name all the kinds of dogs you know of").
- linking a node to its components fits the intuition that it is easier to determine the parts of something ("What do you do when you buy a ticket?") than to determine when it is used ("Name all the times you buy a ticket").

To go against this "current" of information flow, DMAP-0 uses two techniques:

- the A- and P-markers contain pointers back to their source nodes, which the activation and prediction rules above can use, and
- the cref-links under certain nodes go up the packaging and down the abstraction hierarchy in one step.

In DMAP-0, a node [N1] is cref-linked to [N2], if [N2] packages a specialization of [N1]. For example, in an object hierarchy, there would be a cref link from [animal foot] to [horse], because [horse] packages [hoof], which is a specialization of [animal foot] (see Fig. 13.2).

In a system such as DMAP-0, where a node may have multiple abstractions, and may be packaged more than once by the same node via different roles, a node may have many different cref links. For example, [economic event] is cref-linked to [interest rates rising causes . . .], because the latter concept packages a specialization of [economic event] via the *antecedent* role. [economic event] is also cref-linked to [. . . causes unemployment decrease] because this latter node packages a specialization of [economic event] via the *consequent* role (see Fig. 13.3.

Therefore, the cref links attached to a node [N1] are indexed by three things:

- a node [N3] that is a specialization [N1],

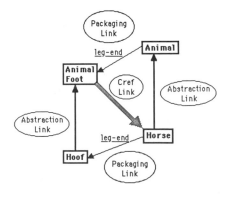

FIG. 13.2.   An example of a concept refinement link in an object hierarchy.

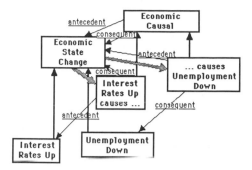

FIG. 13.3.   An example of multiple concept refinement links. Thick vertical lines are abstraction links. Thin diagonal labelled lines are packaging links. Broad textured lines are cref links. Bold-faced words in boxes are concept nodes. Underlined words are role names.

- a role r, and
- a node [N4] that packages [N1] via r.

These three items determine a cref-link from [N1] to [N2], which packages [N3] via r. Note that there may be more than one cref-link with the same set of indices. For example, [animal], *leg-end* and [hoof] would cref-link from [animal foot] to horse, deer, and any other animal with hooves.

When the node [N1] has a P-marker $<[N4],r>$ and an A-marker $<[N3]>$, it uses the information in these markers to index the cref link to [N2]. Then a P-marker $<[N2],r>$ is sent to [N3] and the P-marker on [N1] is removed. In other words, [N4] predicting [N1] is refined to [N2] predicting [N3]. The flow of concept refinement is down the abstraction hierarchy.[4]

A Sample Run.   The DMAP project is part of a larger project investigating knowledge reorganization and learning in the domain of everyday economic reasoning (Riesbeck, 1984). Hence, our interest is not in finding texts best suited to the parser, but in fitting the parser to the texts we have to deal with, namely, real articles from newspapers and magazines.

There is a mismatch, however, between the DMAP approach and the learning project. The learning project is most concerned with reading and understanding new arguments; DMA parsing is most concerned with recognizing old ones. Eventually a DMA parser has to instantiate modified versions of old memories when parsing novel inputs, but the first development goal in DMAP research is pure recognition.

In reconciling this difference in goals, we've reoriented the learning project in

---

[4]MOPTRANS, a "Build and Store" parser (Lytinen, 1984), has a very similar rule, called slot-filler specialization.

what we think is a much more promising direction. The original system would parse the text into small bits, such as "high interest rates limit growth; low growth raises prices," and then try to piece things together. The new system will have "preloaded" in the memory the conceptual representations of various arguments, including information such as who gave the argument, which other ones it supports or contradicts, and so on. The goal of the parser when reading a text with an argument is to find the most relevant existing arguments. Either the new argument will be seen as just another instance of an old one, or it should be entered as a variation of an existing one. The goal of the learning module then becomes to modify existing arguments to incorporate new ones.

The marker passing algorithm described earlier is applied to a memory containing about 40 concept nodes, connected by abstraction, packaging, cross refinement, and concept sequence links. The memory includes a preloaded, preanalyzed representation of the following argument:

Milton Friedman: Interest rates will rise as an inevitable consequence of the monetary explosion. (*The New York Times,* August 4, 1984)

In the memory, this becomes two major structures:

1. Milton Friedman predicts interest rates will rise, which is an instance of an economist making a prediction, and

2. he says that the rise will be caused by the monetary explosion, which is an instance of an economist making an argument.[5]

The portion of memory shown in Fig. 13.4 is for Milton Friedman's prediction that interest rates will rise. The contents of Fig. 13.4 will be enough to follow the trace of the parser in the next section. Concept sequences are inherited in the abstraction hierarchy, so, for example, [Milton Friedman's name] inherits the concept sequence {*first, last*} from [Name].

A Trace of the Parse.   We will now summarize the sequence of marker passing that occurs when "Milton Friedman: Interest rates will rise . . ." is parsed. Our summary follows the sequence that occurs in DMAP-0, using the rules described earlier (Marker Passing). The terms "activate" and "predict" are shorthand for "pass an activation marker to" and "pass a prediction marker to," respectively. Since all predictions in DMAP-0 come from concept sequences, when we say "concept [N1] predicts concept [N2]," we mean that [N1] is a root in a concept pattern, and the concept sequence in that pattern has some element (presumably some role specifier) that predicts [N2].

First, applying Rule P-3 to Fig. 13.4 places prediction markers on the concepts [first name], [name], [actor], [future], and [economic variable], and on the

---

[5]Another item that should be added to the memory is that Friedman claims that there is a monetary explosion.

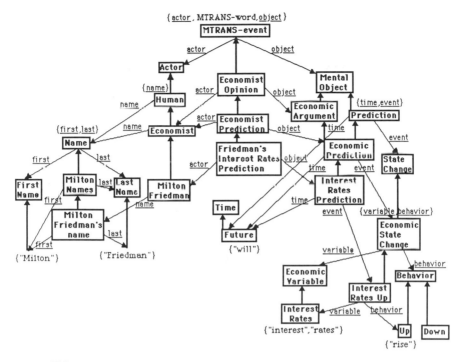

FIG. 13.4. A portion of DMAP-0's Memory Thick vertical lines are abstraction links. Thin diagonal lines are packaging links. Bold-faced words in boxes are concept nodes. Underlined words are role names. Quoted words are lexical items. {item, . . .}'s are concept sequences.

lexical items "Milton," "Friedman," "interest," "will," "rise," because they are the first elements of concept sequences. Note that the word "rates" doesn't get a P-marker because it is not the first element of any concept sequence. DMAP-0 recognizes "rates" only in the context "interest rates," much as some people recognize "lieu" only in the context "in lieu of."

Reading *Milton* activates the "Milton" lexical node (Rule A-1). Activation is passed up to [first name] (Rule A-2), which was predicted by [name]. Using concept refinement, [Milton names] now predicts "Milton" (Rule P-1). Since "Milton" is already activated, the next element of the sequence, [last name], is predicted (Rule P-2).

Reading "Friedman" activates "Friedman" (Rule A-1). Activation is passed up to [last name] (Rule A-2), which was predicted by [Milton names]. Using concept refinement, [Milton Friedman name] now predicts "Friedman" (Rule P-1). Since this is already activated and is the last element of the sequence, [Milton Friedman name] is activated (Rule A-3). The activation is passed to [name] (Rule A-2), which was predicted by [human]. After concept refinement,

[Milton Friedman] now predicts [Milton Friedman name] (Rule P-1). [Milton Friedman name] is already activated and is the only element in the concept sequence for [Milton Friedman], so [Milton Friedman] is activated (Rule A-3). This activation is passed to [economist], [human], and [actor] (Rule A-2). [actor] was predicted by MTRANS-EVENT, that is, by the sequence {*actor*, MTRANS-WORD, *object*}. After several applications of concept refinement, starting with MTRANS-EVENT, [Friedman's interest rates prediction] now predicts [Milton Friedman] (Rule P-1). [Milton Friedman] is already activated, so MTRANS-WORD is predicted (Rule P-2).

Reading ":" activates MTRANS-WORD (Rule A-1), so the concept sequence now predicts [Interest rates prediction] (Rule P-2).

Reading "interest" activates the "interest" node (Rule A-1), which was predicted by the concept sequence for [interest rates]. "Rates" is now predicted (Rule P-2).

Reading "rates" activates the "rates" node (Rule A-1), completing the concept sequence and activating [interest rates] (Rule A-3). Activation goes up to [economic variable] (Rule A-2), which was predicted by [economic state], i.e., by {*variable, behavior*}. Using concept refinement, [interest rates up] now predicts [interest rates] (Rule P-1), which is already activated, so [up] is predicted (Rule P-2).

Reading "will" activates [future] (Rule A-1), which was predicted by [prediction], i.e., by {*time, event*}. Since [future] is already activated, [state change] is predicted (Rule P-2).

Reading "rise" activates [up] node (Rule A-1), which was predicted by the sequence for [interest rates up]. This sequence is completed, so [interest rates up] is activated (Rule A-3), activating [economic state change] and [state change] (Rule A-2). [state change] was predicted by [prediction]. Using concept refinement, [interest rates prediction] now predicts [interest rates up] (Rule P-1). [interest rates up] is already activated, the sequence is complete, and so [interest rates prediction] is activated (Rule A-3). This was predicted by [Friedman's interest rates prediction], the sequence is complete, so [Friedman's interest rates prediction] is activated (Rule A-3), sending activation to [economist prediction], [economist opinion] and MTRANS-EVENT (Rule A-2).

If the sentence ended here, this activated node would be the "parse" of the sentence. If the sentence continued to link the interest rate rise with monetary expansion, then the causal node would be activated as well, yielding two elements to the "parse." In any case, the parse is eventually the activation of the node or nodes indicating a *recognition* of a previously stored Friedman argument.

Indexing Partial Information.   What happens if DMAP-0 parses "An economist says that interest rates will rise?" A Build and Store parser would build a new structure, representing the statement that an economist has predicted a rise in interest rates. DMAP-0, however, using the rules and memory described earlier, will recognize this as Friedman's prediction. The parse of the sentence, the final state of memory, will be the same as it was when the example in the previous section was parsed.

Is this a bug or a feature? We think it is a feature. If some argument is identified with someone, then hearing that argument should be sufficient to retrieve the name of the person who gives that argument. DMAP-0 overdoes it in assuming that the person giving the argument is in fact Milton Friedman, but DMAP-0 is doing the right thing to access Milton Friedman's relationship to this argument.

RECENT DMAP RESEARCH

DMA parsing may be an idea whose time has returned. A number of projects have started with a marked similarity to the foregoing ideas, though their inspirations do not follow so directly from Quillian (1969).

One source of interest arises from lexical access studies suggesting that all senses of ambiguous words (or at least all common senses) are briefly considered and then, in context, are quickly resolved. Granger, Eiselt, and Holbrook (1984) are attempting to merge integrated parsing models (Dyer, 1983; Lebowitz, 1980) with psychological lexical access data (Swinney & Hakes, 1976). Their research on ATLAST (A Three-level Language Analysis SysTem) is focusing primarily on problems of disambiguation. Their parser is broken into three parallel processes:

1. the Lexical Capsulizer forms syntactic groups for the Filter and triggers inferences in the Proposer
2. the Proposer makes connecting inferences using a form of spreading activation
3. the Filter inhibits unpromising inference chains in the Proposer

In TLC terms, the initial connections are made by the Proposer, and the form tests are made by the Filter, using information passed to it by the Capsulizer.

Another DMAP project is Hahn and Reimer's (1983) TOPIC (Text Oriented Procedures for Information management and Condensation of expository texts). TOPIC uses spreading activation to connect concepts together. One (of many) problems to be overcome is to handle correctly the cohesive effects of anaphoric references. For example, in the text sequence:

. . . provided by *micros*. Nevertheless, these *machines* . . .

the anaphoric "machines" should really increase the activation level for "micros." To do this, as well as other tasks, Hahn and Reimer use a variant of word-experts (Small, 1980) to correct activation levels in various circumstances. Specifically, word-expert parsing is used to: fix incorrect activations; take into account linguistic contiguity relations; and provide indicators of text constituents.

A third project with similar characteristics is Charniak's (1985)—not to be confused with the earlier project (Hirst & Charniak, 1982). Like DMAP, Charniak's model is explicitly inspired by Quillian's TLC. The marker passer in Charniak's parser searches a frame-based memory for possible interpretations of texts. Syntactic and inferential means are used to filter out the implausible paths. The parser produces a logical form, so the system is a "Build and Store" model.[6]

DMAP is NOT Disambiguation with Marker Passing

Recently, there has been a fair amount of interest in using spreading activation or marker passing to attack the problem of disambiguation (Hirst & Charniak, 1982, Waltz & Pollack, 1984). The idea is this: When presented with a sentence with several ambiguous words, such as "The plane was by the terminal," the parser finds plausible word senses by spreading markers from all possible senses and seeing where intersections occur. Thus "plane" might mean "airplane," "carpenter's plane" or "Euclidean plane," while "terminal" might mean "computer terminal" or "airplane terminal." Spreading markers from "airplane" and "airplane terminal" would meet, resolving the ambiguity, before markers from the other senses found each other. There are many unsolved problems with this approach, including the basic problem of guaranteeing that the right markers meet first.

DMAP is definitely not disambiguation with marker passing. In DMAP, marker passing is not an appendage to a standard parser. Marker passing *IS* the parsing process. Marker passing is not being done to find the (shortest, strongest, whatever) path between two nodes; it is being used to find the most specific organizing structure in memory. "Airplane" and "airplane terminal" would be connected if a schema could be found that put airplanes by airplane terminals.

The Connectionist work (Feldman & Ballard, 1982) is also currently focusing on the disambiguation problem (Cottrell, 1984), though here it is intended that eventually all aspects of parsing will be included in the same spreading activation framework. The Connectionist project is much more difficult, since they are deliberately limiting the allowable set of mechanisms. They do not have access to the kinds of structured markers we are quite willing to invoke.

---

[6]Charniak believes that the distinction between Build and Store and Recognize and Record is no more than an implementation detail (personal communication).

PROBLEMS

There are many problems to be solved, both with DMAP-0 and with this approach in general. Most of these problems are well known to researchers into spreading activation and marker passing models.

Exploiting Semantic Connections

DMAP-0 integrates language knowledge into memory with its concept pattern sequences. They are the primary source of marker passing control information and do a good job of directing traffic in the system.

The problem is that the concept sequences are currently the only source of marker passing control in DMAP-0. Unlike TLC, DMAP-0 does not take arbitrary sequences of concept nodes and find connections between them. As a result, DMAP-0 cannot do something we think is very important for it to do, namely, recognize conceptual structures given a few scattered key clues. DMAP-0 recognizes concept sequences, not concept structures.

Individuation

A standard problem in spreading activation work is dealing with texts that mention two instances of the same object. If "two men meet a third," how should the parser distinguish the multiple activations of the node man? DMAP-0 has to deal with this problem because so many important nodes, such as [economic state change], are referred to many times in any text. DMAP-0 has two solutions:

1. It uses very short-lived activation markers, kept around just long enough to verify predictions. A second or third activation of a node will not encounter prior activations.

2. It has concept structures and sequences that package distinct references to the same concept nodes via different roles. For example, the structure and sequence for a positive feedback loop argument would specify an economic state change, followed by other economic state changes, ending with another reference to the first state change. During parsing, this structure and sequence determines whether a state change in the text is the same as or different from a previously mentioned one.

Instantiation

Activation does not add to memory, it only uses memory. Activations disappear and new ones come in. Somehow, records have to be made of what was activated. These records have to be normal memory structures, because the whole point of this approach is to parse a text once, save it and then, later, recognize through activation references to it by another text.

DMAP-0 has no instantiation facility. This is another serious lack.

Richness of Memory Structure

It is our belief that other attempts to parse by marker passing or spreading activation have used far too sparse and simplistic a model of memory. Besides using static nets that cannot record new events, the nets have usually represented only the domain of discourse itself, economics in our case. Memory has to have much more. When I read an economic argument, I am aware not only of the economic elements, but of the structure of the argument, the apparent expertise of the writer, the political stance implied by certain arguments, the publication in which the argument appears, the arguments which have appeared before on the same topic, how controversial the issue is, and so on.

DMAP-0 has only a cursory knowledge of argument structure.

CONCLUSIONS

Many years ago, Schank (1973) criticized syntactic analyses of sentences as placing too little emphasis on the obvious differences between a sentence such as "John's can of beans was edible" and "John's love of Mary was harmful." Such a criticism does not argue against syntactic structures per se, but it does argue that the real action lies elsewhere.

We would like to make the same kind of criticism of conceptual analysers. There are obvious differences in how readers understood the text "Mr. Reagan said, 'Yes, I have no plans for a tax increase' " when it appeared several months before the 1984 presidential elections and in how readers understand "John said, 'Yes, I have no plans for a picnic' " when it appears in a linguistics article. It is immediately recognized that the first sentence has to do with politics, elections, possible tax hikes, and so on. It is also immediately recognized that the second sentence has nothing to do with picnics, but with syntactic structures, possible ambiguities, linguistic argument style, and so on. A Build and Store conceptual analyzer would not see any significant difference between these two sentences until the Store operation occurred. Just as Schank (1973) felt that a can of beans differs in important ways from love of another, so we feel that there is an important difference in the understanding of a text that is about something, as opposed to a text that is simply good English.

We have presented arguments for the Recognize and Record model of parsing, which views parsing as primarily a problem of recognizing what nodes in memory a text is referring to, not as a problem of building a meaning structure for the text. The Direct Memory Access Parser DMAP-0 is an example of such a parser. Inspired by Quillian's Teachable Language Comprehender, DMAP-0 uses marker passing to recognize economic arguments.

Our hope is that, even on a serial machine, a DMA parser will be fast, because it builds smaller and fewer intermediate structures, and robust, because, in a reasonable memory, it should always find some node at some level of abstraction to handle the input text, even if only to represent "This text appears to be about things I don't understand."

DMAP-0 leaves unsolved many serious problems, especially the problem of how to remember what has been parsed, but it is a foundation on which we plan to do a great deal of further experiments.

ACKNOWLEDGMENTS

This work was funded in part by the Air Force Office of Scientific Research under contract F49620-82-K-0010.

REFERENCES

Becker, J. D. (1975). The phrasal lexicon. In R. C. Schank & B. L. Nash-Webber (Eds.), *Theoretical Issues in Natural Language Processing* (pp. 60–63). Cambridge, MA.

Birnbaum, L., & Selfridge, M. (1981). Conceptual analysis of natural language. In R. C. Schank & C. K. Riesbeck (Eds.), *Inside computer understanding*. Hillsdale, NJ: Lawrence Erlbaum Associates.

Charniak, E. (1985). *A single-semantic-process theory of parsing*. Unpublished manuscript.

Collins, A., & Quillian, M. R. (1969). Retrieval time from semantic memory. *Journal of Verbal Learning and Verbal Behavior, 9*, 432–438.

Cottrell, G. W. (1984). A model of lexical access of ambiguous words. *Proceedings of the National Conference on Artificial Intelligence* (pp. 61–67). Austin, TX.

Dyer, M. G. (1983). *In-depth understanding*. Cambridge, MA: MIT Press.

Fahlman, S. E. (1979). *NETL: A system for representing and using real-world knowledge*. Cambridge, MA: MIT Press.

Feldman, J. A., & Ballard, D. (1982). Connectionist models and their properties. *Cognitive Science, 6*(3), 205–254.

Granger, R. H., Eiselt, K. P., & Holbrook, J. K. (1984). The parallel organization of lexical, syntactic, and pragmatic inference processes. *Proceedings of the First Annual Workshop on Theoretical Issues in Conceptual Information Processing, 97–106*, Atlanta, GA.

Hahn, U., & Reimer, U. (1983, November). *Word expert parsing: An approach to text parsing with a distributed lexical grammar*. Bericht TOPIC 6/83, Universitat Konstanz.

Hirst, G., & Charniak, E. (1982). Word sense and case slot disambiguation. *Proceedings of the National Conference on Artificial Intelligence* (pp. 95–98). Pittsburgh, PA.

Kolodner, J. L. (1984). *Retrieval and organizational strategies in conceptual memory*. Hillsdale, NJ: Lawrence Erlbaum Associates.

Lebowitz, M. (1980, October). *Generalization and memory in an integrated understanding system* (Research Rep. No. 186). Unpublished docotral dissertation, Yale University.

Lytinen, S. (1984, November). *The organization of knowledge in a multi-lingual, integrated parser* (Research Rep. No. 340). Unpublished doctoral dissertation, Yale University.

Quillian, M. R. (1969). *The teachable language comprehender* (BBN Scientific Report 10). Cambridge MA: Bolt Beranek & Newman.

Riesbeck, C. K. (1978). An expectation-driven production system for natural language understanding. In D. A. Waterman & F. Hayes-Roth (Eds.), *Pattern-directed inference systems.* New York: Academic Press.

Riesbeck, C. K. (1984). Knowledge reorganization and reasoning style. *International Journal of Man-Machine Studies, 20,* 45–61.

Schank, R. C. (1973). Identification of conceptualizations underlying natural language. In R. C. Schank & K. M. Colby (Eds.), *Computer models of thought and language.* San Francisco: W. H. Freeman.

Schank, R. C. (1982). *Dynamic memory: A theory of learning in computers and people.* New York: Cambridge University Press.

Small, S. (1980, September). *Word expert parsing: A theory of distributed word-based natural language understanding.*(TR-954). Unpublished doctoral dissertation, University of Maryland.

Swinney, D. A., & Hakes, D. T. (1976). Effects of prior context upon lexical access during sentence comprehension. *Journal of Verbal Learning and Verbal Behavior, 15,* 681–689.

Waltz, D. L., & Pollack, J. B. (1984). Phenomenologically plausible parsing. In *Proceedings of the National Conference on Artificial Intelligence* (pp. 335–339), Austin, TX.

Wilensky, R. (1981). A knowledge-based approach to language processing. In *Proceedings of the Seventh International Joint Conference on Artificial Intelligence,* 25–30.

14

Parsing with Parallelism: A Spreading-Activation Model of Inference Processing During Text Understanding

Richard H. Granger
Kurt P. Eiselt
Jennifer K. Holbrook
Irvine Computational Intelligence Project
University of California, Irvine

ABSTRACT

The past decade of research in natural language processing has universally recognized that because natural language input is almost always ambiguous with respect to its pragmatic implications, its syntactic parse, and even its lexical analysis, that is, choice of correct word-sense for an ambiguous word, processing natural language input requires decisions about word meanings, syntactic structure, and pragmatic inferences. The lexical, syntactic, and pragmatic levels of inferencing are not as disparate as they have often been treated in both psychological and artificial intelligence research. In fact, these three levels of analysis interact to form a joint interpretation of text.

ATLAST (A Three-level Language Analysis SysTem) is an implemented integration of human language understanding at the lexical, the syntactic, and the pragmatic levels. For psychological validity, ATLAST is based on results of experiments with human subjects. The ATLAST model uses a new architecture which was developed to incorporate three features: *spreading activation memory, two-stage syntactic analysis*, and *parallel processing of syntax and semantics*. It is also a new framework within which to interpret and tackle unsolved problems through implementation and experimentation.

INTRODUCTION

The past decade of research in natural language processing has universally recognized that because natural language input is almost always ambiguous with respect to its pragmatic implications, its syntactic parse, and even its lexical analysis (i.e., choice of correct meaning, or word-sense, for an ambiguous word), processing natural language input requires decisions about word meanings, syntactic structure, and pragmatic inferences. The lexical, syntactic, and pragmatic levels of inferencing are not as disparate as they have often been treated in both psychological and artificial intelligence research. Furthermore, these three levels of analysis interact to form an interpretation of text. For example, the choice of a word-sense affects subsequent pragmatic inference decisions or syntactic structure decisions.

ATLAST (A Three-level Language Analysis SysTem) is a computer model of how humans parse and interpret text. For psychological validity, ATLAST is based on results of experiments with human subjects. ATLAST is also an implemented integration of language understanding at the lexical, syntactic, and pragmatic levels. It uses a new architecture which consists of three processes, developed to incorporate three features: *spreading activation memory, two-stage syntactic analysis,* and *parallel processing of syntax and semantics.* Each of the processes is involved in all levels of text interpretation. The new architecture divides the abilities of the three processes in such a way that ATLAST not only processes texts that people understand, but has difficulty with texts that cause human readers difficulty. The model employs the results of studies of many inference phenomena from several different fields of research. This approach helps solve many of the problems associated with inference decisions at all levels of processing. It is also a new framework within which to interpret and tackle unsolved problems through implementation and psychological experimentation.

BACKGROUND

Our Previous Work, Briefly

The ATLAST model is a descendant of our earlier work on pragmatic ambiguity. We had worked on models that could supplant erroneous inferences with correct ones, and models which could come up with several different plausible interpretations of text events based on different pieces of world knowledge (Granger, 1980; Granger, 1981; Granger, Eiselt, & Holbrook, 1983; Schulenburg, 1982). As we worked on these models, we observed that the different levels of inferencing have much in common. Many pragmatic inferences are triggered by individual words, which reinforced our belief in a close relationship between the lexical and pragmatic levels. For instance, consider the following examples of ambiguity at the lexical level:

[1] The CIA called in an inspector to check for bugs. The secretaries had reported seeing roaches.
[2] The CIA called in an inspector to check for bugs. The secretaries had reported seeing microphones.

The word *bugs* is ambiguous in both texts until the second sentence, yet the first sentence of each text implies an unambiguous reading. In text [1], the "spy" meaning of *bugs* initially appears to be more appropriate than the "insect" meaning. In text [2], both sentences suggest the "spy" reading. In a reading of these texts, the *pragmatic* inferences drawn from the first sentence are based on the *lexical* inferences made originally. The interpretation of the stories' events thus depend on which meaning of the word is selected.

Lexical Access

Because of the interdependence between inference levels, theories about pragmatic inference mechanisms must include theories about *lexical access* processes. Lexical access, the process by which a word's meaning is extracted from its phonological or orthographic code, must include some means for selecting the most appropriate meaning for the context in which the word appears. The recent research on lexical access has led to some interesting conclusions.

Essentially, when an ambiguous word is seen with no context (that is, alone) all meanings of the word are accessed. Then, after about a 600 msec delay, a default meaning is selected, and the other meanings are no longer available (Warren, 1977). If a word is in a context, i.e., a sentence or phrase that biases towards one of the meanings, another counterintuitive process occurs: all meanings of an ambiguous word are accessed initially, and context is subsequently consulted to determine the most appropriate meaning (see Fig. 14.1; see also Lucas, 1983; Swinney & Hakes, 1976; Tanenhaus, Seidenberg, & Leiman, 1979). As lexical access occurs, all meanings are primed regardless of syntactic category, for example, "post the letter" versus "the fence post". This bottom-up-first, top-down-next process is used whether context is available either before or after the ambiguous word is presented.

It has been suggested that when an ambiguous word is presented after biasing context, meanings that are inappropriate to context are actively suppressed (Tanenhaus et al. 1979). That is, they fade away much more quickly than if there had been no context at all. Hence, disambiguation would involve not only the identification of the correct meaning, but the immediate erasure of accessed but inappropriate meanings. The erasure is a special process that can work only with context.

We have proposed a modified version of the active suppression theory. We call the modified theory *conditional retention* (Granger, Holbrook, & Eiselt, 1984). The conditional retention theory states that all meanings of an ambiguous word are retained until it is clear that one or more meanings are appropriate to the whole context. If an ambiguous word appears in isolation, no meaning is inappropriate; therefore, no meanings are suppressed. In a single sentence, if an ambiguous word appears preceding a context that suggests only one meaning of the word, all other meanings will be actively suppressed after the text has been read. The same is true for an ambiguous word that appears in a single sentence

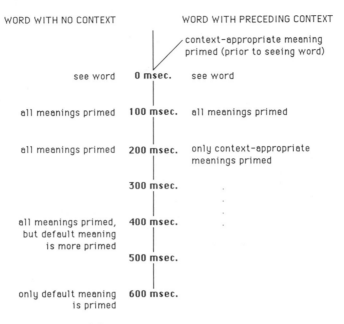

FIG. 14.1.   Lexical access timeline.

after a context: all meanings are activated, and those that do not fit the context will be actively suppressed. However, if an ambiguous word appears within context—if text both precedes and follows the ambiguous word—a meaning will initially be selected that fits the context preceding the word. Those meanings that do not fit the preceding context will not be actively suppressed until the rest of the context is available for final interpretation. Conditional retention explains why humans can understand texts with initially misleading contexts, as was pointed out in example [1] cited earlier, whereas active suppression does not. Furthermore, experimental evidence from human subjects indicates that conditional retention provides a better explanation of human behavior than active suppression. (For a short discussion of some of the experimental evidence, see Appendix I.)

Because the lexical access findings indicate that all meanings are facilitated at first, with one meaning finally chosen, it seems as though all possibilities are pursued simultaneously in memory and are evaluated on the basis of a best fit with the current context. It cannot be true that correct word-senses are chosen by pursuing each possiblity in turn until one fits the current context well. If this were so, only one meaning would ever be facilitated when no context is available.

Inference as Memory Retrieval

Lexical access can be described as the retrieval of, evaluation of, and decision about specific, competing memories. The memories in this case are word-senses.

In the same way, pragmatic inference decisions also depend on the retrieval and evaluation of competing memories—in this case, memories of events and event sequences. With both lexical and pragmatic memories, the evaluation consists of choosing the memory which most closely fits the current context. The choice is made through various evaluation metrics that seem to be available at both levels.

Spreading activation is a memory organization scheme that offers the ability to pursue many inference paths simultaneously and has been employed in a number of models (e.g., Charniak, 1983; Fahlman, 1979; Quillian, 1968). We use a spreading activation process in ATLAST to make inferences at the lexical, syntactic, and pragmatic levels. A serious problem with spreading activation is that it can quickly lead to a combinatorial explosion of inferences if it has no inherent restrictions on which inferences will be pursued or on how far an inference will be pursued. We have addressed this problem within our system by having a separate process evaluate the inference paths that are activated, thus controlling which inference paths will be pursued and which will be abandoned. The use of a spreading activation process for inference pursuit and another process for the evaluation of inferences has led to a new architecture for processing and understanding text.

THE NEW ARCHITECTURE

The ATLAST model consists of three major processes: the *Lexical Capsulizer,* the *Proposer,* and the *Filter.* These processes run in parallel. These three processes were developed to incorporate three features: *spreading activation memory, two-stage syntactic analysis,* and *parallel processing of syntax and semantics.* Each of these features reflects a decision on how to make the model as psychologically valid as possible.

Activation and Inhibition

The first decision to affect ATLAST's architecture was the use of a spreading activation memory process, which we called the Proposer. As discussed earlier, spreading activation allows several inference paths to be pursued simultaneously, which is apparently the way the human inference mechanism works. The Proposer has no inherent restrictions on which inference paths to follow and which to ignore.

Each path is pursued by the Proposer until inhibited by the Filter, a process that runs concurrently with the Proposer. Using a set of evaluation metrics such as parsimony, cohesion, and specificity, the Filter evaluates each inference path (Granger, 1980; Wilensky, 1983). The metrics are plausibility indicators for making decisions about which inferences are to be pursued, and for recognizing which inference paths intersect. In most cases, the Filter will be able to detect and inhibit pursuit of particular inference paths as soon as they are proposed. In this way, the parallel operation of the Proposer and the Filter allows the concurrent pursuit of alternative inferences without suffering from the combinatorial explosion effects of pursuing too many inference paths. Though the idea of beginning pursuit on all inference paths instead of just the appropriate ones may seem both counterintuitive and counterproductive, there are two arguments for using this approach. First, it seems impossible to determine which inferences may be appropriate without first evaluating all inference possibilities; second, this approach is consistent with experimental studies of human behavior (Granger et al. 1984).

Two-Stage Syntactic Analysis

The second decision we made was to divide *intraphrasal* and *interphrasal* syntactic decisions between two processes. The division allowed ATLAST to parse sentences that humans are able to parse, but also caused ATLAST to be unable to parse sentences that humans are unable to parse. One type of sentence that causes both ATLAST and human readers difficulty is the *garden path* sentence, such as text [3]:

[3] The horse raced past the barn fell.

A system that worked out all syntactic possibilities would have no problem understanding such a sentence; when it came to the word *raced,* it would not make a decision as to whether *raced* begins a modifying clause or is the main verb. However, humans do make such a decision: they decide that *raced* is the main verb (the more common usage); but they are wrong, and they cannot parse the sentence. A parser that makes initial *intra*phrasal decisions and later *inter*phrasal decisions has the same problem that humans have (cf. Frazier & Fodor, 1978).

ATLAST has a *Lexical Capsulizer,* which provides initial syntactic groupings, or capsules, of words in a text. The Capsulizer activates much of the information immediately available about a given word, including how it can be used syntactically, phrases associated with the word, and so on. The syntactic information is accumulated by the Capsulizer as it processes words to make initial decisions about syntactic relationships within phrases (intraphrasal syntax). The Filter, on the other hand, contains inference evaluation rules, which include syntactic information as well as metrics for lexical and pragmatic inference decisions, so that the Filter can make decisions about the syntactic relationships between phrases (interphrasal syntax).

At this point, it may seem that the Filter does an unusual amount of work and that it would be more useful to split the Filter into two separate processes: one that evaluates pragmatic inferences, and one that makes interphrasal syntax decisions. However, the kinds of decisions the Filter makes for guiding the

Proposer's search are the same kinds of decisions necessary for making interphrasal decisions; both tasks are simply a matter of applying evaluation metrics. In fact, many of the Filter's decisions about the Proposer's possible inference paths are based in part on syntactic considerations (e.g., possible meanings of a word are limited by the syntactic category of each meaning). The Filter is using the Proposer's suggestions to fill missing parts of the interpretation, which include such syntactic considerations as actor, object, and action. Thus, interphrasal syntax works better within the Filter than as a separate process.

Concurrent Operation of Syntax and Semantics

The third decision that affected ATLAST's architecture was to have concurrent operation of syntactic analysis and pragmatic inference generation. To see the advantage of such parallelism, consider text [4]:

[4] The boy genius athlete was given a medal.

As an understander processes this text, it is unclear whether *boy* will be a noun or a modifier. The understander might guess, but it is equally unclear which of the two *genius* will be and which of the two *athlete* will be, until the word *was* is processed. (See Gershman, 1977, for a thorough discussion of noun group analysis.) Yet introspection indicates that an understander does not wait unitl a syntactic category is assigned to a word before beginning to build up a representation of the situation so far. Furthermore, once the sentence has been parsed through the word *was*, it is still not clear whether the words preceding the word *was* make up an actor or an object (compare with "The boy genius athlete was running"), but an understander knows that the words up to *was* constitute a noun phrase. Thus, as has been pointed out by many other researchers (e.g., Charniak, 1983; Lebowitz, 1982; Schank & Riesbeck, 1981), syntactic decisions need not be made before semantic possibilities are explored.

The Processes and Their Functions

We have introduced ATLAST's three major processes: the Lexical Capsulizer, the Proposer, and the Filter (see Fig. 14.2). Each of the decisions previously discussed contributed to the design of the three processes and their functions. In keeping with the two-stage syntactic analysis, the Lexical Capsulizer provides initial capsules of words in a text using intraphrasal syntactic rules. The Capsulizer recognizes a word by checking a letter string against entries in the lexicon and noticing a match. The Capsulizer activates all the syntactic information about a given word. The syntactic information is accumulated by the Capsulizer as it processes words to make intra-phrasal syntactic decisions. These decisions

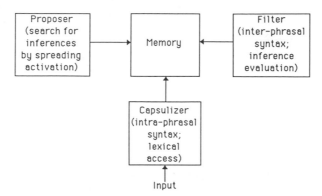

FIG. 14.2.   The organization of ATLAST's major components.

are made available to the Filter (via the capsules), which uses the information to perform such tasks as differentiating between actors and objects.

The Proposer, which is the spreading activation mechanism, can be thought of as an emergent property of the memory organization. When a match is found between a letter string from the text and the lexicon, the Proposer triggers the alternate meanings of the word and pursues all possible inference paths from the associations with each meaning simultaneously. The inference paths lead to associated higher level memory organization packets (MOPs) (Schank, 1982; Kolodner, 1984). Each path is pursued until it is inhibited by the Filter.

The Filter, which runs concurrently with the Capsulizer and the Proposer, inhibits apparently unfruitful searches by the Proposer without expunging them, and allows the Proposer to pursue promising inference paths. The Filter applies evaluation metrics; the metrics are plausibility indicators for making decisions about which inferences are to be pursued, and for recognizing when inference paths intersect. When no more text is available, the Filter expunges, or rejects, all currently inhibited inferences.

The Filter also maintains the various connections between the episodes that make up the alternative interpretations. The Filter makes interphrasal syntactic decisions using appropriate evaluation metrics. These metrics include rules about filling in slots in the representation, such as the actor and object slots. They also include rules that have to do with agreement of tense, number, and gender, as well as keeping track of referents across phrases, understanding when a phrase is modifying another phrase, and so forth.

The Proposer, the Filter, and the Capsulizer all run simultaneously, although they may or may not be working on the same information at the same moment. For example, the Filter cannot evaluate an inference path until the Proposer begins to pursue it. The Proposer cannot begin pursuing inference paths until the Capsulizer finds a match between a letter string and a word in the lexicon. However, the concurrent operation of the three processes allows quick evaluation and inhibition of inferences, easy maintenance of alternative interpretations of text and, thus, easy supplanting of incorrect interpretations (Granger, 1980), and fast, correct parsing of texts with which human readers have no trouble. In addition, the split syntax means that ATLAST has difficulty parsing some of the same types of texts that humans do.

Other models of language comprehension have tried to integrate some of the levels of inference behavior. There are models that integrate the syntactic and pragmatic levels (e.g., Dyer, 1982; Lebowitz, 1980), as well as models that integrate lexical access and syntactic parsing (e.g., Small, Cottrell, & Shastri, 1982). ATLAST is an implemented integration of language understanding on the lexical, syntactic, and pragmatic levels (cf. Charniak, 1983).

ATLAST: THE PROGRAM

What follows is actual annotated run-time output from the ATLAST prototype program. This example illustrates primarily how ATLAST disambiguates between two possible meanings of the word "bugs" in the text, "The CIA checked for bugs." In the interest of brevity and clarity, we use a very short text and just enough of a knowledge base to process this example. ATLAST is written in UCI-LISP on a DECSYSTEM-20, so the parallelism so important to the theory is necessarily simulated in its implementation.

Processing begins

Input text is: (THE CIA CHECKED FOR BUGS *PERIOD*)

Capsulizer:
   Retrieving lexical entry: THE
   No MOPs will be activated from lexical entry
   Begin sentence
   Begin noun phrase

Proposer:
   No activity

Filter:
   No activity
      The first word, *the,* is processed by ATLAST. Though the Capsulizer
      recognizes that this marks the beginning of a noun phrase, there are no
      relevant structures in memory to be activated. Thus, the Proposer and the
      Filter are idle at this time.

Capsulizer:
   Retrieving lexical entry: CIA

Proposer:
Initializing CENTRAL-INTELLIGENCE-AGENCY
Spreading from CENTRAL-INTELLIGENCE-AGENCY
Activating SPY-AGENCY

Filter:
No activity
In this cycle, the memory structure CENTRAL-INTELLIGENCE-AGEN-CY is activated as a result of reading "CIA." The Proposer then begins to search along the links leading from CENTRAL-INTELLIGENCE-AGEN-CY for related memory structures, thus activating the more general SPY-AGENCY.

Capsulizer:
Retrieving lexical entry: CHECKED
Sending capsule
End noun phrase
Begin verb phrase

Proposer:
Initializing SEARCH
Spreading from SEARCH
Activating REMOVE
Spreading from SPY-AGENCY
Activating GET-OTHERS-SECRETS
Activating PRESERVE-OWN-SECRETS
Activating GENERIC-EMPLOYER

Filter:
ACTOR slot filled by CENTRAL-INTELLIGENCE-AGENCY
The next word, *checked,* terminates the noun phrase and begins a verb phrase. The Capsulizer sends a capsule consisting of the word-senses initially activated by the noun phrase, CENTRAL-INTELLIGENCE-AGEN-CY, to the Filter. The Filter, looking for an actor for this sentence, fills the slot with this noun-phrase capsule.

Capsulizer:
Retrieving lexical entry: FOR
No MOPs will be activated from lexical entry
Sending capsule
Begin prepositional phrase

Proposer:
Spreading from REMOVE
Activating REMOVE-OTHERS-LISTENING-DEVICE
Activating REMOVE-HEALTH-HAZARD

Spreading from GENERIC-EMPLOYER
    Activating PRESERVE-HEALTHY-ENVIRONMENT
    Activating MANAGEMENT
Spreading from PRESERVE-OWN-SECRETS
    Found connections at REMOVE-OTHERS-LISTENING-DEVICE
        Path from CENTRAL-INTELLIGENCE-AGENCY to SEARCH
    No MOPs activated from PRESERVE-OWN-SECRETS
Spreading from GET-OTHERS-SECRETS
    Activating PLANT-OWN-LISTENING-DEVICE

Filter:
    New path discovered: IPATH0
        Path from CENTRAL-INTELLIGENCE-AGENCY to SEARCH
        CENTRAL-INTELLIGENCE-AGENCY is a special case of SPY-AGEN-CY
        SPY-AGENCY has the goal PRESERVE-OWN-SECRETS
        PRESERVE-OWN-SECRETS has the plan REMOVE-OTHERS-LISTEN-ING-DEVICE.
        REMOVE-OTHERS-LISTENING-DEVICE is a special case of REMOVE
        REMOVE has the preconditon SEARCH
    ACTION slot filled by SEARCH

    The preposition *for* does not activate any new memory structures, but it does begin a modifying prepositional phrase. The Capsulizer sends the verb component of the verb phrase (SEARCH) to the Filter, which then assigns the capsule to the action slot.

    The Proposer, looking for intersections among the "wavefronts" of spreading activation, finds a connection, or inference path (IPATH0), between CENTRAL-INTELLIGENCE-AGENCY and SEARCH and notifies the Filter. The Filter knows of only one inference path at this time, so there is no basis for comparison and evaluation of inference paths yet.

Capsulizer:
    Retrieving lexical entry: BUGS

Proposer:
    Initializing INSECT
    Initializing MICROPHONE
    Spreading from INSECT
        Found connections at REMOVE-HEALTH-HAZARD
            Path from INSECT to SEARCH
        No MOPs activated from INSECT
    Spreading from MICROPHONE
        Found connections at PLANT-OWN-LISTENING-DEVICE
            Path from MICROPHONE to CENTRAL-INTELLIGENCE-AGENCY

Found connections at REMOVE-OTHERS-LISTENING-DEVICE
   Path from MICROPHONE to CENTRAL-INTELLIGENCE-AGENCY
   Path from MICROPHONE to SEARCH
No MOPs activated from MICROPHONE
Spreading from REMOVE-HEALTH-HAZARD
   Found connections at PRESERVE-HEALTHY-ENVIRONMENT
     Path from SEARCH to CENTRAL-INTELLIGENCE-AGENCY
   Found connections at INSECT
     Path from SEARCH to INSECT
No MOPs activated from REMOVE-HEALTH-HAZARD
Spreading from REMOVE-OTHERS-LISTENING-DEVICE
   Found connections at PRESERVE-OWN-SECRETS
     Path from SEARCH to CENTRAL-INTELLIGENCE-AGENCY
   Found connections at MICROPHONE
     Path from SEARCH to MICROPHONE
No MOPs activated from REMOVE-OTHERS-LISTENING-DEVICE
Spreading from PLANT-OWN-LISTENING-DEVICE
   Found connections at MICROPHONE
     Path from CENTRAL-INTELLIGENCE-AGENCY to SEARCH
     Path from CENTRAL-INTELLIGENCE-AGENCY to MICROPHONE
   No MOPs activated from PLANT-OWN-LISTENING-DEVICE
Spreading from MANAGEMENT
   No MOPs activated from MANAGEMENT
Spreading from PRESERVE-HEALTHY-ENVIRONMENT
   Found connections at REMOVE-HEALTH-HAZARD
     Path from CENTRAL-INTELLIGENCE-AGENCY to INSECT
     Path from CENTRAL-INTELLIGENCE-AGENCY to SEARCH
   No MOPs activated from PRESERVE-HEALTHY-ENVIRONMENT

Filter:
  New path discovered: IPATH1
    Path from CENTRAL-INTELLIGENCE-AGENCY to SEARCH
      CENTRAL-INTELLIGENCE-AGENCY is a special case of SPY-AGENCY
      SPY-AGENCY can be viewed as GENERIC-EMPLOYER
      GENERIC-EMPLOYER has the goal PRESERVE-HEALTHY-ENVIRONMENT
      PRESERVE-HEALTHY-ENVIRONMENT has the plan REMOVE-HEALTH-HAZARD
      REMOVE-HEALTH-HAZARD is a special case of REMOVE
      REMOVE has the precondition SEARCH
  New path discovered: IPATH2
    Path from CENTRAL-INTELLIGENCE-AGENCY to INSECT

CENTRAL-INTELLIGENCE-AGENCY is a special case of SPY-AGENCY

SPY-AGENCY can be viewed as GENERIC-EMPLOYER

GENERIC-EMPLOYER has the goal PRESERVE-HEALTHY-ENVIRONMENT

PRESERVE-HEALTHY-ENVIRONMENT has the plan REMOVE-HEALTH-HAZARD

REMOVE-HEALTH-HAZARD has the role-filler INSECT

New path discovered: IPATH3

Path from CENTRAL-INTELLIGENCE-AGENCY to MICROPHONE

CENTRAL-INTELLIGENCE-AGENCY is a special case of SPY-AGENCY

SPY-AGENCY has the goal GET-OTHERS-SECRETS

GET-OTHERS-SECRETS has the plan PLANT-OWN-LISTENING-DEVICE

PLANT-OWN-LISTENING-DEVICE has the role-filler MICROPHONE

New Path discovered: IPATH4

Path from CENTRAL-INTELLIGENCE-AGENCY to SEARCH

CENTRAL-INTELLIGENCE-AGENCY is a special case of SPY-AGENCY

SPY-AGENCY has the goal GET-OTHERS-SECRETS

GET-OTHERS-SECRETS has the plan PLANT-OWN-LISTENING-DEVICE

PLANT-OWN-LISTENING-DEVICE has the role-filler MICROPHONE

MICROPHONE is a role-filler of REMOVE-OTHERS-LISTENING-DEVICE

REMOVE-OTHERS-LISTENING-DEVICE is a special case of REMOVE

REMOVE has the precondition SEARCH

New path discovered: IPATH5

Path from SEARCH to MICROPHONE

SEARCH is a precondition of REMOVE

REMOVE has the special case REMOVE-OTHERS-LISTENING-DEVICE

REMOVE-OTHERS-LISTENING-DEVICE has the role-filler MICROPHONE

New path discovered: IPATH6

Path from SEARCH to INSECT

SEARCH is a precondition of REMOVE

REMOVE has the special case REMOVE-HEALTH-HAZARD

REMOVE-HEALTH-HAZARD has the role-filler INSECT

New path discovered: IPATH7

Path from MICROPHONE to CENTRAL-INTELLIGENCE-AGENCY

MICROPHONE is a role-filler of REMOVE-OTHERS-LISTENING-

DEVICE
REMOVE-OTHERS-LISTENING-DEVICE is a plan of PRESERVE-OWN-SECRETS
PRESERVE-OWN-SECRETS is a goal of SPY-AGENCY
SPY-AGENCY has the special case CENTRAL-INTELLIGENCE-AGENCY
Parsimony metric—IPATH7 explains more input than IPATH3
Specificity metric—IPATH4 more specific than IPATH1
Parsimony metric—IPATH0 shorter than IPATH4

The Capsulizer reads the ambiguous word *bugs,* which results in the activation of two word-senses: INSECT and MICROPHONE. The Proposer's search has uncovered several new inference paths. When two different inference paths connect the same two word-senses, the Filter applies inference evaluation metrics to the two paths to determine which of the two provides the better explanation of the input text. The rejected paths are "deactivated," or ignored, until later text results in activating that path again.

Capsulizer:
Retrieving lexical entry: *PERIOD*
No MOPs will be activated from lexical entry
Sending capsule
End prepositional phrase
End verb phrase
End sentence

Proposer:
No activity

Filter:
OBJECT has competing slot fillers: INSECT vs. MICROPHONE
Specificity metric—IPATH7 more specific than IPATH2
Parsimony metric—IPATH5 explains more input than IPATH6
Word-sense ambiguity resolution: MICROPHONE vs. INSECT
All paths through INSECT have been deactivated
The ambiguity is resolved—MICROPHONE selected
OBJECT slot filled by MICROPHONE

The Capsulizer encounters the end of the text and sends to the Filter a capsule containing the word-senses activated by the prepositional phrase. The Filter determines that the capsule contains the object of the action SEARCH, and that this object is ambiguous. The Filter attempts to resolve this ambiguity by applying the inference evaluation metrics to the remaining active inference paths. Because MICROPHONE and INSECT are now known to be competing word-senses, the Filter treats IPATH7 and IPATH2 as competing inference paths. That is, although IPATH7 connects MICRO-PHONE to CENTRAL-INTELLIGENCE-AGENCY and IPATH2 connects INSECT to CENTRAL-INTELLIGENCE-AGENCY, the two different paths are evaluated as if they connected the same two word-senses because INSECT and MICROPHONE were activated by the same lexical entry (*bugs*). For this same reason, IPATH5 is evaluated against IPATH6. This evaluation results in the two remaining inference paths containing INSECT to be deactivated, so the Filter resolves the ambiguity in favor of MICRO-PHONE. Below is the active memory structure after all processing has ended, followed by the pointers into the structure.

Processing completed

    Active memory structure:
      Path from MICROPHONE to CENTRAL-INTELLIGENCE-AGENCY
        MICROPHONE is a role-filler of REMOVE-OTHERS-LISTENING-DEVICE
        REMOVE-OTHERS-LISTENING-DEVICE is a plan of PRESERVE-OWN-SECRETS
        PRESERVE-OWN-SECRETS is a goal of SPY-AGENCY
        SPY-AGENCY has the special case CENTRAL-INTELLIGENCE-AGENCY
      Path from SEARCH to MICROPHONE
        SEARCH is a precondition of REMOVE
        REMOVE has the special case REMOVE-OTHERS-LISTENING-DEVICE
        REMOVE-OTHERS-LISTENING-DEVICE has the role-filler MICRO-PHONE
      Path from CENTRAL-INTELLIGENCE-AGENCY to SEARCH
        CENTRAL-INTELLIGENCE-AGENCY is a special case of SPY-AGENCY
        SPY-AGENCY has the goal PRESERVE-OWN-SECRETS
        PRESERVE-OWN-SECRETS has the plan REMOVE-OTHERS-LIS-TENING-DEVICE
        REMOVE-OTHERS-LISTENING-DEVICE is a special case of RE-MOVE
        REMOVE has the precondition SEARCH
    Pointers to memory structure:
      Actor: CENTRAL-INTELLIGENCE-AGENCY
      Action: SEARCH
      Object: MICROPHONE

SUMMARY AND CONCLUSIONS

As a model of the behavior of human inference processes during text understanding, ATLAST is quite different from those proposed to date (e.g., Dyer, 1982; Riesbeck, 1982; Lebowitz, 1980). The features that distinguish the ATLAST model from others can be summarized as follows:

1. ATLAST unifies inference processing at three distinct levels: the lexical, syntactic, and pragmatic levels.
2. The separation of intraphrasal and interphrasal syntactic analysis enables ATLAST to process texts which humans understand and to make the same mistakes a human understander makes.
3. The use of a spreading-activation memory model allows ATLAST to pursue competing inference paths simultaneously until syntactic or semantic information suggests otherwise. Previous models of inference decision processes either left a loose end or chose a default inference when faced with an ambiguity (DeJong, 1979; Dyer, 1982; Granger, 1980; Granger, 1981; Lebowitz, 1980; Wilensky, 1983).
4. The concurrent operation of ATLAST's Capsulizer, Proposer, and Filter permits pragmatic interpretations to be evaluated independently of syntactic decisions. This parallel organization also allows immediate evaluation and inhibition of competing inference paths, thus minimizing combinatorial explosion effects.
5. ATLAST conforms to the results of controlled experiments on human subjects.

Future Work

The ATLAST framework has been applied only to relatively short texts. We will be applying ATLAST to longer texts as well, to look at such factors as the "distance" between inference points, which we believe will also affect inference processes, especially at the pragmatic level. We will also be applying ATLAST to different types of text to discover further rules for inference processing.

The model makes several predictions about what kind of behavior to expect from human readers. Because ATLAST is meant to be a model of human behavior, and not simply a program which can read texts, ATLAST has difficulty parsing certain kinds of text, which human readers also find very difficult to parse. The causes of ATLAST's difficulties are predictions of the causes of human readers' difficulties. We are currently designing and running several experiments on human subjects to allow us to test these predictions. We are designing more lexical access experiments to decide how disambiguation occurs with longer texts. We are also designing lexical access experiments with different experimental methodologies to strengthen the claims we make. We are making more specific predictions, which will allow us to divide more accurately the roles of the Capsulizer, the Proposer, and the Filter in disambiguation. We are also designing experiments to test our predictions about why garden path sentences are so difficult for human readers. Still another set of proposed experiments has to do with devising and testing various evaluation metrics, and testing what happens when the evaluation metrics conflict with one another.

ATLAST is a model of language understanding that employs the results of studies of many inference phenomena from several different fields of research. This approach helps solve many of the problems associated with inference decisions at all levels of processing. It is also a new framework within which to interpret and tackle unsolved problems through implementation and psychological experimentation.

ACKNOWLEDGMENTS

This research was supported in part by the National Science Foundation under grant IST-81-20685 and by the Naval Ocean Systems Center under contracts N00123-81-C-1078 and N66001-83-C-0255.

REFERENCES

Charniak, E. (1983). Passing markers: A theory of contextual influence in language comprehension. *Cognitive Science, 7,* 171–190.

DeJong, G. F. (1979). *Skimming stories in real time: An experiment in integrated understanding.* (Research Rep. No. 158). Unpublished doctoral dissertation, Yale University, New Haven, CT, Department of Computer Science.

Dyer, M. G. (1982). *In-depth understanding: A computer model of integrated parsing for narrative comprehension.* (Research Rep. No. 219). Unpublished doctoral dissertation, Yale University, New Haven, CT, Department of Computer Sciecnce.

Fahlman, S. E. (1979). *NETL: A system for representing and using real-world knowledge.* Cambridge, MA: MIT Press.

Frazier, L., & Fodor, J. D. (1978). The sausage machine: A new two-stage parsing model. *Cognition, 6,* 291–325.

Gershman, A. V. (1977). Conceptual analysis of noun groups in English. *Proceedings of the Fifth International Joint Conference on Artificial Intelligence,* Cambridge, MA.

Granger, R. H. (1980). *When expectation fails: Towards a self-correcting inference system* (Tech. Rep. #162) University of California, Irvine, Department of Information and Computer Science.

Granger, R. H. (1981). *Directing and re-directing inference pursuit: Extra-textual influences on text interpretation.* (Tech. Rep. No. 171) University of California, Irvine, Department of Information and Computer Science.

Granger, R. H., Eiselt, K. P., & Holbrook, J. K. (1983). STRATEGIST: A program that models strategy-driven and content-driven inference behavior. *Proceedings of the National Conference on Artificial Intelligence,* Washington, DC.

Granger, R. H., Holbrook, J. K., & Eiselt, K. P. (1984). Interaction effects between word-level and text-level inferences: On-line processing of ambiguous words in context. *Proceedings of the Sixth Annual Conference of the Cognitive Science Society,* Boulder, CO.

Hudson, S., & Tanenhaus, M. (1984). Ambiguity resolution in the absence of contextual bias. *Proceedings of the Sixth Annual Conference of the Cognitive Science Society,* Boulder, CO.

Kolodner, J. L. (1984). *Retrieval and organizational strategies in memory: A computer model.* Hillsdale, NJ: Lawrence Erlbaum Assocaites.

Lebowitz, M. (1980). *Generalization and memory in an integrated understanding system.* (Res. Rep. No. 186). Unpublished doctoral dissertation. Yale University, New Haven, CT, Department of Computer Science.

Lebowitz, M. (1982). *Limited parallel parsing.* Department of Computer Science, Columbia University, New York.

Lucas, M. (1983). Lexical access during sentence comprehension: Frequency and context effects. *Proceedings of the Fifth Annual Conference of the Cognitive Science Society,* Rochester, NY.

Quillian, M. R. (1968). Semantic memory. In M. Minsky (Ed.), *Semantic information processing.* Cambridge, MA: MIT Press.

Riesbeck, C. K. (1982). Realistic language comprehension. In W. G. Lehnert & M. H. Ringle (Eds.), *Strategies for natural language processing.* Hillsdale, NJ: Lawrence Erlbaum Associates.

Schank, R. C. (1982). *Dynamic memory: A theory of reminding and learning in computers and people.* New York: Cambridge University Press.

Schank, R. C., & Riesbeck, C. K. (1981). *Inside computer understanding.* Hillsdale, NJ: Lawrence Erlbaum Associates.

Schulenburg, D. A. (1982). *Generating alternate interpretations: Directing inference during story understanding.* Unpublished Master's thesis, University of California, Irvine.

Small, S., Cottrell, G., & Shastri, L. (1982). Toward connectionist parsing. *Proceedings of the National Conference on Artificial Intelligence,* Pittsburgh, PA.

Swinney, D. A., & Hakes, D. T. (1976). Effects of prior context upon lexical access during sentence comprehension. *Journal of Verbal Learning and Verbal Behavior, 15,* 681–689.

Tanenhaus, M., Leiman, J., & Seidenberg, M. (1979). Evidence for multiple stages in processing of ambiguous words in syntactic contexts. *Journal of Verbal Learning and Verbal Behavior, 18,* 427–440.

Warren, R. E. (1977). Time and the spread of activation in memory. *Journal of Experimental Psychology: Human Learning and Memory, 3* (4), 458–466.

Wilensky, R. (1983). *Planning and understanding.* Reading, MA: Addison-Wesley.

APPENDIX I: CONDITIONAL RETENTION EXPERIMENT

One of the experiments we ran had subjects read two-sentence texts such as texts [1] and [2], introduced earlier:

[1] The CIA called in an inspector to check for bugs. The secretaries had reported seeing roaches.

[2] The CIA called in an inspector to check for bugs. The secretaries had reported seeing microphones.

The last word in the first sentence of each of the texts was ambiguous (bugs). The second sentence was always written in such a way that only the last word would disambiguate the text. For example, in text [1], the disambiguating word is *roaches*. In text [2], it is *microphones*. Immediately after the subjects read a text, they saw a pair of words. Each word was related to one of the meanings of the

TABLE 14.1
Results of the Word Choice Experiment

	Type of Text			
	Distractor Items (Lexically Unambiguous)	Neutral/Bias (1 Context)	Bias/Same Bias (1 Context)	Bias/Different Bias (2 Contexts)
Error Rate	0%	7%	7%	54%

*Described as the context type of the first sentence followed by the context type of the second sentence. A context could be *neutral* with respect to selecting the meaning of the ambiguous word, or *biased toward* one or the other meaning of the ambiguous word.

ambiguous word, (e.g., *ant* and *spy*). The subjects were to choose the word most closely related to the story's events. They did this as quickly as possible because they thought they were being timed on their decision. After subjects had chosen one of the words, they answered several questions related to the story events.

Active suppression would predict that for stories in which the two sentences were biased toward different interpretations (*conflicting context* stories, such as text [1]), understanding would be difficult, because the initially inappropriate meaning, which is necessary to understand the story, is suppressed after the first sentence. If understanding is difficult, then answers to story comprehension questions should have a high error rate. Furthermore, active suppression would predict that when subjects had to choose between the two words, the choice would be easy, because the inappropriate meanings would have been suppressed, so that the correct meaning would be the only one primed. (If the subjects were not making their choice as quickly as possible, the error rate should in fact increase because the story interpretation difficulty should interfere.)

The conditional retention theory makes opposite predictions. Understanding the conflicting context stories should be easy, because both meanings are available. Thus, answering the comprehension questions should be easy. However, the error rate for the word-choice task should be high because both meanings are still available, resulting in confusion. The results of this experiment are in Tables 14.1 and 14.2.

TABLE 14.2
Results of the Question Answering Experiment

	Type of Text			
	Distractor Items (Lexically Unambiguous)	Neutral/Bias (1 Context)	Bias/Same Bias (1 Context)	Bias/Different Bias (2 Contexts)
Error Rate	3.75%	6.25%	2.2%	4.9%

In the word-choice task, the difference in error rate between the two-context condition and the other conditions was highly significant. However, the difference in error rate between the other conditions is not significant. This is exactly what conditional retention would predict. In the question-answering task, the difference in error rate between all four conditions was insignificant. This, too, is what conditional retention would predict. The results of this experiment agree with the conditional retention theory. We are also testing the conditional retention theory using several other methodologies. Experiments done by Hudson and Tanenhaus (1984) using a different methodology, confirm some parts of our results. Their experiments, however, were not designed to test for conditional retention, so they did not control for some of the important variables which would be necessary for a full confirmation.

Author Index

247

Subject Index